Commander

Commander

*The Life and Exploits of
Britain's Greatest Frigate Captain*

STEPHEN TAYLOR

W. W. NORTON & COMPANY

NEW YORK LONDON

For information about permission to reproduce selections from this book,
write to Permissions, W. W. Norton & Company, Inc.,
500 Fifth Avenue, New York, NY 10110

For information about special discounts for bulk purchases, please contact
W. W. Norton Special Sales at specialsales@wwnorton.com or 800-233-4830

Manufacturing by Courier Westford
Production manager: Louise Mattarelliano

Library of Congress Cataloging-in-Publication Data

Taylor, Stephen, 1948–
Commander : the life and exploits of Britain's greatest frigate
captain / Stephen Taylor. — 1st American ed.
p. cm.
Includes bibliographical references and index.
ISBN 978-0-393-07164-1 (hardcover)
1. Exmouth, Edward Pellew, Viscount, 1757–1833. 2. Great Britain.
Royal Navy. Officers—Biography. 3. Great Britain—History, Naval—18th
century. 4. Great Britain—History, Naval—19th century. 5. Frigates—Great
Britain—History—18th century. 6. Frigates—Great Britain—History—
19th century. I. Title.
DA87.1.E9T39 2012
359.0092–dc23
[B]
                              2012027783

W. W. Norton & Company, Inc.
500 Fifth Avenue, New York, N.Y. 10110
www.wwnorton.com

W. W. Norton & Company Ltd.
Castle House, 75/76 Wells Street, London W1T 3QT

1 2 3 4 5 6 7 8 9 0

To the Memory of My Mother

Contents

⊷⊶

Illustrations

———◆◆◆———

Plates

—∞∞∞—

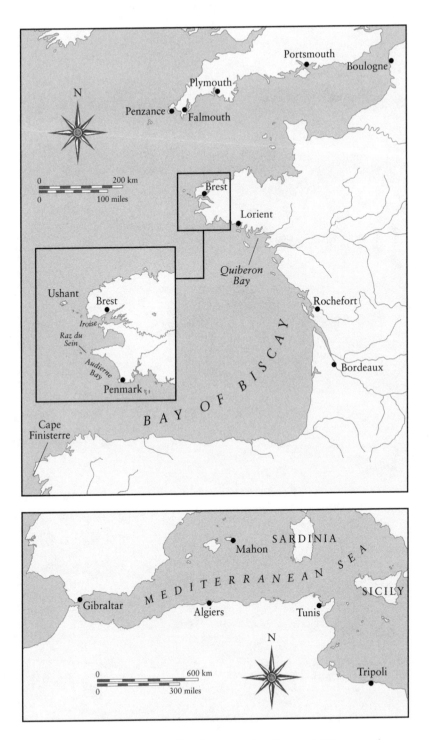

Edward Pellew's seas of endeavour: the Channel, Biscay and
Mediterranean.

Introduction

Sea officers pose a more than usually daunting prospect to the biographer. Though we may be drawn to maritime subjects by the grandeur of the sea and the drama of life on it, the technicalities of sail are a challenge to both writer and reader, while the blue-coated personalities who commanded tall ships can appear leaden – obscured by nautical jargon and a milieu now strange to us. Perhaps for this reason, fiction has been more successful than biography at bringing such men to life; the name of Hornblower is probably recognised by more general readers than that of Hawke, Aubrey more than Anson. Nelson, as in all things, is the exception, but that is because Nelson represents themes seemingly bigger than even the sea – transfiguration and martyrdom, not to mention sex and scandal.

Edward Pellew actually bestrides both worlds – as Hornblower's fictional mentor and as captain of the famed *Indefatigable*; and if his name is now better known from the novels of C. S. Forester than for his true exploits, these still resonated grandly enough in his own time. Pellew can be fairly described as the greatest frigate captain in the age of sail, an incomparable seaman, ferociously combative yet chivalrous, and with a gift for performing eye-catching feats in public. Later in life he commanded a fleet in a bloody and crusading operation to free European slaves in Barbary.

Yet Pellew is a neglected figure, even in the somewhat rarefied field of naval studies. Despite the wealth of available material, his paradoxical spirit – pugnacious but tender, acquisitive yet generous – may have stood in the way of biographers. While they have extolled the doings of Pellew the commander, they seemed to me as I started to explore his life, to have missed much of Pellew the man.

I should admit to having been initially drawn more to the man than the commander. In studying his letters for my last book, *Storm and Conquest*, I was struck by their warmth. While his education was scanty and his hand so atrocious it can defy transcription, they have an intimacy and a sensibility that are strikingly modern. His love for his men, as well as his friends and fellow officers, was as transparent as his desire for glory and honour. His nature, like his courage, had nothing to do with English *sangfroid*. It was hot-blooded, elemental. Throughout a long life he campaigned on behalf of individuals he saw as victims of injustice.

His flaws were of a part with this emotional temperament. Left fatherless at the age of eight, with a mother and five siblings, Pellew fought his way from the very bottom of the Navy to the top, and then covered the tracks of his rise from penniless youth to fleet command and a viscountcy. But the scars of childhood distress were never erased and he pursued wealth almost as avidly as he did an enemy frigate. Although there was nothing unusual in this, Pellew's awkwardness – on top of his impoverished origins he was a clannish Cornishman – attracted the wrong kind of attention. He had none of Nelson's gift for effortless politicking and, as an outsider with a talent for antagonising his better-born peers, he made many foes. Another boyhood legacy was a fierce protectiveness of his younger brother, a fellow officer whose fallibility he helped to conceal, just as he promoted his sons' careers well beyond their abilities. In any matter of family, Pellew was blindly and dangerously partisan.

There are two previous biographies. The first was commissioned by his elder brother as an exercise in reflected glory soon after Pellew's death – and published in 1835 in defiance of his beloved wife Susan who denied its author, Edward Osler, access to his papers. Although pure hagiography, the book divided the family. Pellew's most devoted son, George, scrawled objections on virtually every page, inserting corrections and observations gleaned from Pellew's confidant and right-hand man, John Gaze. He then spent years transcribing his father's papers and making notes for an approved biographer.

Almost a century passed without one being found. Eventually Pellew's descendants passed his papers to the National Maritime Museum at Greenwich on the understanding that its director, Geoffrey Callender, would write the new, long-awaited life. Callender, however, was overworked and passed the task to a promising if opinionated graduate, Cyril Northcote Parkinson, just starting a career as a maritime historian. Within a year Parkinson produced a substantial book, *Edward Pellew, Viscount Exmouth*, which was published in 1934 and has remained the standard work.

Parkinson had a prodigious intellect – though he is remembered today more for the aphorism of Parkinson's Law than his contribution to maritime studies – but the life of Pellew, his first foray as an author, was far from his best work. Written in haste, it is wordy, condescending (particularly considering that it came from the pen of a 23-year-old) and simply wrong in some respects, notably in underestimating the difficulty of Pellew's early years, his attitude to discipline and the nature of the resentment for which he became a target.

The materials for a reappraisal are extensive. The Exmouth papers at Greenwich alone run to thirty-three boxes, each containing hundreds of letters, left in the order in which Parkinson examined them eighty years ago and uncatalogued until recently. The Admiralty Records, the logs and musters of Pellew's ships, were ignored by Parkinson but give insights into Pellew's methods. The papers of his friends and enemies, scattered in archives around the country, illuminate the jealousies and feuds that dogged him.

Some finds had the thrill of discovery about them. I visited the house where he spent the last years of his life – now the offices of Teignmouth Town Council, but intact enough to imagine a coach drawing up outside and being met by a pigtailed figure in shabby livery, one of the old admiral's tars retained as a footman. I also wrote to the 10th Viscount Exmouth, telling him of my interest. Generously, he sent me the family copy of Osler's biography, with George Pellew's angry scratchings in the margins; and he suggested a visit to a farm west of Exeter. Leaving the Canonteign valley and the doomed estate that devoured the family fortune, I followed a lane that petered out in a yard and was taken to a barn with a tractor and a mountain of objects covered by tarpaulins. One of these was peeled away to expose a pile of metal trunks with, painted on the sides, 'Lord Exmouth, Personal Papers'. Inside were the documents compiled by George Pellew for the proposed life of his father.

From these various resources emerged details that added further human dimensions to the portrait. Perhaps the most surprising was the extent to which Pellew's warrior spirit was scarred by his own countrymen. In more than thirty-six years at sea, most of them at war and exposed in action, he was never wounded by enemy fire; but he suffered repeatedly from the sneering and sniping of his enemies at home, a battering which left him wary and suspicious. Beneath the tough officer exterior lay an unexpectedly vulnerable soul.

Biographers run the risk of identifying themselves too closely with their subjects, of imputing to them qualities and characteristics that did not exist, particularly when these might add to their appeal. I have therefore hesitated to make a connection with fiction and a character popular from novels set in the age of Nelson. Repeatedly, however, I have been drawn back to similarities between Edward Pellew and Patrick O'Brian's creation, Jack Aubrey. Both were fighting captains *sans pareil* in single-ship actions. Both were gunnery experts who drilled their every ship for accuracy and speed of fire. Both happened to be strong swimmers with a penchant for going overboard to rescue clumsy or drunken hands. Both sustained warm friendships with gallant enemy captains. Both nurtured entourages of followers who accompanied them devotedly from ship to ship. They were genial hosts at dinners in the great cabin, fond of wine and company, yet implacable and utterly single-minded in battle. They were also unworldly fellows who made a hash of dealing with their superiors. Big men who tended to bulk in later years, they were loving husbands and fathers, yet with an eye that might roam.

O'Brian was touchily guarded about his inspiration for Aubrey. While openly drawing on the exploits of another frigate captain, Thomas Cochrane, he was disdainful of the man himself, insisting that the real model for Aubrey's character was his own brother. Readers will judge for themselves whether O'Brian was ignorant of his hero's resonance with Pellew. Either way, he deserves to be remembered, for a life of adventure in the age of sail, and as a man thought by his contemporaries to be the greatest sea officer of his time.

North Africa, 1816

A year after Waterloo, while the citizens of Europe were looking forward to their first spring at peace in twenty years, a Royal Navy fleet came to anchor where the Sahara Desert meets the Mediterranean Sea. It was a warm morning and a sense of drowsy tranquillity prevailed as a ship's boat carrying a trio of blue-coated officers, including an extremely tall but stout man in the golden markings of an admiral, put off and was rowed towards the white walls of Tunis.

The naval force commanded by Lord Exmouth was an imposing one, but – at the outset at least – his visit to the Barbary States had no whiff of conflict about it. Indeed, Restoration comedy might have been closer the mark. When the admiral arrived at the Bardo palace it was to find Princess Caroline of Brunswick and a party of aristocratic pleasure-seekers as guests of the Bey. On a cruise, bound for the sights of Athens and Constantinople, the estranged and increasingly rotund wife of the Prince Regent was living in sumptuous style, waited on by slaves and admitted to the company of the harem where, it was unkindly said, she felt thoroughly at home. Her presence in Barbary could only embarrass the British side in what was a highly sensitive diplomatic mission.

On 12 March the Navy party entered the Bardo, a citadel of high arches, colonnades and fountains, coming by way of courtyards studded with Byzantine mosaics to the Bey's presence. The officers had a reassuring glimpse of the Princess making a discreet departure by a side door 'to take her farewell of the ladies of the harem', before they were set on a divan, with coffee and sherbet, to explain the purpose of the visit.

Lord Exmouth had been a commanding presence on Navy vessels for almost forty years and he spoke in terms which, translated, came close to an ultimatum. For centuries, he said, the states of Europe had been dismayed to see their citizens captured by corsairs and brought to Barbary as slaves. Now they required that all Christian slaves should be set free.

This speech might have led to trouble then and there; but the Bey, one of the Navy party noted, was a languid fellow, 'never in his life known to show any semblance of exertion, except one night when he got out of his bed to murder his brother'. Moreover, Exmouth was, in effect, acting as an intermediary for Naples and Sicily, the European states that had suffered most at the hands of Barbary pirates, and was offering a final ransom payment on their behalf for the slaves' freedom. When Exmouth left the palace it was with the freedom of hundreds of Europeans assured, and the Bey's promise that enslavement would cease.

Two weeks later, a similar agreement was reached in Tripoli that set at liberty hundreds more European fishermen and sailors. Proceeding to his next destination, Algiers, Exmouth was in high spirits in reporting to the Admiralty:

> I sincerely hope we have finally smoked the horrors of Christian Slavery. We have released 2,500 poor creatures and left the Dungeons empty – I hope for ever.

The author of these words, the subject of this story, cut an improbably bucolic figure on the 98-gun flagship *Boyne*. A red-faced giant with a round hat on his head, given to wandering his quarterdeck in bare feet, a scarf around his ample waist, he resembled more a rustic from his native Cornwall than a great naval commander. In truth, however, his peculiar appearance was of a part with a reputation grown somewhat dusty. His early glory as the most dashing and successful frigate captain in the Navy's history was a distant memory. The high-born sneered about his lowly origins. Senior officers gossiped about his cupidity and nepotism, younger ones grumbled that he was critical and ill-tempered. For all the resonance of his title, Lord

Exmouth of Canonteign was somehow a lesser figure than his earlier persona, Sir Edward Pellew.

As Pellew himself had reflected over years of pacing various quarterdecks, it was a curious business, this question of reputation. A decade earlier, the *Naval Chronicle*, noting the absurd renown of a single naval commander, had lamented:

> that ill-judged and overweening popularity which tends to make a Demi-god of Lord Nelson at the expense of all other officers in the service, many of whom possess equal merit and equal abilities and equal gallantry.

The author had a point; but Trafalgar followed just a few weeks later and the apotheosis of Nelson was complete. Since then Pellew had pondered wryly on the fragility of status, his own diminished by passing years and human jealousy, and though he had only admiration for the great man envied him the timing and manner of his end. Often he yearned for death in battle himself: 'How sweetly could I give up Life in such a cause.'

Comparing himself with Nelson was not vainglorious. They were contemporaries and had gone to sea as boys within a year of one another. Until they were both well into their thirties, the name more likely to be recognised by the public was that of Edward Pellew rather than Horatio Nelson. The reason was Pellew's genius for frigate command. In a trio of ships, *Nymphe*, *Arethusa* and *Indefatigable*, he had established ascendancy over the French in single-ship actions at the start of the Revolutionary wars. Years before the fleet battles that revealed Nelson's greatness, Pellew was lauded by the press – especially *The Times* which kept a keen journalistic eye on his exploits – and had a following that included the King as well as defeated French officers who would testify to his humanity, his graciousness in victory. Frigate captains were public figures, their glamour enhanced by the prize money they had won and the damn-your-eyes swagger that went with it, and at that time none was more striking than Pellew. An athletic, warm-hearted man of commanding presence and generous purse, he did then, rather more than Nelson with his sometimes odd appearance – 'like that of an idiot', thought one female admirer – actually look like a national hero.

Twenty years on, a comparison of their images would have shown Nelson on the *Victory*, a slight yet princely figure, encrusted with gold, majestic in his power; and Exmouth – or Pellew, as we may choose to think of him – a bluff squire in rough calico breeches and, as he acknowledged (with a touch of exaggeration, for he could still reach the masthead quicker than many of his men), 'grey as a badger, fat as a pig and running to belly'.

So where, he might have wondered, as his fleet passed down the North African coast to Algiers on the last stage of his Barbary mission, where had it all started to go wrong? There were no simple answers – the wrath of Spencer? the hatred of Troubridge? – to a question that might itself appear rather trite. How Pellew himself traced his rise and fall is not clear. His private letters, breezy and affectionate, give little hint of the ferocious feuds and intriguing that seemed always just across the horizon. But it is clear that the question had come to trouble him. So is the fact that, while Lord Nelson had become a subject of universal veneration, Lord Exmouth was turning in some quarters into a target for vilification. In reputation, the knight errant had become more a robber baron.

Six weeks later, on 24 June, the fleet returned home to Spithead. From despatches already received at the Admiralty, it was apparent that Algiers had not crowned Exmouth's mission with success. Far from having 'finally smoked the horrors of Christian Slavery', the admiral had to report that Omar Bashaw was a far more formidable personality than the rulers of Tunis or Tripoli and had refused to free any of his European captives. Moreover, it transpired, tempers had been lost on both sides, leading to a complete breakdown in negotiations.

Other more explosive accounts from Algiers were also reaching England. The admiral and his entourage, it was said, had been set upon at the Dey's court – had been manhandled by armed thugs known as janissaries. The British consul had been seized and held hostage. Two of Exmouth's captains had actually been beaten up by a mob while out riding.

For the Navy to have suffered such ignominious treatment was without precedent. An American diplomat in London reported that the affair had 'excited universal indignation'. A view was abroad that such a thing could never have happened in Nelson's time. Exmouth's old rivals in the Navy nodded sagely and gloated quietly. They included Sir Sidney Smith, a flamboyant, capricious fellow with whom he had been on terms of cordial dislike since they were frigate captains twenty years earlier. Sir Sidney had made a personal campaign of Christian slavery, had given his opinion that only he could handle the Barbary rulers and was now reminding anyone who would listen that he'd told 'em so.

Exmouth's political foes weighed in. A satirical newspaper portrayed him as a grasping bumpkin, 'a rude, sturdy, boisterous and impudent seaman; a sort of bifrons or Front de Boeuf fellow . . . who always scents out what is to be got and obtains about double his share of it'. The implication was clear: lord or not, little else could be expected from one who had started out a ship's boy from Cornwall.

Four days into this turmoil of recrimination, fresh tidings brought a real bombshell.

Bad as the treatment of the Navy party was, far worse had occurred a few days later. On 23 May, hundreds of Sicilian fishermen, given an assurance of British protection, came ashore north of Algiers to celebrate Ascension Day. The Dey's soldiers arrived to detain them and gunfire broke out. About 200 honorary British citizens had been massacred.

Within a week of his return, Exmouth was on a coach back to Spithead. If he had his critics at the Admiralty, he had supporters too and they had given him one last mission: to punish the Algerines and liberate all Christian slaves. That he would fail seemed quite probable. He had seen no real fighting for almost twenty years, had never commanded a major fleet action and, if it came to conflict, he would be attempting the most ambitious attack of its kind since the Battle of Copenhagen. Yet he exulted as he went.

Few realised that Exmouth's final campaign was also a personal crusade. Like any seaman, he was familiar with the lateen sails of the Barbary xebecs that preyed on vulnerable European and American vessels. Quite how many Christians had been taken into slavery over the previous three centuries was, and remains, uncertain, although academic studies have put it at well over a million. Thanks to naval power, British seamen were by and large safe. But there had been a time when the xebecs had ranged far to the north. When Edward Pellew was a lad, Cornish folklore was rich in tales of corsairing raids on land and sea in which some 10,000 seamen and coastal residents had been enslaved. Among them was Thomas Pellow, a ship's boy who spent twenty-three years in Barbary, returning home to write a memoir of his captivity and dying a few years before Edward's birth. Thomas had been kin, a member of an extended Cornish clan.

So Lord Exmouth had his cause – and he had his challenge. Algiers was a walled citadel, with cannon bristling from fortified batteries. Nelson, victor of Copenhagen, had declared that the minimum force needed to subdue it would be ten ships of the line. Exmouth had made his own assessment, based on a study of the port, and was setting out with five.

He knew the risks. He had wealth, title, estate and family, but what mattered now was reputation and here was one last chance to reclaim it. Should he fail, he had no wish to return; privately he had expressed more than once a desire to die on his quarterdeck.

That he contemplated such a fate is indicated by the last letter he wrote a few hours before sailing. Dated 20 July and addressed to his eldest son, Pownoll, it began, 'When this reaches you the Father who loves you will be no more . . .'

It was a fond and touching farewell from a man for whom family and the Royal Navy had always rivalled one another in importance. However, it also tends to raise a suspicion that Exmouth may have been considering death in battle as an alternative to disgrace, rather than as the final, sublime glory won by Nelson. A single line at the last hinted at the demons that beset and haunted him:

> I have been <u>basely & vilely belied</u>, but Truth will at last prevail for I am innocent.

PART ONE
EMERGENCE

A Turbulent Boy, 1757–1775

It may be said of more than one great seafarer that he was born to the sea, but the life of Edward Pellew was virtually defined by it. He was born beside the sea, he died by the sea, and for all but a few months of the seventy-seven years in between he was either on it or in sight of it. He had taken his first steps on the quarterdeck of his father's brig as a small boy. So it was perhaps appropriate that his earliest rite of passage, one marking a disastrous turn in his family's fortunes, was a voyage.

In the spring of 1765 – some fifty years before the events previously described – a widow and her six children were preparing for a journey across southern England. Following the death of her husband, Constantia Pellew was returning to her family home and faced the daunting prospect of transporting her little brood the entire breadth of the land, from Dover in the south-east, to Penzance in the extreme south-west, a distance of 300 miles through the countryside, by coach and cart. In the event, because of Samuel Pellew's seafaring connections, word was passed around the taverns of Dover and they were found a far easier passage down the coast, by sea.

Edward Pellew and his sister Catherine had been born in Dover eight years earlier, on 19 April 1757. Although a twin, he grew sturdily and proved his fighting spirit early on by surviving a bout of smallpox with no worse effect than a pockmarked face. His father's death was a sterner test. Samuel Pellew had been a captain in the maritime postal service based at Dover, a member of a powerful seafaring clan and a somewhat piratical figure: packet captains were not always respectable, being sometimes complicit in smuggling and other illegal profiteering; but they were usually prosperous.[1] Samuel's death cost the family their sense of well-being, and any assurance as to the future. His widow had no option but to turn to her parents for support.

The tiny thatched cottage where Edward spent the next five years still stands on the western outskirts of Penzance, a charming relic of the sort favoured as a retreat by today's urban dwellers. Even then it was no hovel. Though snug for its nine occupants, it was quite substantial for one of the tenants of the Lord of Alverton Manor: the six children slept above a barn, there were two small bedrooms for Constantia and her parents, and a fire kept them warm around the table downstairs. Nor did the children experience other aspects of the grinding poverty known to most families deprived of their breadwinner, for Constantia's father was not without means. In a home where both food and education were available, they were far from being consigned to the lowest order of English society.

Over those years Edward harvested apples for tenant farmers, herded cows and attended school. But a boy used to gazing out on an infinite blue was never content looking in on farms and orchards; and, progressively, he sought to escape from this pastoral, back to the soothing of the sea. Much more painful than their new austerity was evidence of his family's continued disintegration.

Constantia is described in family memoirs as a woman of extraordinary spirit. That may have been a euphemism for heartlessness, or at least a lack of emotional connection with her six children. Still a relatively young widow, she married secondly a Penzance man named Samuel Woodis, a gardener and a mercer – and a bit of a chancer; and because he would not accept her offspring under his roof she moved away from them, which seemed like another abandonment. The match was a bad one, 'imprudent' it was said. Woodis had little money and may have hoped to profit by the connection. If so he miscalculated. Constantia's father, Edward Langford, wrote her out of his will and she and her new husband later ran into financial difficulties.[2]

The distress of Constantia's children was far greater. One said that, by the marriage, she 'deprived [them] of their remaining parent and threw them upon the world with scanty resources, and almost without a friend'.[3] The effect on Edward – aged ten when his mother left the cottage at Alverton – can be seen as a thread running through his life: in boyhood it was reflected in a kind of bewildered pugnacity; in adulthood it endured as a fierce loyalty to family that over-rode all other considerations.

Tales attaching to the early years of historical figures, of bold deeds that chime with the known man, are properly regarded with suspicion. In Edward Pellew's case, though, the folklore has some resonance, combining accounts of boyish escapades with hints of a darker side. He was a strapping, boisterous lad, quick with his fists and known for using them against others twice his size. At the same time he lorded it over smaller ones, and while he would also act as their protector, they had to demonstrate fealty; already, it might be said, he exhibited the tendencies of a ship's commander. Many years later, an old schoolfellow still harboured ambivalent feelings about the boy who had gone on to win national renown, writing: 'I confess I rather stood in awe of him; though with his high spirit he had a very kind heart'; and, more revealingly: 'Pellew would never suffer the weak to be trampled upon . . . But I think he once thrashed me.'[4]

Among these vulnerable boys in the background we may glimpse the first of Edward's dependants, and a key figure in his life – his younger brother Israel.

They were four brothers in all. Samuel stood apart, being the eldest and receiving the benefit of what financial means there were. Edward, the second-born, took the two youngest, Israel and John, under his wing. Well into adulthood Israel remained there, overshadowed in every way by the brother sixteen months his senior. In this intense boyhood, the two sisters, Catherine and Jane, are rarely visible. The children grew up under the hand of their grandmother, Katherine, with the patriarchal figure of her husband in the background.

Had he been a boy in any other part of England, Edward's visceral connection to the sea might have lain dormant; but Cornwall had an especially rich seafaring tradition, based on its fishing grounds and on its south-west exposure, which opened on shipping lanes leading to the great world beyond. This hinterland was a life-shaping force in other ways too. Cornish folk had in their isolation a regional identity that many saw as a kind of nationhood – a language, a local pride and yet strangely also an ardent loyalty to the distant Crown that had been manifested during the Civil War. Even 'the lower classes', local historians asserted, 'employed in pursuits which require observation and judgment, and familiarized to danger in their mines and fisheries, are peculiarly thoughtful and intrepid'. Similar qualities were doubtless to be found among common folk elsewhere. What still makes this relevant is how it resonates with the character of young Pellew.

While Edward's schooling was desultory he was clearly bright, although in his state of rebellion that went barely noticed. He would abscond regularly from school to go down to the fishing quay at Penzance, where his toughness was admired and, a childhood friend recalled, he was 'taught to be a famous boxer by his friends the sailors'. Here, too, restored to the water, Ned 'would spring into the first boat he found afloat, cast off the painter, and away to sea'.[5] Unusually among seamen, he became a strong swimmer, and his affinity with the sea was enlarged – for it would please him not only to be on it, but in it.

Matters came to a head when he was sent away to the grammar school in Truro and, perhaps because this was one upheaval too many, became a fist-flailing fury. After various scraps, he beat another boy badly enough to be sentenced to a flogging by the head. Rather than submit, he ran away, back to Alverton, where he announced he was going to sea. He was thirteen.

The decision was not welcomed by his grandfather. That devout old man had hoped he would go into trade, and if his admonition, as related by family lore, sounds somewhat apocryphal – 'Do you know that you may be answerable to God

Cape Cornwall from Land's End. This scene, a few miles from where
Edward Pellew grew up, would greet him throughout his life as he
was homeward bound.

for every enemy you kill? And if I can read your character you
will kill a great many!' – it is clear the boy went to sea without
help from him. Langford established trusts of £200 for each
grandchild, but until Pellew reached his majority he would have
no financial support.[6] In a Navy officer's career, that signified.

The day after Christmas in 1770 a sturdy adolescent came on
board the frigate *Juno* at Spithead. A gale bringing rain blew
across the deck and it was very, very cold.[7] Below he was met by
a sight that to modern eyes would have resembled a grotesquerie
by Hogarth.

The gundeck of a 32-gun frigate was home along its 130-
foot length to some 200 men. It was unlit and unheated, and
they were by and large unwashed. As well as being gloomy and
bitterly cold, it was damp, fetid and so cramped the men had, in
effect, to sleep in shifts. Each hammock was allowed a width of
14 inches – although because of the watch system the men had
in theory 28 inches in which to spread themselves. A ship of war

was still one of the most crowded habitats to be found anywhere in the supposedly civilised world. When the Portsmouth women came on board it was for reasons of space as well as discretion that their services were enjoyed between the carriages of the guns. Scarcely more room was available forward on the foc'sle, where were found the off-watch leisure area and the 'heads', where men squatted over the bows and defecated directly into the sea.

Virtually every Englishman who rose to high command in the great age of sail entered this hugger-mugger as a boy. Three weeks after Pellew, a twelve-year-old midshipman named Horatio Nelson joined his first ship at the Nore.[8] What sets Pellew apart in such company is that at a time when either fortune or patronage was a prerequisite for promotion, he began with neither. Because this runs counter to the accepted version of his entry to the Navy provided by his biographer Northcote Parkinson, and because it is a key to the man who became Lord Exmouth, it needs exploring.[9]

Quite how Pellew came to be on the *Juno* at all is uncertain, but it would seem that, in the autumn of 1770, her captain, John Stott, was recruiting hands on a visit to his native Cornwall when they met. Now, it has been said that the Pellew clan in Flushing were involved in this vital first step and that, moreover, their influence secured protection from Stott for the boy, ensuring his passage to the quarterdeck. There is no evidence for this. While the Pellews were an established seafaring family, the fortune made by Samuel's father as a merchant captain had been dissipated; the Pellew family in general, living a day's journey from Penzance, seem to have taken no great interest in Samuel's children at this time. The Pellew name may have counted for something with Stott at their meeting, but the lad joining the *Juno* received no preference from her captain.

That tends to be confirmed by the ship's muster. Boys marked for advancement entered as midshipmen or captain's servants, starting an apprenticeship in which they would do time in the tops while being spared more rigorous service. On the *Juno*, no fewer than seven boys had been designated as captain's servants, and not all were well-connected. Some had come from the Marine Society, a charity founded partly to get urchins off the streets and give them an occupation.[10] Edward Pellew entered as the purser's servant, making him more junior than even the lowliest of these.[11]

Another sign of his low ranking is seen in an entry stating that he had been provided with 'slops' (clothes), at a cost to his master, the purser, of 13 shillings and twopence.[12] In short, he entered with virtually no clothes, and no money, as well as no status. All these factors tell against Northcote Parkinson's conclusion, that 'it would be a mistake to suppose that he started his naval career under peculiar difficulties . . . His social position was rather above than below the average. He was poor but only moderately so.'[13]

In the raw world of the lower deck, Pellew could look after himself. But what mattered most in the career of a young sea officer was 'interest', in other words influential relatives, and he had none of those. Among the Navy's natural hierarchy he was, and would always be, an outsider.

To start with, he and Nelson did have one thing in common. Both had entered in a general mobilisation arising from a crisis after Spain's seizure of the Falkland Islands, a British colony so insignificant (as Samuel Johnson pointed out at the time) few had ever heard of it. But if Pellew's imagination was fired with visions of battle and glory, he was to be rapidly disabused. The *Juno* stayed at Spithead for another three months, during which he discovered that routine rather than action was the regular part of a seaman's life. This time was notable in one respect, however, for marking the start of a lifelong friendship.

Frank Cole was the same age as Pellew. Although without his physical advantages – he seems to have been somewhat sickly – he was better connected, and had entered as captain's servant. More significantly he was Cornish, hailing from Marazion, a fishing village across the bay from Penzance, and over the next five years Edward and Frank became inseparables.

Companionship is a neglected aspect of the seafarer's world. In our time Jack Tar's life has become synonymous with misery. The general perception is of a form of slavery defined by press gang and lash, disease and drunkenness, and it bears noting, therefore, that most seamen embraced it willingly, some heartily. Beyond the simple incentives – free food and drink, and medical care of sorts – lay the prospect of adventure, prize money and membership of a proud and powerful tribe.

That tribalism now enfolded Pellew, providing the security lacking in his life so far, as well as the fellowship of shared endeavour and a theatre for his abilities. From the time he went to sea, boyish belligerence gave way to aspects of his nature that were its more true counterpoint, warmth of heart and generosity of spirit. While he would make enemies – and often dangerously potent ones – his real and greater gift was for friendship.

After agonisingly dull months and false starts at anchor, the *Juno* sailed in the spring of 1771 and immediately Pellew was liberated. From scraping the ship's sides and holystoning decks, he went aloft and found what he was born for.

Of the qualities required by an able seaman in the age of sail, one in particular stands out: physical prowess. Climbing ratlines to the yardarms and inching out along them, unfurling a weight of billowing canvas and hauling it in, balancing on footropes while swaying eighty feet above the sea – and all in conditions ranging from light squalls to sail-shredding gales – took not only nerve but strength and agility.

Still only thirteen, Pellew was big enough to pass for sixteen in the *Juno*'s muster book.[14] He was also naturally athletic, revelling in exertion, and his title of purser's servant was nominal, his duties a mere stepping stone to the real business of becoming an able seaman. It was not long before he was to be seen racing to the tops and out on the yards, performing gymnastic feats with a wild-eyed exhilaration which, enacted in front of gnarled older hands, may first have been regarded with tolerant amusement, but in time won fond admiration. A lieutenant, recalling how the boy Pellew used to sport in the tops, marvelled: 'He was like a squirrel.'[15]

One of the better descriptions of life on the lower deck was left by an able seaman of the time (for if tars were usually illiterate there are notable exceptions):

> A vessel of war contains a little community of human beings, isolated, for the time being, from the rest of mankind. This community is governed by laws peculiar to itself . . . Each task has its man, and each man his place. A ship contains a set of human machinery, in which every man is a wheel, a band or a crank, all moving with wonderful regularity and precision to the will of its machinist – the all-powerful captain.[16]

The all-powerful captain . . . In the first of these omnipotent characters to figure in his life, Pellew was fortunate. John Stott might have paid little attention to the Cornish boys, left to make their way among the seamen, rated ordinary and able, the gunners, carpenters, sailmakers and the rest; but he was a decent commander, which is to say an able seafarer who kept his men busy, seldom lashed them and identified ability.[17] When Pellew and Cole came to his notice for their talents he rewarded them by promotion; and later, when he did punish them, it is fair to assume there was good reason.

The *Juno* was accompanied by the *Florida*, a supply ship, and the sloop *Hound*, a slow dog that had to be hastened along by signals from the frigate's cannon. Nevertheless, after sailing from Tenerife on 16 May, they made steady south-westerly progress, through intermittent squalls which kept hands occupied in the tops and the discovery of a leak in *Juno*'s hull that required days of exertion at the pumps until it could be located and made good. Completion of the Atlantic crossing was recorded by the log on 17 July, 'Southward of the Sugar Loaf Hill. Distance of the shore 3 leagues. Moderate and clear.'

Trivial in itself, entries like this, recording *Juno*'s arrival in Rio, are revealing of a larger picture. Every day of Pellew's service

– or any other seafarer's – is recorded in journal form, a diary of events dramatic or mundane, showing his exact whereabouts and doings, whether handling foresails in his youth or commanding a man of war in his prime. Ship's logs may tell us what men ate on a given day, who suffered the captain's displeasure and was flogged, and who died and was seen over the side by his shipmates (who would then auction his few possessions among themselves). The logs cast a light into hidden corners of battle and exploration and all the smaller dramas of the wooden world hundreds of years ago.

It was a ship's log that recorded the prosaic end to the first Falklands crisis. Spain had backed down even before the departure from Spithead of *Juno* and her consorts, and when they came in sight of Saunders Island in mid-September, the final act was a formality.[18]

> September 16: At noon the captain & a party of Marines went on shore and took possession of Port Egmont. The Marines after hoisting His Majesty's colours fired 3 volleys of small arms.

It was more anti-climax than high drama, but Pellew and his friend Cole could at least console themselves that they had been in at the end. Among the other ships mobilised for war, the *Raisonable* (with young Midshipman Nelson) never stirred from Chatham.

To top off Pellew's first sea adventure, the *Juno* flew home, studding sails filled, coming in sight of the Lizard, England's southernmost point, on a hazy winter's day. On 12 December, the log records, the crew was paid off and 300 pounds of fresh beef and 30 butts of beer were received on board. So, too, no doubt, were boatloads of women from Portsmouth – and the gundeck was filled with cheer and tobacco smoke as they fiddled and danced and drank. Savouring it all were the boys, Pellew and Cole. They were home for Christmas.

Pellew returned to Penzance at the end of 1771 to find the family circumstances had taken a turn for the better. His grandfather

Edward Langford had prospered, and Pellew's elder brother Samuel, now aged sixteen, was being educated for a medical career. The old man's disapproval of the sea life may have lost its edge, for Edward's younger brother, thirteen-year-old Israel, had just followed him into the Navy, while the youngest, John, twelve, was set on joining the Army. With Edward's twin Catherine and Jane, nine, they could all gather beside the festive hearth to hear of his adventures.

It is unlikely that their mother, Constantia, joined them. She had by now produced another set of twins, but her husband, Samuel Woodis, was, it seems, still ostracised by her family and his business may already have been in trouble.[19]

Whatever the ups and downs of this return home, Pellew's paramount concern was when it would end so he might get back to sea. Seamen then did not join the Navy, they signed on to a ship, and the passing of the Falklands crisis meant an end to mobilisation. Britain was at peace with the world, stringency was in the air and Pellew was far from being the only young fellow eyeing his prospects with anxiety. Many others with far weightier backing than he, midshipmen and higher, found themselves ashore and unable to find a ship.

Fortunately, his old captain had a new command. By summer Stott was back in Cornwall, recruiting again, and signed on not only Pellew but Cole as well.[20] Stott had been given the *Alarm*, a 32-gun frigate with an innovative copper-sheathed hull that lent her speed. Her most recent captain had been one John Jervis. (It was a small world, this Navy. Jervis – the future Lord St Vincent – was to play a significant role in Pellew's life, first as his ardent supporter, later as an implacable foe.)

Pellew was back at Spithead on 3 August, coming on board just in time to be given six months' pay in advance and two weeks' leave of absence with the rest of the crew.[21] Having passed his fifteenth birthday, he was perhaps also of an age to appreciate some of the earthier pleasures offered in the lanes and taverns of Portsmouth.

*

A few weeks after sailing in the *Alarm*, Pellew was rated able. Now the complete seaman, he wore loose canvas breeches known as trowsers, a white checked linen shirt with a bright knotted handkerchief at the neck, and a blue double-breasted jacket. A second jacket, coated with tar for waterproofing in foul weather, had earned the British seaman his popular name, Jack Tar. Six months later, aged sixteen, Pellew was made up to master's mate.[22] Whether because he had performed outstandingly in his captain's eyes, or Stott was favouring a fellow Cornish native, this was a meteoric rise.

The *Alarm* was bound for the Mediterranean, calling at ports which were to become familiar – Lisbon, Gibraltar, Mahon, Leghorn (Livorno), Genoa, and, because a state of peace existed with France, Toulon and Ajaccio (where a toddler named Napoleon was taking his first steps towards European domination). A year into their cruise, she came to anchor off Algiers and Pellew was presented with his first view of this formidable bastion.

Barbary – the name came from the Arabic word Berber for the inhabitants of North Africa – occupied a dark place in the minds of seamen. Algiers was the most powerful of the Barbary States, with a fearsome reputation among the people of the Mediterranean, some 175,000 of whom had been enslaved over the previous century, even though the corsairs' power was by then on the wane.[23] But when their reach was greatest, in the seventeenth century, Barbary corsairs had ventured as far north as the British Isles and British seamen, too, had seen thousands of their number taken into shackles on galleys, the great majority from Cornwall and the West Country.[24] Among them was Thomas Pellow.

Thomas was a fairly typical member of the Pellew clan – other variations of the name, French in origin, included Pellaw, Pellor and Peliew. Born near Falmouth and with seafaring connections, he was eleven when he joined an uncle's ship, bound for Genoa in 1715 but captured by corsairs off Cape Finisterre. Just what occurred over the twenty-three years he spent as a captive in

Barbary, whether or not he embroidered his experiences, has been the subject of debate among historians; but by Pellow's own admission he enjoyed sufficient freedom after converting to Islam and joining the Sultan's army of European renegades that he married and eventually was able to escape and return to Cornwall. In writing about his sufferings, Pellow tended to pass over these ambiguities while making much of 'the *Manners* and *Customs* of the Moors, the astonishing *Tyranny* and *Cruelty* of their Emperors'. The result became a best-seller in a genre now known as the captivity narrative.[25] This epic cannot have escaped the attention of one who was not only a fellow seaman but a kinsman; nor would it have failed to impress him. Long before it became his mission to eradicate Christian slavery, Edward Pellew was aware of the slaves' plight.

There was no inkling of trouble when the *Alarm* put in at Algiers in October 1773. A peace treaty had existed for almost a century and Britain kept a consul at the court of the Dey. Underlying tensions became clear, however, when the consul was rowed out, bearing a letter to Stott from the Dey demanding that any slaves escaping to the ship should be returned.[26] A veiled threat was offset by a cordial gesture, as the log records:

October 16: Rec'd a present from the Dey for the Ship's company – 3 Small Bullocks, 9 Sheep, some bread and vegetables.

While these offerings were eaten Stott went ashore for an audience with the Dey, whose warmth turned to wrath when the captain refused to undertake to return slaves seeking sanctuary. Stott was dismissed. Next day, the consul came on board. He had been expelled.

This spat, one of many to come, had no enduring impact on diplomatic ties with Barbary. On the lower deck, though, the Dey's capricious despotism was remembered by the young Pellew. The Navy was still some years from fashioning British mastery at sea, and for the time being its seamen remained as susceptible to the utterly unpredictable as any others.

*

Five years after taking ship together as boys, Pellew and Cole had become as close in their respective careers as they were in friendship. They were both eighteen and had risen in virtually simultaneous promotions, first being rated able, then master's mates and finally midshipmen. This last was the most significant, especially for one with so little influence as Pellew, for it marked him as a potential officer. At this point an incident occurred that led to Stott sending the pair simultaneously from the ship in disgrace.

Two versions of what happened while the *Alarm* was at Mahon in August 1774 have been passed down. Both are partial to Pellew (coming as they did from his family) and neither is very convincing. The ship's records, often revealing, do not help, for the muster is opaque and the log for the relevant period has disappeared.

At the bottom of it, seemingly, was a mistress whom Captain Stott kept on the *Alarm*. According to the first version, Cole had an altercation with the lady after driving her pet fowl off the quarterdeck.[27] The second is that Cole drew a lewd caricature of her and was found by the captain chortling over it, schoolboy fashion, with Pellew.[28] The common feature is that Cole was the object of Stott's wrath, that the captain turned him out of the ship, and that Pellew only went because he insisted gallantly on sharing his friend's fate.

This does not quite square with the little surviving evidence. Pellew and Cole are noted in the muster as having been discharged 'in lieu', which clarifies nothing.[29] But both came to Stott's attention again a few years later, when each was being examined for lieutenant. Cole was able to produce 'journals and certificates of diligence' from previous captains – including, presumably, Stott. However, Pellew was not. Admiralty records show the board was told his 'want of journals and captain's certificates' could be overlooked under a special dispensation.[30] There was good reason for this, because he had just become a hero. But the question does arise why Stott did not provide a certificate for one who had served him well for five years; the most likely conclusion is that, whatever passed between the captain's mistress and the two mids, Pellew rather than Cole was the culprit.

The cause was not, however, serious enough to warrant the opprobrium of the *Alarm*'s two aristocratic lieutenants, Keppel and Seymour, who treated it all as a prank and helped the errant youths with money and advice when they were sent ashore at Mahon. They got home by signing on aboard a merchantman.

Pellew and Cole would stay the closest of friends, and serve together again as captains. But at this point their careers diverged. Pellew was poised for a life-changing twist of fortune . . . and his first taste of war.

2.

War for the Lakes, 1776–1780

⊶⊷

While Pellew was learning the ropes in the Mediterranean, world-shaking events had been unfolding across the Atlantic. By the time he reached home, late in 1775, tensions between the American colonists and the Crown had turned to conflict. He may have been in time to hear of George III's declaration to Parliament on 26 October that the rebellious colonists were intent on 'establishing an independent empire'; he was certainly among the Navy's early recruits as it prepared for war.

He was, however, starting over again – at the bottom. Though there might have been no lasting disgrace arising from his dismissal by Stott, there could be no question of picking up where he had left the *Alarm*, as a midshipman with the potential for promotion. At Chatham, on a bitter day in February 1776, twenty-two men described in the muster as 'the Totnes volunteers' came aboard the frigate *Blonde*. They were a motley crew, drawn from Devon and Cornwall and including six landsmen – which is to say complete lubbers – as well as a few experienced hands. Their chief distinction was having entered freely rather than being rounded up in a press. Among them was Ned Pellew. He was back in the tops as a common seaman, rated able.[1]

But fate had thrown him a wild card. The *Blonde*'s captain was one Philemon Pownoll, a rising star among a brilliant new officer generation. Pownoll was more than just a dashing commander – though his part in taking one of the richest prizes in history, the Spanish treasure ship *Hermione* in 1762 with a mere sloop, was no small distinction.[2] He was an innovator. Not all his experiments were successful, notably his attempt to distil potable water from the sea. However, in observing talent on the lower deck, and giving it the incentive to shine, he was well ahead of his time.

Pellew came to his attention early on, possibly through the young man's increasingly theatrical bent. The story was told how, just before the *Blonde* sailed for America, carrying General John Burgoyne, the Army commander came on board and was astonished to see, among the hands manning the tops in salute, one performing a handstand out on a yardarm.[3] This first glimpse was the start of an improbable but warm association between the general and a lowly seaman. Aged twenty, Pellew had entered his manhood. Big, confident and with a touch of the show-off about him, the 'squirrel' was becoming a lion.

Pownoll soon took note. Within weeks of entering the *Blonde*, Pellew was among a few able hands identified by the captain for advancement. He was briefly made up to midshipman, then reduced to master's mate two months later, while another hand was given a trial as midshipman.[4] Pownoll, it seems, thought Pellew's exuberance required tempering. It is a mark of his wisdom that Pellew himself later recognised Pownoll had been right.

On 5 April, the *Blonde* sailed in convoy with twenty transport ships, carrying troops to war – not in America, but Canada.

The American Revolution was the making of Edward Pellew. He would be unique among British seamen in being commended for gallantry in a battle fought not at sea but on a lake; and for going on to win his spurs with the Army. Arguably, no other naval officer would have desired such landlubberly distinctions. They were crucial, however, to the rise of one who was ever the outsider.

His duties took him far inland. He was often to be found felling, dragging, hauling or carrying timber across an unruly landscape of forests, rapids and snow. The terrain was tough, the conditions were brutal – hunger and hardship were constant, and months were spent in icebound isolation amid temperatures falling to -30 °C. All this was almost a sideshow to events further south, where George Washington was conducting the war against William Howe, the British commander. But the battle for the lakes on the Canada border seemed crucial enough at the time, and though it was never going to affect the eventual outcome, it might have delayed it.

British strategy was based on the principle of isolating New England from the rest of the rebellious colonies. The key to this, in turn, was controlling the waterways running north to south between Quebec and New York – the St Lawrence–Lake Champlain–Hudson corridor. The previous December, an American army had crossed the Maine wilderness to attack Quebec – a bold project which, though it ended in defeat, left the force still in effect besieging the British stronghold. On 8 June 1776, a few days after *Blonde* came to off Quebec, delivering Burgoyne's army, the siege was lifted and the Americans retreated to Montreal.

With matters thus in the balance, and just a few months in hand before winter again froze the waterways, Burgoyne's objective was to drive the Americans from Canada and shift his troops the 120-mile length of Lake Champlain from north to south, then to pursue the rebels down the Hudson, all the way to New York. His chief obstacle was a maritime force under Benedict Arnold which had established control of the lake. On its shores a race now began as the Navy embarked on a boat-building programme that would enable them to match the Americans. To this end, men were sent from the fleet off Canada for what became known as the Lakes Service.

By 12 August the *Blonde* had edged up the St Lawrence to Trois Rivières, a former French settlement seized six years earlier as Britain consolidated its control over Quebec. Here a longboat put off and Captain Pownoll wrote in his log: 'Sent a mate and 15 men for the service of the Lakes.'[5] Pellew was the mate, and this was his chance.

His commanding officer was Lieutenant John Schanck. A latecomer to the Navy with an artisan background and now in his late thirties, Schanck was a curiosity. He had none of the polish associated with the officer class and, like Pellew, was without connections. His gifts were for carpentry and ship design, and both were fully exploited on Lake Champlain. A rudimentary shipyard had been established at St John's (now St Jean), the northernmost navigable point of the lake, where, with 700 seamen and Marines, Schanck was supervising the construction of a flotilla to do battle for Champlain.

It was a prodigious feat. The shipyard lay thirty miles south-east of Montreal and was cut off from it by a series of rapids, so everything required at St John's in the way of stores and equipment had to be carried across the last twelve miles. So did a ship, the *Inflexible*, of 180 tons, and two schooners, *Maria* and *Carleton*, which were brought up the river from Montreal to a spot called Chambly, then dismantled, manhandled around the rapids to St John's and reassembled. Guns for these vessels, including some 24-pounders, had likewise to be carried. To the fore during this remarkable exercise was the *Blonde*'s strapping master's mate. Lieutenant Schank noticed him soon enough. And such was Pellew's activity and – that especially naval quality – zeal, he became Schanck's right-hand man. Here was the start of another lifelong friendship.

Here, too, was a worthy outlet for Pellew's athleticism. At St John's, where every day counted and vessels were taking shape beside Lake Champlain even as the summer slipped away, more was at stake than mere display. By mid-September the *Inflexible* had been relaunched and Pellew was high on a tripod sheer, trying to raise the mainmast, when the entire assembly collapsed. He had time just to leap clear, so instead of falling to almost certain death on the deck, he plunged into the water. 'Pellew! He's gone!' Schank exclaimed, for it was taken for granted seamen were not swimmers. Then a head burst clear of the water and, to cheers, Pellew swam back to the side.[6]

In addition to rebuilding the ship and two schooners, Schanck's corps hewed and raised a flotilla of almost thirty fighting vessels out of the surrounding forests by October. Surveying their handiwork, their commander, Sir Charles Douglas, the senior

Navy officer in Canada, declared that it 'almost exceeds belief'. Morale might have been boosted by the optimistic if flawed reports received about events to the south – 'of our troops beating the rebels at New York and taking their general, Lee, prisoner'.[7] But there was also an aspect of the lakes campaign that showed British tars at their best. Douglas wrote that they had:

> ... far beyond the limits of their duty, exerted themselves to the utmost on this great and toilsome occasion; nor has a man of that profession uttered a single word expressive of discontent amid all the hardships they have undergone.[8]

Their exertions had, nevertheless, occupied the entire summer. When it sailed from St John's on 9 October, the flotilla was certainly strong enough for its purpose, to win control of the lake from Benedict Arnold's naval force. The question was whether it was already too late in the year for the overall objective to be achieved.

Pellew had won the approbation of one, fairly junior, officer at St John's. Thanks to his first battle, he came to the attention of a far more influential circle. A small-scale operation with a good deal at stake was a fine theatre in which to be seen as able, courageous and zealous, and he seized his moment.

The flotilla proceeding south on Lake Champlain under a following wind was led by Captain Thomas Pringle in the schooner, *Maria*. The second schooner, *Carleton*, was in the hands of twenty men from the *Blonde*, including Pellew, under Lieutenant James Dacres. As senior lieutenant, and in recognition of his labours at St John's, Schanck had the *Inflexible*. In their wake came twenty-five gunboats and dozens of bateaux carrying troops.

Arnold, the American commodore, had formed up his flotilla line of battle in a narrow strait between the western shore of Lake Champlain and the little island of Valcour. His fifteen armed vessels, including three schooners, were not only outnumbered but outgunned, with their heaviest weapons 18-pounders against

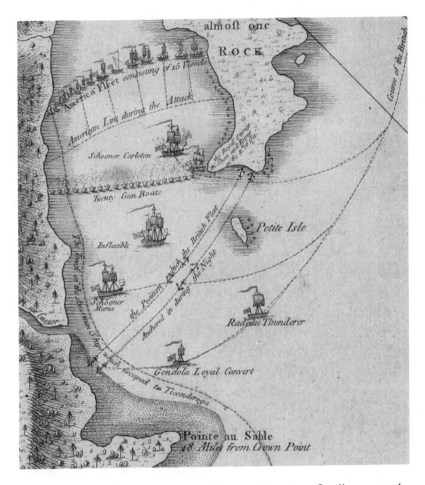

The action on Lake Champlain where an American flotilla emerged from the strait off Valcour Island to confront British vessels was Pellew's first experience of battle.

24-pounders. Pringle, however, came close to squandering his advantage. Early on the morning of 11 October, he passed to the east of the island without discovering the Americans. It took two of Arnold's schooners to emerge from the strait, firing their guns, to attract his attention. But now the British flotilla had to work up against the wind to come to action.

The gunboats, single-masted and easier to manoeuvre, were first into position, and suffered severely under the Americans' fire while the larger vessels were still battling against the wind. It was the *Carleton* that came to their relief. Soon after noon, and long before *Inflexible* and *Maria* could get up, Dacres inserted his schooner in front of the gunboats and dropped anchor opposite the Americans. *Carleton* began to engage broadside-to-broadside with a line of schooners, galleys, gondolas and a cutter – her 6-pounders set against double the number of 12-pounders.

Within minutes of finding himself in battle for the first time, Pellew had men falling around him. Dacres went down, then the second-in-command, Brown. And in that moment he was not only in action, he was in command.

Few first-hand records exist of the Battle of Valcour Island and the only source for Pellew's part in it is Sir Charles Douglas, who was not even there and was relying on what he had learnt from those who were. What can be said is the mate's conduct made a profound impression on all of them.

The *Carleton* remained blazing away from her position, 'nearly in the middle of the rebel half-moon, anchored with a spring on her cable'.[9] Her hands had been together on the *Blonde*, they knew one another and they trusted the shipmate who had taken command. Their gunnery was also good enough to hit vessels in the American line repeatedly, including the schooner *Revenge*. At the same time, the *Carleton* was coming under additional fire from riflemen on the shore and would suffer a frightful rate of casualties – 70 per cent. But they stayed in position, exchanging blow for blow while being steadily withered, until Pringle observed their plight while striving vainly to work the *Maria* up into the strait and signalled Pellew to withdraw.

This posed a new test. Although the cable holding *Carleton* at anchor was cut, she would not come round. Pellew, rather than order one of his fellows into danger, then exposed himself by going out on the bowsprit to pull the jib around to catch the wind. Still she stayed broadside on, receiving fire, until two of the gunboats came up to the rescue. Again Pellew himself swung out on the bowsprit, casting them a rope so she might be towed clear.

In the meantime, while *Carleton*'s gunners kept their posts, the outcome had been resolved by Schanck's perseverance in *Inflexible*. Coming up with the American vessels late in the afternoon, she introduced 24-pounders to the battle, at which, Douglas reported, 'Five broadsides silenced their whole line.'[10]

That night Arnold withdrew under the cover of a fog blanketing the lake, but his escape was brief. Pringle caught up with him at the southern end and a two-hour action sealed matters. Of Arnold's fifteen vessels, all but four were sunk, taken or burned.

The Battle of Valcour Island was the US Navy's first action. Though it counted as a defeat, Arnold had held up the British and left eighty dead against forty Americans. Crucially, his presence on the lake had thwarted an army advance down the Hudson towards New York until another winter had passed.

For Pellew, too, it was a transforming encounter. A mere rating, he had taken command, exposed himself repeatedly throughout and demonstrated judgement as well as the sort of hot courage that swung battles. He had also shown another quality – luck. Despite his size and his prominence, he had come through unscathed while eight out of the *Carleton*'s crew of twenty were dead and six wounded. In a highly superstitious fraternity, that counted.

He had also seized his moment. Exhilaration at victory and survival was followed by recognition in the form of high praise from Dacres, who survived his wound, and Sir Guy Carleton, the Governor of Quebec, who had observed the action from the flagship. Their reports elicited a letter to Pellew from Douglas, the Navy commander in Quebec:

> The account I have received of your behaviour on board the Carleton schooner in different actions with the Rebels on the Lakes, gives me the warmest satisfaction, and I shall not fail to represent it in the strongest terms to the Earl of Sandwich and also to my Lord Howe and recommend you as well deserving a Commission for your Gallantry.[11]

Pellew could have had no stronger endorsement. Sandwich was First Lord at the Admiralty, Vice-Admiral Howe the Navy commander in America. With testimonials in such exalted quarters, Pellew's promotion to lieutenant was almost assured on his return home. As another savage winter closed in, forcing suspension of hostilities, a glow of achievement sustained him.

He spent the winter of 1776 in Quebec. A large part of the British contingent sailed home, including his own ship, the *Blonde*, taking Burgoyne with her. Pellew had been appointed to command of the *Carleton*, but because she was frozen on the lake he repaired down the St Lawrence where, for the time being, he was entered temporarily on the *Garland*.[12]

Whether his sudden rise to prominence brought with it privileges – access to the relative comforts of the Governor's circle – is not clear. In terms of rank he remained a lowly master's mate, and it is more probable that, as the temperature plummeted to -20 °C in November, he was among the crewmen clustered below decks, beating their hands and huddling together as the river froze over, relieved only by the meagre comforts indicated in the *Garland*'s log:

> Got on board 3 stoves to preserve the People from inclemency of the weather. Abundance of snow. Ice in the river.[13]

It got still colder. Ice froze all activity besides the business of staying warm. But one of Pellew's skills may have been nourished in an otherwise barren winter. He was still with Schanck, and Schanck had a special knowledge of what made a good sailing ship – and how even a bad ship could be made better. As a captain, Pellew would demonstrate a grasp of ship design which may have been instilled over grim, cold evenings with Schanck.

Another bond was also in the making. Pellew had probably met Alexander Broughton while they were still on the lakes. Broughton was senior not only in rank and age – a midshipman and five years older – but came from a quite different class, a wealthy and well-connected Staffordshire family. Whether their friendship would have flourished at sea, even in the comparatively egalitarian environment of the Navy, is an open question. But

Broughton had engaged in all the hardships at St John's – 'ship-building, house-making, cutting down and drawing timber, etc' – as well as serving in the action at Valcour, and had suffered so acutely 'being much exposed to the rain and cold, with severe duty night and day' that his health never entirely recovered.[14] With their shared privations, the strongest friendship of Pellew's life began.

It was not until Burgoyne's return in the spring of 1777 that Quebec operations were resumed. Pellew was reunited at the same time with his brother, John. Aged just seventeen, the youngest of the Pellew boys had arrived with Burgoyne's forces, a plain foot soldier in a regiment recruited in the West Country. He had joined the military in as lowly a role as his older brother had begun his naval career.[15]

If Burgoyne did not immediately recognise the acrobat of the yardarm, he was soon reminded of him as Pellew, commanding the *Carleton* again, helped to land an army of 7,000 men, along with artillery, on the south shore of Lake Champlain for an attack on the Fort Ticonderoga garrison. Burgoyne noted Pellew's new status among his fellows and decided he could be useful on the waterways with a company of seamen. Rather than an officer, it was the master's mate who was asked to accompany the troops and command the Navy contingent.

The operation was doomed before it began. Fatally, no orders had been issued to the British forces in New York to advance up the Hudson to join Burgoyne and so, although the American soldiers were soon driven from Ticonderoga, their retreat created an illusion. There were plenty more where they were going. Burgoyne's army was floundering south, into the arms of a superior force.

Once they left the lake, Pellew and his tars operated on the Hudson, transporting provisions and scouting, while the army moved overland. Sustaining a force of such a size across so extended a line became increasingly challenging. The terrain was tough, disease broke out, desertions began. In six weeks after taking Ticonderoga, the army advanced barely seventy miles before reaching the Hudson, where Pellew and his party were building a bridge. As Burgoyne said to him wryly later, Pellew's bridge would carry them all to disaster.

On crossing the Hudson, they came to a place called Saratoga and the American line where the first of two battles was fought on 18 September. Burgoyne kept the field but lost 600 men, and over the next two weeks was surrounded as American reinforcements arrived on the scene. Amid skirmishing prior to the second battle, John Pellew was killed.

Pellew never wrote about the impact of this tragedy on him and family history is equally silent on the subject. Edward was not close, it is known, to the eldest boy, Samuel, but during the upheavals of their boyhood years he had become devoted to the younger, Israel.[16] Given his powerfully paternalistic bent, he would have felt bitterly the loss of another vulnerable and even younger sibling.

Edward threw himself into the final days of the Quebec army with reckless abandon and a last flourish which took place, fittingly enough, on the Hudson, where the Americans had seized a barge containing 650 barrels of provisions – two thirds of what Burgoyne had left. With a small party in boats, Pellew crossed the river under fire, boarded the barge and recaptured it. According to a witness, the rope broke as they were towing it back – at which Pellew plunged in with another line, secured it, and brought the barge safely in.[17]

Burgoyne himself was watching and wrote to Pellew, congratulating him on:

> . . . the Gallantry and address with which you conducted your attack . . . The Courage displayed by your little party was deserving of the success which attended it; and I send you my sincere thanks, together with that of the Army for the important service you have rendered.[18]

Ultimately, it made no difference. Burgoyne was left with fewer than 4,000 men, outnumbered roughly three to one, cut off and facing another winter without supplies. The council he summoned on 13 October, and to which Pellew was invited, had no option but to accept surrender. Pellew argued that the naval corps ought to be exempt and he should be allowed to lead the tars through the American line, back to Quebec, but was over-ruled.

Burgoyne did, however, grant him one last honour. After the surrender on 17 October, Pellew was sent home with dispatches, sparing him the sufferings of the army during their winter captivity, and allowing him to arrive in London while his exploits were fresh in memory.

The young man who presented himself at the Admiralty in December 1777 cut an unusually bold figure for a master's mate. He had left England a plain seaman, rated able, twenty months earlier. He returned with accolades from the great and powerful, testimonials which claimed attention and, for a while, received it. Howe, the Navy commander in America, had praised 'Your gallant behaviour'.[19] From the Admiralty, Lord Sandwich had written: 'You have been spoken to me for your good conduct in various services in so handsome a manner that I shall receive great pleasure in promoting you to Lieutenant.'[20]

Now, as well as his testimonial from Burgoyne, he brought a valedictory paean from Sir Guy Carleton, describing him as '. . . a young man to whose Gallantry and Merit during two severe Campaigns in this country I cannot do justice'.[21]

Few cases illustrate so clearly why a naval career held out such attractions to able and ambitious commoners in eighteenth-century England. When the Army remained in the control of aristocrats and wealth, Pellew was proof of what might be achieved in the Navy by everyman. Yet, though distinctive, he is at this point still a relatively one-dimensional figure. We see a man of formidable strength and stamina, his youthful bumptiousness channelled into an ardour for service, one who showed not so much courage under fire as utter fearlessness. The voice of the inner man would take more time to emerge.

Pellew would write constantly during his naval life. In addition to a vast body of official correspondence, a good number of personal letters show another side to the man of action – one who wrote vividly and affectionately to friends, fondly to family (albeit in a hand that constantly tests the reader's deciphering skills). However, none of these survive from his early years, and we are left to imagine the terms in which he related his adventures to old friends, like Frank Cole, or his promotion to new ones, like Schanck.

On his return he also renewed contact with another new friend. Alexander Broughton – unlike Schanck, Cole or Pellew himself – came from a high-born family. Still, the bond between them would develop to the point that Pellew could write to 'My Dear Alex . . . my dearest, best of friends', in chatty, confidential tones, as one equal to another. And unlike his other friendships, this one endured in the form of a correspondence more revealing of his nature than any other.[22]

He was duly made lieutenant, but that did not in itself bring further active service. Although he now had advocates he still lacked the ingredient crucial to rapid advancement – 'interest', or the patronage of an influential figure. After France joined the war on the American side, Lord Sandwich had been besieged by petitions for postings. Despite his own aristocratic background, Sandwich had a keen eye for merit and was more impartial in promoting officers than any of his predecessors. But no First Lord could be regardless of interest. That is clear from the dispatch with which he advanced the career of another young officer, for while Horatio Nelson showed charm and ability in rising from lieutenant to captain, he had not yet demonstrated his spectacular gifts for fleet command. What he did have was an uncle, Captain Maurice Suckling, who took the boy on his ship as a midshipman and further shaped his career from a senior post at the Navy Board.[23]

Pellew's euphoria at his own promotion did not last. His first officer posting was to probably the most miserable vessel he ever served in. The *Princess Amelia* was a guardship and, as such, she never stirred from her moorings at Spithead in the ten months he was in her, but took on and disgorged a stream of men – prisoners (Americans and French), and pressed hands in their hundreds. As a lieutenant, Pellew was in all probability engaged in boarding outward-bound ships with a press gang – such as the East Indiamen intercepted on 18 March – and although he would have had no qualms about the practice, the subsequent conduct of resentful men demonstrated it was not the best method to recruit hands. Floggings for fighting and attempted desertion took place regularly on the *Princess Amelia*.[24]

On 5 June 1778 Pellew presented himself in London for the formality of his lieutenant's examination. He could not, as we have seen, produce a certificate of diligence from Captain Stott, but he had more than made up for his discreditable conduct on the *Alarm*, and as for the other requirements – that he could 'Splice, Knot, Reef and Sail and is qualified to the duty of an Able Seaman' – few candidates could have been better practised.[25]

For the first time, too, he had some real money of his own. In April he had reached his majority, and received the legacy from his grandfather, Edward Langford, which came with interest to £293 5s. 5d.[26]

But how he yearned for another ship. Evidence of his frustration can be seen in efforts made on his behalf by his mother, Constantia. She had been drawn back towards the children of her first marriage by the troubled circumstances of the second and was lobbying for her sons in the only way she could – by petitioning a distant figure who had once helped their father. 'A mother begs you to take to your protection the sons of her Pellew who whilst he lived you honoured with your friendship,' she wrote. Edward was 'impatient of such an inactive life' as he was having on the *Princess Amelia*.[27] There is no evidence anything came of it.

Finally, after almost a year, he did get another ship. The *Licorne* was no plum, but she was a frigate, she was on active service and her captain, Henry Bellew, was an able officer who liked nothing more than exercising her in the chase of every sail to come in sight. Significantly, she also had on board Pellew's younger brother, Israel.

It is extremely unlikely that Edward Pellew found himself serving with another of his brothers through mere coincidence. Although Israel had followed Edward to sea, he had little of his brother's ability and none of his magnetism, being a dogged timeserver with an occasionally overbearing manner. As they rose together through the ranks, his career would be advanced more than once by his older brother, and Israel's presence on the *Licorne*, as captain's servant, was probably the first of these services. Pellew, while he started out with no interest himself, never hesitated to promote members of his own family, or those of close friends. Although this was almost certainly a legacy of his early insecurity, there can be no question but that, time and again, he was guilty of nepotism of an order conspicuous even in a service where it was standard practice.

The start of 1779 saw the *Licorne* cruising the Channel. Regular entries in the log – 'Made sail in Chace . . . proved a Bristol privateer' – indicate that her new lieutenant was kept as busy as the crew. The rewards were greater when, in accompanying an Atlantic convoy, they sighted a large ship coming up by the stern and stood to the south to meet her.

> At half past 3 came alongside of her and after 28 minutes engaging, she struck. Found her to be L'Audacieux privateer 24 guns from Bayonne.[28]

It could only have come as a relief. Nine years after entering the Navy, Lieutenant Edward Pellew had finally seen real action on the high seas.

Even more gratifying was the upshot of an encounter in Plymouth, where a new frigate put in while the *Licorne* was at anchor. She was the *Apollo*, and her commander was Captain Philemon Pownoll. The young lieutenant did not hesitate before hastening across to see his former captain, to relate his recent adventures and press his suit.[29] When Pownoll was next in need of an officer, he accordingly requested that it should be Lieutenant

Pellew. Here, finally, was the fruit of endeavour – service under a masterly captain in one of the finest frigates afloat. He stepped on to *Apollo*'s quarterdeck in April 1780, a few days short of his twenty-third birthday.

3.

Patronage Lost and Won, 1780–1792

It began as another summer's day off the Dutch coast. Wind blew in fresh gales from the west, flicking cream off the top of waves that alternated between shades of blue and grey each time the sun came and went in the sky. Ostend lay some twelve miles to the south-west, clear enough on such a day for a church steeple to be visible from the *Apollo*'s quarterdeck.

The first excitement occurred in the mid-morning when a strange sail was sighted, starting a chase that ended with a warning volley from the frigate's 12-pounders, at which the stranger came to and identified herself as an English cutter.[1] Such exercises were standard practice. They kept a ship's crew in fighting trim for real action.

Two months had passed since Pellew joined the *Apollo*, and while she had been at sea for less than half of that time, he had been learning at the shoulder of his captain for all of it. In a squadron of four frigates, they had cruised the Channel, hunting for French prizes. A few weeks earlier *Apollo* had set after a 24-gun enemy privateer and chased her all the way in to Cherbourg until 'shots from the fort [were] going over us and through our sail'.[2]

Captain and first lieutenant were on deck that morning of 15 June – big men both in blue and gold. Although Pownoll was not quite Pellew's size, he had, to judge from his reputation and Sir Joshua Reynolds's portrait, an unmistakable air of command. Scarcely had the cutter been sent on her way than another strange sail was sighted in the south-west, bearing up the coast towards them. She spotted them at the same time and tacked away to the south, running for Ostend under a following wind. It was near midday.

Pownoll's first thought was that he had come upon another privateer. In fact, she was the *Stanislaus*, a French frigate of 32 guns, but although having the same broadside weight as the *Apollo*, she was intent on escape. Her efforts seemed in vain because the *Apollo* was more skilfully handled and, with the wind behind, was coming up very fast. The log recorded: 'All clear for action at noon.'

Drawing ahead, Pownoll gave orders to tack, with the aim of crossing the *Stanislaus*'s line. She was having none of it, and while raising her colours and firing a broadside, went off on a different tack to escape. *Apollo* tacked again and, within an hour, 'Came up alongside of him & began the Action, he running right in for the Land.'

Her captain may have been reluctant, but there was nothing wrong with the *Stanislaus*'s gunnery. Another broadside aimed at disabling the *Apollo*'s rigging carried away braces and clew garnets. At the same time it felled a blue-jacketed figure standing by the gangway.

What caused Pownoll's death – ball, shot or a flying shard of timber – is not recorded. The log – which ended with the ghostly inscription 'by Capt Philemon Pownoll, Deceased' – stated only: 'Our Captain was killed & the 1st Lieutenant Mr Pellew continued the action.'

There is a story, perhaps apocryphal, that as Pownoll lay, shot through the body, he had time to whisper to his kneeling lieutenant, 'Pellew, I know you won't give His Majesty's ship away.'[3] His death was not, in any event, lingering. For a second time, Pellew had succeeded to command in battle.

Apollo's guns had shredded the French sails but, as her own manoeuvrability was affected, Pellew found he was still overrunning the enemy frigate because he could not slow by hauling in the courses. Flying along, all he could do was 'sheer across his hawse, first on one bow, then the other, raking him as we crossed'.[4] In answer, the *Stanislaus* kept up her own fire, so *Apollo*'s masts were 'much wounded, the rigging very much torn'. Her hull had also been holed and sea was pouring in.

The race ended as they approached Ostend where, Pellew had been warned, shoals guarded the harbour entry. No sooner had he tacked away than the *Stanislaus* struck hard, her foremast and maintop toppling with the impact. Grounded, she lay at his mercy. At this point she fired a gun, to claim the protection of a neutral port, and was answered by cannons from the Dutch garrison. Reminded of the observations of neutrality, Pellew wrote, 'I did not think myself justified in renewing the attack.'[5]

His account of the action, the first surviving words from his pen, was contained in a draft letter to Lord Sandwich at the Admiralty devoted largely to Pownoll's death.

> The ship's company have lost a father. I have lost much more, a father and a friend united. Never, my Lord, was grief more poignant than that we all feel for our adored commander. Mine is inexpressible. The friend who brought me up, pushed me through the service, is now no more! It was ever my study, and will always be so, to pursue his glorious footsteps.[6]

There can be no doubt Pellew's grief was heartfelt; but Pownoll's death at forty-five was a disaster in more ways than one for his 23-year-old lieutenant. For the first time he had acquired a patron, and a brilliant one at that. Pownoll would have risen to flag rank, taking his protégé with him and thus creating a new officer generation. It was the Navy's way of doing things, and if it has a whiff of favouritism to modern sensibilities the point is worth making that it was successful because merit usually prevailed. An officer would not weaken his own circle and damage his reputation by advancing an incompetent.[7] From the assurance of being Pownoll's man, Pellew found himself staring into a wilderness – as is apparent from the tone of his letter to Sandwich:

> Unassisted by friends, unconnected with the great, and unsupported by the world, I must throw myself totally on your Lordship's generosity . . . Permit me to hope that you will extend to me that protection which I have lost in my dear departed benefactor.

There was a good deal more in the same vein, a résumé of the campaign in which he had won honour, a reminder of the great and good who had commended him. Pellew, it is evident, came closer to real terror at this time than ever he did in action. He agonised over the letter for days, crossing out passages and correcting himself repeatedly in such a way as to show that his schooling, while limited, had not been wasted. It also says something for his dignity, and his courage, that in the end it seems he did not send the letter at all.[8]

His late captain's memory was always revered in Pellew's household. He called his first-born son Pownoll and spoke of his namesake with something like awe, so in family lore the name resonated down the generations. More than once he said that but for 'a guide so kind and judicious as Captain Pownoll', his own judgement 'not yet matured by experience, might have carried him into mistakes'.[9] If anything this was an understatement. The wild boy sent from the *Alarm* in dishonour had been first salvaged from obscurity by Pownoll, then set on the path to self-discovery.

Pellew was also fortunate, however, in serving a First Lord who, though he was a gambler and a rake, was alive to the realities of the service and sensitive to its interests. Lord Sandwich still remembered the young officer and wrote to him directly after Pownoll's death, 'condoling with you on the loss of your much-lamented Patron and Friend', and promising: 'I mean to give you immediate promotion as a reward for your Gallant conduct.'[10] He was duly made up to master and commander, entitling him to a ship of his own.

Not that Pellew – as an officer in the 'tarpaulin' rather than 'gentleman' tradition – received any further favour.[11] His first command was a sloop, the *Hazard*, and she was aptly named for it turned out she was a threat to anyone who sailed in her.

Over the next two years, up to the peace of 1782, Pellew knew little but frustration. With the rank of master and commander it was expected he would serve a further apprenticeship, honing his skills in an inferior vessel, before being promoted to post-captain. In the *Hazard* and then the *Pelican* he certainly did that.

He began with high enthusiasm, and a boyish, almost effusive, sense of gratitude towards the Lords of the Admiralty for his promotion. After hanging around in town for a few days in the hopes of an audience, he wrote:

> My Lords, I hope I shall not be thought obtrusive ... by requesting admission to your Lordships' presence personally to express the unbounded gratitude my <u>heart</u> is big with – for your great goodness in giving me <u>promotion</u>.[12]

Reality set in on confronting his sloop. The *Hazard* was elderly and slow, a 'wretched excuse for a man of war', he called her.[13] She handled like a leaky barrel, making escape laughably easy for the smugglers she was supposed to hunt off the north-east coast, and in heavy weather shipped water so badly she became downright dangerous. On one occasion a pilot flatly refused to take charge of her, while in a storm off Whitby one November night she came so close to sinking that Pellew had to order all the guns and swivels to be heaved overboard to lighten her and, when that was not sufficient, sent the spare anchor and booms after them.[14] More often, she was undergoing repairs just to keep her afloat. After six months the risk posed by this dog of a vessel was recognised and she was removed from service.

There followed more than a year ashore while Pellew awaited another command, fulminating at his 'disgraceful inactivity'.[15] Money was a concern too. The inheritance from his grandfather had not been large to start with, and it was now all but gone. 'My finances are not equal to the expenses of London,' he wrote to the Admiralty. Becoming bolder, he went on. 'In justice to myself I feel it necessary to say how very irksome and painful I find my present indolent situation.'[16]

The family rallied round. His mother Constantia fired off petitions to anyone she thought might help. 'The present fixture by no means suits his active temper,' she wrote. 'A frigate is the wish of his heart. Can you, Sir, assist me in recommending him to Lord Sandwich?'[17] These well-meaning efforts afforded Pellew no little embarrassment, as his own letter to the intended patron made clear: 'Fortune not <u>interest</u> was attendant when my mother addressed you, Sir.'[18]

What perhaps kept him in mind at the Admiralty was his desire to be doing something – anything – in preference to nothing. Whereas most unemployed commanders, especially those with money or interest, were unwilling to jeopardise their status by accepting any post more lowly than their last, he pleaded for service 'as a Volunteer . . . in any capacity your Lordships may direct'.[19] Here, it could be inferred, was an officer whose zeal was not compromised by false notions of honour.

When finally a command came it was in the shape of the *Pelican*, a second sloop and no great improvement on the first, though she was at least seaworthy and provided him with some action. Off Plymouth, in the spring of 1782, they encountered a lugger which was more sluggish still and turned out to be a French privateer with four 4-pounders.[20] A meagre prize she might have been, but she was Pellew's first and she was his own.

A few weeks later he followed up by running in under a battery on the Brittany shore and driving aground three French vessels. This raid attracted further attention and, on being commended for 'Gallant and Seaman-like Conduct . . . in the service to which your universal good Character and conduct do Credit', he was promoted to post-captain.[21]

As such, he had charge of a frigate, the *Artois*, for six weeks in the summer, and in a sharp exchange took a 22-gun French raider, the *Prince de Robecq*, off Cork. His delight was unbounded. 'She is almost new and the most complete privateer I ever saw,' he crowed.[22]

While still savouring his laurels he suffered another setback. The American colonies had won their independence, and in the winter of 1782 treaties were signed with Spain and France. The peace would last a decade, during which much of the Navy was disbanded.

*

Few young captains had sufficient influence to retain a command in peacetime. One who did was Horatio Nelson, aged twenty-four. Despite a record that at this point glittered rather more brightly, Edward Pellew, aged twenty-five, did not. In a year after the peace, the number of ships in commission was cut from 200 to 140. Their captains were sent ashore on half pay.[23]

Pellew's career is set here in the context of Nelson's for illustration rather then comparison as in their respective paths and personalities they could scarcely have been more different: Pellew admired the great man's qualities and at one point hoped to become his follower; Nelson, for his part, was respectful but wary, declining to accept him among his 'band of brothers', perhaps because he sensed that as an equally strong character Pellew would be hard to handle.

Their differences are as evident in an era of peace as they were in war.

Both made visits to France in 1783, Nelson ostensibly to learn the language, Pellew because he suffered from the seaman's curse, rheumatism, and was advised to spend the winter in Marseilles and 'avoid the punishments cold weather afflicts me with'.[24] The fruits of Nelson's tour were scant. He hated the French in war, disliked them in peace and made little headway with their tongue. Pellew had – like many Cornishmen – Gallic antecedents, which translated into a natural affinity with the French. He admired French ideas of chivalry, befriended former foes among them, and learnt the language.[25]

The attitudes of the two men were just as distinct when it came to women, love and matrimony. Nelson's affair with Emma Hamilton is almost synonymous with the man himself; less so is his heartless treatment of his wife, Fanny. Pellew certainly knew temptation and was not unswervingly faithful after his marriage. Few sea captains were; but he was a devoted husband, and a hopelessly adoring father.

Pellew probably met Susan Frowde soon after coming ashore in 1782, when he was spending much of his time hunting – he was a decent shot and keen horseman – and walking the countryside simply to keep himself occupied. He would recall that he had 'roused my Wife out of a snug Corner in a little retired village before she had ever heard a Gun or seen the Sea', so it appears their first encounter took place by chance in the hamlet of East Knoyle in her native Wiltshire, a rustic hunting ground for the country set.[26] She was aged about seventeen.

Susan was the daughter of James Frowde, a local gentleman entitled to the usage of Esquire and with extensive lands to his name. Navy captains were usually thought respectable suitors, although whether Edward Pellew fitted Jane Austen's genteel model for the type is another matter. He was, by his own memorable admission, a 'Pockmarked, Ugly, Uninteresting and Uneducated Cub'.[27] Susan's family, devout and with a strong clerical tradition, played little part in their subsequent life together and, while this does not signify in itself, there is a sense of haste about their courtship that was more a part of his world than hers. When they married, at East Knoyle in the spring of 1783, she was eighteen, he a worldly twenty-six.

As a young woman, she was described by one of their familiars as 'the fascinating Susan, full of vivacity – pleasing to all'.[28] Of her demeanour there is no other record; as to disposition, she turned out to be a paragon of a sea officer's wife: a partner, domestic manager and friend.

Of the many hundreds of letters they exchanged over his life at sea just a few scraps survive, and those are Susan's only.[29] But these reveal a sensible as well as tender confidante, able to offer a distant husband comfort in bad times and assurance that she had family matters under control. While he won victories and fortunes, she made children and homes. As Pellew wrote to his friend Broughton some twenty-five years after their marriage: 'I would not part with her for the *Princess Charlotte*.* Don't tell her so or I shall never be able to manage her.'[30] The masculine bonhomie is entirely transparent. With Susan he would fashion a family life as central to him as the sea.

---

* The *Princess Charlotte* was the biggest man of war afloat, a 100-gun ship of the line.

Their early years together were hard. The figure of the half-pay sea captain is an unhappy one in period fiction and Pellew still had some of the turbulence of his youth about him. What he owned to be 'a vile passion of temper' was not improved by rheumatic pain and inactivity. Nor did it help that his family's finances were in trouble again, the fortune of his grandfather Edward Langford having recently been lost.[31] Hopes for a revival rested for the time being on Pellew's elder brother, Samuel.

Investment in Samuel's education had paid off and, having qualified as a surgeon, he was practising in Truro, a day or so from Penzance in their native Cornwall. For a few months, such was their financial state, the newly-married Pellews went to live with him. But another change in fortune – one that touched the entire Pellew clan – was signalled by Samuel's appointment as Collector of Customs at the nearby port of Falmouth in 1784. Samuel had won the favour of the local aristocrat, Lord Falmouth, who arranged his placement in this lucrative and influential post. His lordship perhaps took account of the stir being created by Samuel's younger brother and marked him as a coming man. But Samuel rather than Edward was almost certainly the initial beneficiary of Falmouth's sponsorship.[32] This may account for Samuel's proprietorial attitude in later life, when he basked in his brother's glory and, on his death, promoted a biography in defiance of Susan's wishes.[33]

The family attachment was always to the West Country, but from this time the Pellews' association with Penzance diminished while that with the Falmouth area grew. Edward and Susan made a home in the village of Flushing, opposite Falmouth harbour, and all six of their children were born in these parts, five of them before he went to war again. The first, Emma, arrived in January 1785, the second, Pownoll, the following year.

Lessons from these years ashore distilled Pellew's attitude towards patronage. That he had, more than once, come close to losing his way, that fatherhood stirred in him the need to provide – these reinforced his understanding of the natural order. With neither subtlety nor guilt, he had started to cultivate Lord

Falmouth and was mixing in local affairs. In short order, he became a burgess, an alderman and a magistrate, all posts lying, in effect, within his lordship's gift. It was fortunate Pellew's politics – ardent royalist, gut-instinct conservative – chimed with those of his benefactor. He carried to his grave a philosophy shaped mainly on the quarterdeck, amounting to the divine right of kings and, to a lesser extent, sea captains. By the same measure, those invested with such responsibility had an absolute duty to do the right thing by their people.

Although his activities ashore are less apparent, the captain was visible around and about in the countryside – off shooting woodcock, riding to hounds and meeting, among others, his old friend, Frank Cole, who had come through their shared escapade on the *Alarm* unscathed, risen to the rank of master and commander and was back living at Marazion.

A new friend was even closer at hand. William Kempthorne, captain of the packet *Antelope*, lived with his family next to the Pellews with whom they became so intimate that a door was knocked between the two houses to connect them. After Kempthorne's early death his family would turn, naturally, to the captain who lived next door.

Then there was his closest friend of all. Alexander Broughton's Navy career had ended – it was usually said because of the rheumatism brought on by his sufferings on the lakes. Yet there were other factors too. While Broughton had entered with all the prospects that went with influence, he had somehow fallen short of the mark. Once, in their later years, Pellew tried to reassure his friend, who evidently felt a burden of failure. 'You had no impediment but your interest,' he wrote. 'You had too many friends of power who fed your expectations without carrying you over the difficulties every officer meets in early Life.'[34]

An unlikely comradeship flourished, at first perhaps for pragmatic reasons. Broughton had not only means, which he put to use in profitable ventures, but the connections that took him to those hubs of higher English society, Windsor and Bath. Pellew's glory as a national figure lay ahead of him, but he had shown what he was capable of and, as a captain, could already attract a following. Yet always there was a sense of brotherhood. Broughton, too, had married and was living no great distance away, at Teignmouth in Devon. The young couples exchanged visits, along with letters combining news of domestic affairs and births – 'whether Mrs Pellew be in the straw or out of it, I hope she is well' – with matters ranging from horses to politics. The Pellews and Broughtons were never neighbours, and the amount of time the two men actually spent in one another's company in almost thirty years of friendship was not great because Pellew was so often at sea. The bond was deepened rather by the letters that were, for Pellew at least, a channel for confidences and reflection, and a form of companionship when command cut him off from intimacy with those around him. 'My Dear Alex' became the one man with whom he could communicate, writing with an easy fondness, as if 'conversing with the friend of my heart who I have so long loved and respected'.[35]

An acquaintance of this time remarked of Pellew: 'In every undertaking by sea or land his whole mind was in it.'[36] And, after four years, the energy he had devoted ashore to nurturing a new patron bore fruit. Lord Falmouth had influence at the Admiralty as well as in local affairs, which almost certainly explains why, early in 1786, Captain Pellew was given a 32-gun frigate, the *Winchelsea*.

The officer who came up the side at Spithead on 27 April – it was a clear spring day – had just turned twenty-nine. Entering his maturity, Pellew retained what the American historian A. T. Mahan described as 'an animal energy not to be repressed, the exulting prowess of a giant delighting to run his course'.[37] Below he found his new realm. The captain's cabin on a frigate was an unimpressive space – a sleeping pod with room for just a cot, a desk and a chest, and beside it the aft gallery cabin, with a table that might accommodate six diners or serve for briefings. Yet this little area was a domain that would henceforth put him at a distance from everyone else on board.

The captain's privilege was also to be seen in the *Winchelsea*'s crew. Pellew had with him thirty Cornish youths – his first followers – two of whom stand out: Christopher Cole was eighteen, brother of his boyhood friend Frank; Richard Pearse, nineteen, was a family friend.

They set into the Atlantic, bound for Newfoundland. Ahead lay weeks of fair blue-water sailing, the captain at the taffrail, the thrum of wind in the rigging above and the creak of timbers all around. Here at last he had claimed his element. Cole recalled their first voyage for the captain's 'kindness of heart and cheerfulness of manner'. On the Newfoundland station – where a naval officer usually served as colonial governor and British vessels engaged profitably in cod fishing – a year of hard sailing followed, mainly on convoy duty and patrolling the dangerously exposed east coast. It was an appropriate time for Cole to observe the athleticism for which Pellew had become celebrated:

> Whenever there was exertion required aloft, to preserve sail or a mast, the captain was foremost at the work, apparently as a mere matter of amusement; and there was not a man in the ship who could equal him in personal activity.
>
> I remember one night . . . on gaining the main-topsail yard, the most active and daring of our party hesitated to go out upon it, as the sail was flapping about violently, making it a service of great danger. A voice was heard amidst the roaring of the gale from the extreme end of the yardarm, calling upon us to exert ourselves to save the sail. A man said, 'Why, that's the captain – how the Devil did he get there?' The fact was that the instant he had given us orders to go aloft he laid down his speaking trumpet, and clambered like a cat by the rigging over the backs of the seamen and before they reached the maintop he was at the topmast-head, and from thence by the topsail-lift, a single rope, he reached the situation he was in.
>
> In the course of this year we visited every harbour, nook and corner on the east coast of Newfoundland that the ship could be squeezed into; and the seamanship displayed by the captain in working the ship in some most difficult cases was not lost upon the officers and crew. I have often heard the most active seamen, when doubting the possibility of doing what he ordered to be

done finish by saying, 'Well, he never orders us to do what he won't do himself.[38]

Cole's recollection of Pellew diving overboard in full uniform to save one of the ship's boys from drowning is likewise part of a well-attested canon. His strength as a swimmer was often spoken of and, much like his athleticism in the tops, became a form of prowess in which he revelled. Though not all these incidents were recorded, there seem to have been at least four instances of Pellew plunging to the rescue of hands fallen overboard.

Even at this early stage he was quick to perceive means to improve his ship's sailing qualities – in the *Winchelsea*'s case lowering her bowsprit, which proved fragile on a number of occasions when she was under a press of sail in bad weather.[39] Time and again Pellew would see to the heart of a ship's physical demons and make appropriate recommendations for exorcising them.

Finding the right formula for the crew's emotional well-being was more complex and the *Winchelsea* was not always contented in their two and a half years together. Pellew was still finding his way as a leader and there were testing elements on board, notably an unstable first lieutenant, a corrupt purser and some difficult men. In all things at sea, however, a captain was responsible for what happened on his ship.

Contrary to what Northcote Parkinson had to say, Pellew's instinctive attitude to discipline was mild rather than strict.[40] He was never an enthusiastic flogger. During eight months in his two first commands, *Hazard* and *Pelican*, not a single man was beaten, and to start with his hand on the *Winchelsea* was similarly light. In a year, there were a dozen floggings among a crew of more than 200 – which was few for a ship of her size. The tone of the log started to change as she sailed home from Newfoundland. One entry records a sentence on a quartermaster:

> . . . 1 dozen for drunkenness, 1 dozen for wilful neglect of duty when cunning the ship, 1 dozen for disobedience of orders & 1 dozen for mutinous expressions when under punishment.[41]

Back at Spithead, the purser, Thomas Croxton, was found to have siphoned off rations. Bad or inadequate food was a guaranteed recipe for discontent and an incensed Pellew insisted Croxton should not only be court-martialled but submitted to a civil court for fraud. The dismissal of the master for tampering with a logbook and a surgeon's mate for fighting were further signs all was not well.

Pellew made a hasty visit home to Flushing that spring, when Susan conceived their third child, before returning to the ship at Plymouth. After a few weeks cruising off Ireland, the *Winchelsea* returned to the Newfoundland station, and again trouble began.

First to be flogged was a cook's assistant who was perhaps fortunate to escape with two dozen lashes for 'embezzlement of stores'. But over the next eighteen months, there were another fifty-five occasions when men were stripped to the waist, braced against a grating and beaten – roughly two every three weeks. This was partly attributable to a cabal of tough hands: one man who often felt the cat on his back, an Irishman named Edward Powell, was a raging bull of a fellow, drunken and riotous. However, there were also problems further up the chain of command, at least by the time of their return from Newfoundland. As they approached Spithead, Pellew wrote in the log: 'Confined Lieutenant Gordon of Marines for rioting and Lieutenant Northey for contempt.'[42]

Alexander Gordon and James Northey were taken to Haslar hospital, having suffered the kind of dementia that could assail those left isolated, melancholy or simply overwhelmed by sea life. It was a sombre end to Pellew's command. A few days later, in February 1789, the ship was paid off and he found himself ashore again.

A second revolution began across the Channel later that year and set in train conflicts which, apart from a short interlude, lasted from 1793 until 1815 and overshadowed even the American war. This struggle was to be the making of British sea power and a rich seam of history – along with the future Lord Exmouth. He was there from the very start, thanks to the startlingly forthright way in which he exercised his influence with the then Lord Falmouth.

By the summer of 1792 he was desperate enough to have turned to farming. Command of a second frigate on the Newfoundland station, the *Salisbury*, had ended with the ship being paid off and, to provide for his growing family, Pellew had taken them to land at Treverry owned by his brother Samuel. The fact that the farm commanded high ground looking out to sea may have been an even greater source of exasperation than his failed attempts to make something from the soil. He was, by his own account of it, a hopelessly inept farmer even by seamen's standards. (He later admitted selling a cow owned by a neighbour to a butcher in the belief it was his own.) Worse, he felt he was becoming 'an object of contemptuous pity' even to those in his employ.[43] For a man used by now to respect and control of his own little world, this was intolerable.

Solace at this time came from his brood. He and Susan had four children: Emma, now aged seven; Pownoll, six; Julia, four; and a second son for whom he asked his best friend to stand as godfather. While replying that 'there is no child for whom I would so soon attend at the font as yours', Broughton declined, on the ground that he was no moral exemplar, while at the same time suggesting that the boy be given two of his family names.[44] He was accordingly christened Fleetwood Broughton Pellew over a bitterly cold yet joyful Christmas with the Broughtons. Aptly, he was his father's favourite, and turned out his greatest sadness. Pellew was a doting patriarch to all his children, the girls no less than the boys. Fleetwood, though, was special – 'the flower of my flock', as his father once called him.

His other hope lay in the increasing likelihood of war with France. For some time he had sustained a polite bombardment of Lord Falmouth, which now intensified. He wanted a ship, he wrote to his benefactor, and he wanted one for his brother Israel, too. Falmouth complied 'by applying to Lord Chatham in the manner you desire, with what probability of success I can't say'.[45] That there should have been any response at all was a small miracle because Chatham, the new First Lord, was in the habit of taking letters home and forgetting all about them.[46] That a mere captain should lay siege to an aristocrat like Falmouth in such direct terms might also seem surprising, but they were now part of an interdependent society.

Under the parliamentary system, peers like Falmouth relied on strong local supporters and, as an alderman of years' standing, Pellew had been zealous on his behalf. In stepping up his campaign for a ship, Pellew could therefore write, with just a hint of threat, 'I must not bring myself to think you will desert a friend who has so long and faithfully served you.' And, with a questioning of his patron's influence that came dangerously close to insult: 'We must think he [Lord Chatham] wants inclination to serve Your Lordship if he does not comply with such a reasonable request.'

Pellew's outspokenness would one day cost him dear. On this occasion Falmouth merely rebuked the upstart for his 'indelicate insinuations', while accepting 'the reality of your regard for my interest . . . from the many proofs you have given me of it'.[47] Just what these services were was never spelled out. However, the peer was obviously loath to see Pellew posted to a distant station where his value would be lost. It was Pellew who provided the solution:

> Permit me to hope you will follow up the application and ask Lord Chatham to give me the command of *Nymphe* or *Thalea*, both frigates at Portsmouth fit for service.[48]

Both ships were on the Channel station, where he might engage in active service while meeting his obligations to Lord Falmouth in need. The fit was ideal, and so was the timing. On 11 January 1793, Pellew was given the *Nymphe*. Three weeks later France declared war.

4.

A Cornish Chief, 1793–1794

To appreciate the impact that Edward Pellew's exploits had on the British public early in the war, it is as well to recall that the Royal Navy of 1793 was not yet an overwhelmingly dominant force. The name of Nelson was unknown outside naval circles, and those other historical echoes, the Nile, Copenhagen and Trafalgar, had as yet no resonance at all. France and Spain were still held to be formidable naval powers and French ships were universally regarded as superior – faster, better built and better armed.

It happened that the ship sighted by Pellew at her moorings as he came down the parade at Portsmouth on a brittle January day was French, or at least had been until her capture in 1780. The *Nymphe* was big and strong for a frigate of the day – 940 tons and 38 guns – with at least some of the qualities of speed and manoeuvrability associated with the latest French-made ships. A black strip passing around her hull, accentuating the curve of her bow and stern, highlighted her sleek lines. Despite her years she was, in Pellew's eyes, exquisitely named, a true beauty.

The trouble was, she had no hands. Not just insufficient of the 255 men required to make her an effective weapon but, at the point Pellew commissioned her on 15 January, none at all other than the few followers he had brought with him. And, because press gangs had already swept Portsmouth's taverns clear, none were to be found there.

He wrote to the Admiralty, which sent him 150 men. In the meantime he pressed hands from merchant vessels coming to Portsmouth, and in the process acquired another follower. John Gaze, a master's mate and therefore exempt from impressment, related that Pellew summoned him and said: 'I cannot press you, but if you will enter the service I will place you on the quarterdeck and take care of you.'[1] He was as good as his word. Gaze became his right-hand man, one who would be with him to the end of his sailing days.

Still Pellew remained short-handed, informing the Admiralty: 'Nymphe is under every embarrassment with so weak a ship's company.'[2] In desperation, he wrote to his brother Samuel, asking him to recruit in Falmouth whatever men he could. This inauspicious overture was to be the genesis of a legendary crew.

A few weeks later a ship arrived in Portsmouth bearing the fruits of Samuel's efforts. They included a few old hands but many more, perhaps eighty in all, stood out among the seafarers like an alien tribe, and a warlike one at that, for 'they struck terror wherever they went and seemed like an irruption of barbarians'. Fearsome-looking subterraneans, they were 'dressed in the mud-stained smock-frocks and trowsers in which they worked underground, all armed with large clubs and speaking an uncouth jargon which none but themselves could understand'.[3] They were in fact Cornish tin-miners, or tinners. Looking them over, Gaze thought grimly 'a large portion utterly unfit for the service'. Such was the need, however, they were entered in the ship's muster as landsmen.

What Gaze with his purist's eye had missed were qualities besides seamanship. Tars could be, often were, made from men with no connection to the sea, and most ships' companies represented diverse elements from around the country. The tinners already had their own bonds of loyalty – a crucial element in any ship's company – and, as Cornishmen, an affinity with their new chief. Cornwall, as we have seen, had a powerful regional identity, with a Celtic culture attached to mining and fishing. It also had its own tongue – 'the uncouth jargon' referred to.[4] Pellew may well have spoken the language himself, and he certainly felt the sense of commonality – of tribe – that went with it. From this nucleus he shaped a crack frigate crew, one of the ablest in Navy history, who would follow him from ship to ship over the next six years.

This was despite a constant temptation in their path. Pellew's frigates were always based in Falmouth, and on the *Nymphe*'s first visit the lure of homes nearby proved too much for sixteen men. So, at least, the ship's muster relates.[5] Another version, told by Gaze, was that Pellew gave leave to some really hopeless cases, with orders to return a week later – then sailed early.[6] Be that as it may, the ship retained its West Country core. Along with the captain's established Cornish followers, like Richard Pearse, were those among the tinners, such as Theophilus Coad and Ephraim Noy, who had left the mines behind them forever.

Pellew's other concern was guns. *Nymphe*'s main armament, twenty-six 12-pounders, was supplemented by twelve 6-pounders on the upper deck. He was unimpressed by the latter and had taken note of an innovative weapon – a short gun with a large calibre. Carronades, or 'smashers', had been around since the American war, but though they could be manned by small teams, and were lighter than cannon yet devastating at close quarters, the Admiralty took some time to be persuaded of their merits because they were ineffective at any sort of distance.[7] Pellew saw that, in conjunction with 12-pounders, they would provide a formidable broadside and, with a further eye to the *Nymphe*'s stability, had her 6-pounders replaced by twelve 24-pounder carronades, adding 'considerably to her force but also reducing the weight of guns on her upper works'.[8]

The Nymphes learnt the ropes soon enough. Their captain drove his new ship hard, whether in escorting a convoy – racing like a sheepdog beside a flock, firing signal guns to tell the laggards to close up and the leaders to shorten sail – or in gunnery practice. Having acquired the guns he wanted, Pellew drilled his men at running them in and out. This was basic exercise; but Pellew was unusual in also practising gunnery with powder and ball, though the cost may have had to come from his own pocket. In his years of frigate command, Pellew's ships became renowned for ferocious accuracy, whether from cannons or carronades, and for their rate of fire, which would have been as fast as on any ship, almost one round every minute. Gaze's remark on this passion could have been applied by the novelist Patrick O'Brian to his character, Jack Aubrey: 'Capt P always paid particular attention to the great guns. It was his forte to the end.'[9]

While gunnery was the key to *Nymphe*'s success, activity and purpose touched all quarters. From an empty hulk, she had become in a few months a tight ship, yet a contented one. In the year Pellew captained her there were just six floggings.[10]

With fellow captains relations were always more complex, and often more fraught. Pellew's closest friendships – and he was good at friendship – were with other officers, but so were his most bitter enmities. He was not alone in this, for it was only natural that men omnipotent in their own worlds often found it difficult to rub along with one another. Petty rivalries easily developed into rancorous feuds. As Pellew's old Admiralty ally Lord Sandwich remarked:

> Sea officers are apt to be discontented if everything is not done according to their wish. They are exceedingly jealous of one another and ready to find fault with everyone's conduct but their own.[11]

Just as jealousy inflamed these passions, so too did the thorny issue of prize money. Pellew's first dispute with another captain arose soon after he took command of the *Nymphe* and was given orders to hunt the French frigates and privateers then preying on British merchant shipping in the Channel. He was paired with the *Venus*, Captain Jonathan Faulknor, and, as was common among frigate captains, the two agreed to share the proceeds of any prizes.

On 19 May 1793 they sailed from Spithead and had just come in sight of the Channel Islands the next evening when they sighted two frigates and a pair of brigs, which barely paused to raise French colours before hastening away southwards. With the *Venus* some distance astern, *Nymphe* signalled her to close up while shadowing the enemy. Pellew stamped the quarterdeck with impatience, constrained by odds of four against one, as

Venus continued to lag. Faulknor never did come up and Pellew fulminated at having to watch the French gain the shelter of Cherbourg. Faulknor's explanation, that he was short-handed, cut little ice because the *Nymphe* was not fully manned either.

Days later one of the brigs came in sight again, and this time *Nymphe* was alone.

> At half past 4 fired several shot at the chace & boarded her. She proved to be the Sans Culotte privateer of 16 guns & 75 men.[12]

Pellew was carrying home this prize privateer – she had taken four British merchantmen – when he fell in with Faulknor, his ship in disarray, sails riddled, masts tottering, after an encounter with a French frigate, the *Semillante*, in which neither had prevailed. There was no disgrace in an action that cost the *Venus* twenty-two casualties, but so far as Pellew was concerned Faulknor had proved an unimpressive partner and it galled him to be sharing the proceeds of his first prize, some £560, with 'my thick-headed friend'. It was just the start. Egos and prize money were the making of epic feuds among frigate commanders.

He did not have long to wait for his own next test in battle. On 17 June, *Nymphe* put in at Falmouth. This was to be a regular event on Pellew's frigates, a happy blend of private and professional life. As Cornwall's main port, with its anchorage of Carrick Roads, Falmouth was a gateway linking the Atlantic and the Channel, and a crucial frigate base for monitoring the French Navy at Brest. It was also now the Pellew family home. Edward could see Susan and the children, and indulge the Cornish hands with a few days' leave among their own kin.

On this occasion they stayed just one night. That was enough for the last men bringing *Nymphe* up to full strength to be pressed from a merchant vessel, and for Israel Pellew to come on board.[13] Not for the first time, nor the last, Israel's career was in the doldrums and, not for the last time, his brother was doing his best to revive it. Having failed to get Israel a ship through Lord Falmouth, Pellew invited him to join *Nymphe* as a volunteer, in the hope of seeing some action.

According to the ship's muster, a third Pellew was on board too – a seven-year-old boy entered as captain's servant. Pownoll was Pellew's first-born son and one of the two whose careers he tried to forge in his own likeness through an unhappy blend of persuasion, influence and plain nepotism. He was also the first of his sons to disappoint him. Pownoll is a sad figure in Pellew's story. Even in adulthood, the inescapable image is of a small boy, looking out in bewilderment and fright from behind his father's blue jacket.

On 18 June they sailed again, bound for Spithead. As Gaze recalled it, Pellew ordered the officer of the watch to hold a southerly course under easy sail, 'for the chance of seeing something'.[14] At dawn, they saw something.

She lay in the south-west and she was a frigate. The *Nymphe* set off after her and 'made the private signal, which was not answered'. That was enough to establish she was French. Pipes twittered. All hands went to their stations. Guns were run out and decks sanded, bulkheads were stripped down and fires extinguished.

On the *Cleopatre*, Captain Jean Mullon sized up his antagonist. It was usual practice for French ships to avoid confrontation with enemy men of war in order to focus on merchant vessels, but Mullon was an officer of the *ancien régime* who had served in the Indian Ocean with the legendary Admiral Pierre André de Suffren a decade earlier when the British had been bloodied in a series of battles. Mullon sensed another fighter here and, at the start of a new war between their flags, resolved to do battle.

Pellew addressed his men from the quarterdeck. His words were not recorded but he celebrated Cornish pride and told them riches as well as honour were for the taking. At 6 o'clock on a hazy morning with a moderate breeze aloft they came up on *Cleopatre*'s starboard quarter – close enough for captains and crews to observe one another.

Mullon spoke to his men from the gangway, brandishing a revolutionary cap of liberty and drawing shouts of 'Vive la

Republique!' A bareheaded Pellew, waving his hat, cried 'Long
live King George!' and was answered with three cheers.[15] Drums
rolled. At 6.15 he placed the hat back on his head. It was the
signal to open fire.

The two frigates were fairly matched. While *Nymphe* had a
slightly heavier broadside, *Cleopatre* was a crack ship, newly
built, fast and better manned. That mattered less now as they ran
abreast under a soft breeze. What counted was gunnery.

On *Nymphe*, Israel Pellew had command of the after guns on
the main deck. The first broadside from her 12-pounders swept
Cleopatre's quarterdeck, striking the mizzenmast and causing an
explosive dispersal of timber splinters that killed or wounded
about a dozen men.

Mullon had not neglected gunnery either. His reply hit
Nymphe's main and foremasts, and felled a number of hands,
including Richard Pearse, youthful protégé and family friend of
the captain.

The battering of broadsides was not prolonged – perhaps
twenty minutes or so, which allowed for around a dozen volleys.
But it was exceptionally bloody and, as Pellew noted from the

Nymphe's victory over the French *Cleopatre*. The first naval
action of the war catapulted Pellew to fame and was
greeted in Britain as an omen.

terrible wounds of those falling around him, 'God knows, hot enough'.[16] The crucial moment came just after 6.30 when, with gun smoke enfolding the ships, obliterating sea and sky, a ball smashed the *Cleopatre*'s wheel and her mizzenmast fell. Mullon, standing near the helm, was mortally wounded. The other effect was to bring the French head round to starboard, so she came bow-on amidships of the *Nymphe*.

Loss of their captain seemed to unnerve the French. From the *Nymphe*'s main deck all that could be seen amid the ruins of *Cleopatre*'s rigging and fallen mizzen were shattered bodies. As Pellew's boarders surged over her bows they met little resistance before most of the French retreated below. Lieutenant Amherst Morris, leading the boarding party, received the French surrender soon after 7 o'clock.

Pellew had claimed the first victory of the war. At fifty minutes, it was among the sharpest and bloodiest frigate actions yet recorded, and his strategy – 'to make a short affair of it' – had been vindicated. 'We have suffered much . . . but we were all in it, heart and soul,' he wrote home.[17] Here, in embryo, were the guiding principles that carried the Navy to victory again and again over the next decade – to go straight at the enemy and engage hard.

Aftermath brought time for prolonged reflection. That night, moving about the bloody, dark and reeking cockpit serving as the surgeon's theatre, Pellew went offering comfort to the relics of those fifty minutes of mayhem – twenty-nine men in hammocks, some groaning, others shrieking in pain. Then there were the bodies, twenty-three of them, to be sewn up in canvas and watched over the side.

Losses were even higher on the French side – sixty-three casualties including Mullon, who was found dead on his quarter-deck with most of his right side shot away and his commission stuffed in his mouth. He had thought it to be his signal code and tried to save it falling into enemy hands by swallowing it.

Moved by his antagonist's gallantry, Pellew took it upon himself to write to Mullon's widow, in French, lamenting her husband's death and declaring him a brave and fine man. He also gave her his word, '*sur l'honneur d'un officier Anglais*', that Mullon's private effects would be returned to her.[18] A meticulous inventory of the contents of Mullon's cabin showed that these included various coins, a gold watch, one silver candlestick (broken), six pairs of silk stockings and four nightcaps.[19] Mme Mullon replied thanking Pellew for his kindness, 'which I took care should be publicly known as I sent a copy of your letter to the Minister'.[20] The upshot was a Letter of Compliment to him from the revolutionary authorities in Paris, and the beginnings of his reputation among French officers for chivalry.

Samuel Pellew said Mme Mullon's plight at being left with five orphans so moved his brother – an echo perhaps of their own childhood – that 'he sent, with her husband's property, what [financial] assistance his then very limited means enabled him to offer'.[21] Pellew also arranged Mullon's funeral in Portsmouth, which he attended.

He was less taken with *Cleopatre*'s lieutenant. Robert Raffe wrote to him, blaming Mullon for the defeat and requesting an exculpatory letter for himself, as 'without it I am certain I shall be executed on my return'.[22] In reply Pellew said he was happy to declare *Cleopatre* had been bravely defended; but he treated the idea of criticising Mullon with disdain.[23]

Far harder to write were letters of condolence to the families of his own dead, like Samuel Ediall, a midshipman from Truro. In the case of Richard Pearse, he was overcome. Pearse had been with him since *Winchelsea* days, following a similar path to Pellew himself having recently been made up to master's mate, and was twenty-three when he fell. Pellew wrote instead to his brother Samuel: 'I cannot write to Pearse's mother for my life – do send a note; I really cannot. I loved him, poor fellow, and he deserved it.'[24]

Few contemporary British commanders – the tender-hearted Cuthbert Collingwood was a notable exception – would have been so deeply affected. Pellew was a romantic by nature, easily moved and comfortable enough with it to acknowledge a capacity for tears.[25] He retained a bond with the lower deck, and the young on it, partly because of his origins there, but also because of the West Country attachments that ran ashore. In particular cases they went further: the Coles of Marazion, the Smiths of Mevagissey ... they were not just followers; they were neighbours and friends. The intimacy between Pellew and his crew was more profoundly tribal than usual, even for their clannish species. Losses among them marked him. They tempered his enthusiasm for battle with a keen sense of how best to minimise his casualties even as havoc was being wreaked on the enemy. And they required him to be a benefactor to families of the dead.

Kinship was among the strengths of Pellew's ships. It could also be a weakness, exposing him to charges of favouritism as well as nepotism once he rose to higher command. There can be no question he was guilty of both. Reporting the *Cleopatre*'s capture to the Admiralty, Pellew commended the conduct of Israel who, he noted in passing, 'was accidentally on board' during the action.[26] Privately he made it known that his brother had been in charge of the guns. Israel did hold the rank of commander and would have been expected to be closely involved; but practice had brought *Nymphe*'s gunnery to a good state before he joined her.

The next member of his family to benefit from Pellew's manoeuvrings was the seven-year-old boy entered as his servant, although it seems unlikely that Pownoll had been in the *Nymphe* during the action. Pellew was quick to advise Samuel that he and Israel were safe, but made no mention of his son. One explanation is that Pownoll had been left at Falmouth – to keep him out of harm's way even as he was being credited with sea experience.

News of the triumph preceded *Nymphe*'s return to Portsmouth with her prize on 21 June, when she was met with thundering salutes and three cheers from ships at anchor. The Commander-in-Chief, Lord Howe, told Pellew the action would 'set an example for the war' – which may have been even more prescient than he realised.[27]

A naval victory at the outset of the conflict was just what the public wanted. The press took its cue accordingly, reporting: 'When Captain Pellew landed he was received with three cheers from the populace gathered in great numbers, and the church bells congratulated his arrival.'[28] All this added to the lustre of a famous action. *Cleopatre*, it was stated, was absolutely the finest frigate possessed by the French, with a complement of 320 men who had submitted to 250 Englishmen. More than a victory, it was an augury.

The King, just recovered from the first of his bouts of madness, was so delighted that he announced the news from his box at the opera.[29] He then made it known he intended to honour the hero and invited him to a palace levée. On the eve of the reception, however, *The Times* was dismayed to relate that, although Captain Pellew had been offered a knighthood, 'he wishes to decline it'.[30] In fact, Captain Pellew was delighted by the honour, but feared that he was too poor to sustain a title. The King would have none of it.

On a high summer's day, 29 June, a large man in blue and gold, perspiring heavily from the heat and his own nerves, was taken by Lord Chatham in a carriage to St James's Palace and brought before the King. A plain soul, George III was immensely taken with his new champion, introducing him to the Queen as '*our* friend' and waving away his financial anxieties by declaring that Susan would be granted an annuity of £150 from the Privy Purse for any extra household costs.[31] The King could scarcely have imagined what all this meant to a man who was not only a commoner but a passionate monarchist. Israel Pellew, who was present at his brother's insistence, was told he was being made up to post-captain and, overwhelmed, kissed the King's hand.

Later Sir Edward Pellew was entertained by Chatham who, as well as being First Lord at the Admiralty, was eldest son and heir of the late Prime Minister, William Pitt the Elder. Chatham also introduced Pellew to his brother – William Pitt the Younger, himself now Prime Minister and war leader.

A knighthood and fame – all had fallen to Pellew in just ten days. The tale of the boy who rises from the lower deck to command is an enduring one in naval tradition, though more often founded in fable than fact. While the Navy would acquire a reputation for social mobility, Pellew was a glorious exception in his time for the scale of his rise.

It was not only himself that Pellew had refashioned, however. At times of despair he had confided to his brothers a fear that 'the Sun of our Family [will] be out for ever'.[32] He had rekindled his family's fortunes, and that mattered to him no less than his own.

Even as Sir Edward, however, he was not at home with London society, with its clubs, rakes and wits. It was a high time to be in the capital, to mix with the racy set, but it must be noted that he left no mark on it. Nor was he touched by London's cultural life, the visionary mysticism of William Blake, the plays of Richard Sheridan or the caricatures of James Gillray (all of whom were his exact contemporaries). Sir Edward was one of a class of person whose new fame or new money had given rise to a new term. He was, it must be said, a parvenu.

He did have one brush with the arts. He had his portrait painted. Even in this natural celebration of status, tribal instincts prevailed. The artist, John Opie, was spoken of as a self-taught genius. More to the point, he came from Truro and was dubbed the Cornish Wonder.

Pellew's return to his native soil might have provided a setting for Handel's 'See the Conquering Hero Comes', the local boy transfigured by warfare, a blue-coated giant moving among his people as hero and benefactor. His appearance now, aged thirty-six, is less clear, and even Opie's efforts may not be all that illuminating. Seven portraits of Pellew were painted in his lifetime, not one of which looks remotely like another, their only common feature being a sense of physical strength, piercing eyes and a rather magnificent nose. Two portraits actually come from the same period, when he was almost sixty. Samuel Drummond discerned the damn-your-eyes fire-eater of yore, while William

Owen saw a benign old patriarch; in these instances the paradox was at least apt because Pellew was capable of being either. With so many impressions, what he actually looked like remains unclear, although the 1797 portrait by Sir Thomas Lawrence was thought a good likeness and may offer the best idea of him in his prime – a powerfully built, assured man, with a penetrating gaze and that nose.

Susan and the rest of the family had been 'beside ourselves and frantic with Joy', and awaited him in a reunion as intense as any represented by painters of the seafarer's return. Even Samuel was caught up in the fever of the moment:

> Oh my Dear Brother, with what words and with what language can I express to you my Gratitude, my Love, my Adoration for your Conduct . . . The whole Country redounds with your Praise.[33]

At the same time, Pellew set out to repair the wounds caused by their father's death thirty years earlier, when the family divided. His mother Constantia was able to put her financial embarrassments behind her (along with, it seems, her second husband) and, thanks to Pellew, would end her days in Bath, the fashionable retreat of the well-heeled. In a healing gesture, he arranged for Opie, the Cornish Wonder, to paint her portrait as well.[34]

His stay in Falmouth was not prolonged, but it served one other purpose. Men were needed to replace the *Nymphe*'s casualties, and if Pellew had ever experienced difficulties in recruiting hands before he never did again. Men were drawn to his ships as it became known that not only glory awaited those who served with him, but bounty too.

The prize-money was paid at Spithead on 23 December, a delay having been caused by a final falling-out between Pellew and Faulknor of the *Venus*. The latter claimed that their agreement entitled him to a half share not just of the *Sans Culotte* privateer, which he received, but of the *Cleopatre* as well, although his ship had been undergoing repairs at the time. Only after Pellew appealed to the Admiralty, which ruled in his favour, were the

Nymphes paid out. A handsome reward it was too. The *Cleopatre* was assessed at £7,798 17s. 1d, of which a three-eighths share went to Pellew, three-eighths to the officers and petty officers, and two-eighths to the hands.[35]

While still recovering from merrymaking, they shifted from *Nymphe* on Christmas Eve – every man jack. The Admiralty had decided that the rising star should have a frigate worthy of him, and take his people with him. She was the *Arethusa*, and she really was a plum.

His new command also represented a shift in Admiralty strategy. The *Arethusa* joined a squadron of five crack frigates based at Falmouth, patrolling the Channel with orders to protect British trade. In practice, that amounted to hunting down French men-of-war and privateers, and preying on French merchant vessels. It was a golden age from which frigate captains emerged as lions of the sea. While the French shrank from fleet battles and admirals appeared dull dogs by comparison, the exploits of a handful of enterprising officers captured the public eye. None was more prominent, in action after action, than Pellew.

The Navy system had always advanced captains up the command chain according to seniority rather than talent. The frigate squadrons introduced by the Admiralty in 1794 were unique in being able to operate independently and outside the usual fleet command. The ablest young captains were selected for the best available ships – newer and more heavily armed with 18- and even 24-pounders.

Such a combination of talents and egos was liable to produce further explosive results – may indeed have been designed to do so – and it did. Others in these competitive waters included two fine captains, James Saumarez and Richard Keats, both exact contemporaries of Pellew's, and the dashing figure of Sidney Smith. Among these rivals, Keats was rare in becoming a true friend. Pellew's dealings with the flashy, vain Smith were always touchy, while he and Saumarez were to quarrel so furiously that they never spoke again.

These disputes have often been attributed to prize money. Pellew, it is true, had been left with a horror of poverty and even long afterwards, when the raw austerity of his boyhood was but a memory, he had an eye for profit that gave him a reputation for cupidity. But most captains and plenty of admirals were just as avid for riches and some were utterly insatiable. He and Saumarez were never in pursuit of the same prize, and their feud may have been more personal; Saumarez, who won the second frigate victory of the war, felt his reception was relatively subdued and was furious at being asked to pay for his knighthood.[36]

Class played a part as well. Something about Pellew grated with a clique of high-bred officers. This is not an easy matter to define because it has never been clear just how he stood out – possibly some gaucheness of manner, or rough West Country accent. It was not ignorance or literacy, because he was quick and despite his poor education had learnt to write a good letter. What can be said is that while his modest background had been noticed before in a general way, knighthood and sudden prominence attracted a new kind of social sneering. One contemptuous officer called him 'a man of mushroom extraction' – a reference to his rapid emergence from nowhere.[37]

He was assigned to the Western Squadron, commanded by Sir John Borlase Warren of the *Flora*, a flamboyant university-educated dandy with a gambling habit and a reputation for avarice, but adventurous and capable with it. They had served together before on Captain Pownoll's *Apollo*. The squadron was completed by *Melampus*, Captain Thomas Wells, *Concorde*, Sir Richard Strachan, and *Nymphe*, now under Captain George Murray. These were all 36-gun ships, apart from *Nymphe* and *Arethusa* with 38.

Early on 23 April 1794 they were off Guernsey when four strange sail were sighted and identified as three French frigates and a corvette. They included *Pomone* which, at 44 guns, was far the most powerful ship in action that day. Warren signalled: 'Engage without regard to the order of battle'. The *Flora* and

Arethusa were first to come up with *Pomone* and *Babette*, the corvette of 20 guns.

The opening shots were fired just before 6 a.m. For about forty-five minutes, the four ships surged around and between one another without any severe damage being done, before the *Flora* lost her mainmast and dropped astern. With his commodore out of action, Pellew closed with the corvette. *Arethusa*'s carronades quickly destroyed her resistance. He then turned to *Pomone*, coming to within pistol range at 8.30 and raking her repeatedly. In twenty-five minutes one of the finest new French frigates was a ruin, her main and mizzen masts gone overboard and a fire burning on the poop. Just after 9 a.m.:

> They call'd out to us that they had surrendered. Finding the People getting overboard from the fire, brought to & hoisted out the boats to save the People, but happily the fire was extinguished.[38]

The *Arethusa* had just five casualties including one dead. *Pomone* had between eighty and a hundred dead or wounded out of her 350-man complement. Some idea of the terrible effectiveness of the *Arethusa*'s fire can be gathered from the fact that, in a lengthy action, Strachan in the *Concorde* had meantime captured another French frigate, *Engageante*, with a mere twenty casualties on each. The *Pomone* confirmed the reputation of Pellew's ship for lethal firepower and Sir John Warren was warm in his appreciation:

> My Dear Friend . . . I shall always hold myself indebted to you for the noble support you gave me today. God bless you and all yours.[39]

His gratitude was proper. As commodore of the squadron, Warren received the lion's share of the credit, including the Order of the Bath, even though his ship had been left behind after being disabled and two of the three enemy ships captured had surrendered to Pellew. And while two British frigates had taken virtually no part at all, the proceeds were shared among all five, roughly £2,750 for each ship (about £825,000 at today's values).[40]

(The rivalries were none the less keen for that. In 1835, when they were all dead, *The Times* reported a naval dinner tale, of how Strachan had tried to join Pellew in engaging *Pomone* and 'in a supplicating voice, hailed Sir Edward desiring him to bear up a little to enable him to pass to windward but [Pellew], seeing he would lose the vantage ground, answered, "Dicky, I'll see you damned first." Sir Richard then took his hat off and kicked it across the quarterdeck in a rage. Later, after taking *Engageante*, he shouted across to *Arethusa*, "Pellew I forgive you but I never would have if I had not got hold of this frigate."'[41])

The ensuing celebrations of the Arethusas in this windfall year entered seafaring legend. Old hands mustered with their tankards would relate tales of the 'Harrythusers' – of how, on receiving their bounty, five tars hired a coach and horses in Plymouth, loaded it with harlots, grog, a fiddler and an organ-grinder, and careered in triumph around the town for days until the money ran out. The fame of their escapade also gave rise to one of the more joyful images of Navy life, George Cruikshank's etching *Sailors on a Cruise*.

They were presumably back on the *Arethusa* a few months later when Pellew relieved Warren temporarily as commodore of the squadron. Others had joined it in the meantime – notably Sidney Smith in the *Diamond*, Richard Keats in *Galatea* and Edmund Nagle in *Artois*.

An emerging pattern of victory over French ships that were, on paper, superior, was sustained when they sighted another new and formidable frigate, the 44-gun *Revolutionnaire* off Ushant soon after 6 a.m. on 21 October. From the outset of a general chase Nagle's *Artois* justified her reputation as a flyer, coming up first with the Frenchman after about three hours and engaging her until Smith joined in and forced her to strike. The *Arethusa* was hindmost during the chase, which Pellew undoubtedly found galling. But a story that somehow gained currency – that he took umbrage at Nagle being knighted – is not supported by the tone of a letter he wrote to the Admiralty, praising his junior for 'distinguishing himself in a well-conducted action', adding that he hoped he might 'express approbation of an officer of nearly the same standing without being presumptuous'.[42]

Pellew's taking of *Pomone* and *Babette* were never fully acknowledged, although he did receive a letter from the First Lord's office lauding 'an event that adds new lustre to your professional merits'. His status at the Admiralty was such that he could virtually have named his next command, and a more genuinely ambitious captain would have opted for a ship of the line – a 74, say, with the ultimate objective of fleet command. The previous year the relatively unknown Captain Nelson had commissioned the 64-gun *Agamemnon*. For the present Pellew's only interest was another frigate and the prospect of more glory and more riches – in that order – while sustaining the Falmouth connection with his family and his people that enriched his heart. So he wrote to request the ship with which his name would always afterwards be associated – the *Indefatigable*.

5.

Indefatigables, 1795–1796

The *Arethusa* lay at anchor in Carrick Roads. Squalls whistled around her upper works and rain spattered the decks, but, below, her company sat snug in their messes, drinking their beer over plates of fresh stewed beef. It was the evening of 17 November, they were back home in Cornwall, and when Captain Pellew went among them, relating that men from the Admiralty would come aboard in a day or two with their latest instalment of prize money, he was given three cheers.

That Christmas season of 1794, Pellew might have reflected, had a special, golden glow. Most seafarers would have put down so tidal a change to simple fortune or some other mysterious intervention, but since he had become quite devout under Susan's influence he would probably have seen the agency of his happiness as Providence. He had battled for years against contrary elements. Now it was as though a divine force had provided him with a following wind under full sail.

Fundamental to a more prosaic understanding of these fair conditions, however, and scarcely less of a divinity himself, was the First Lord of the Admiralty. Lord Chatham had followed Pellew's meteoric rise with fond approval since having the young captain brought to his attention by Lord Falmouth, and it was Chatham who had accompanied him to the King's levée. The first letter Pellew wrote on reaching home was to Chatham, requesting command of the *Indefatigable*. Within a few days he had his reply: 'With respect to your wishes . . . I shall have great pleasure in meeting them.'[1] At the same time the First Lord indicated Pellew was being given command of his own frigate squadron.

Almost immediately Chatham was replaced. He had brought no great distinction to his office and his brother Pitt the Younger, facing new challenges as revolutionary France over-ran its neighbours, was resolved on transforming the Army and Navy. To the Admiralty came the 2nd Earl of Spencer, a magisterial figure in his own right, member of the Whig aristocracy and brother to Georgiana, the Duchess of Devonshire. While courteous and extremely capable, he had no previous Navy experience and was naturally cautious to start with. When Pellew wrote asking for the *Indefatigable* to be given the guns he now saw as crucial to any ship of his, Spencer replied: 'I cannot quite promise you the Carronades you desire but if it can be done without too much transgressing Rules, you shall have them.'[2]

Bringing the *Indefatigable* to good fighting condition was to occupy months of frustration. She was one of a class of super-frigates known as razees, which is to say a two-deck 64 with the quarterdeck and forecastle removed, in effect reducing her to a 44-gun single-decker – which had consequences for her sailing qualities. Razee design was still evolving. The *Indefatigable* was neither fast nor weatherly, and she rolled in heavy seas. In correctly identifying the reasons for her ungainliness – which involved her centre of gravity, ballast, and the height and location of masts – and turning her into a byword for sailing brilliance, Pellew showed the practical side to his seafaring genius. Early lessons, shipbuilding on the lakes under Schanck, and service in miserable vessels like the *Hazard*, had left him with a sure grasp of how any ship could be improved. In *Indefatigable* he managed this despite the resistance of Navy Board blockheads who obstructed him at every turn, refusing or ignoring requests for longer masts. In this battle Spencer was again ineffectual. It took mishaps in her sister ships, *Anson* and *Magnanime*, to convince the board of her design defects and the need to address them, and even when longer masts were approved Pellew was not allowed to shift them further aft. Some flaws were never rectified. But over four years in her, Pellew honed the *Indefatigable*, grew to love her and brought off a victory that has resonated down naval history.[3]

Manning was resolved more easily. The Arethusas followed their captain almost to a man and became Indefatigables, but there were only 230 of them, and another 100 or so were required for a razee. The numbers were made up in drafts from the Channel Fleet. With hands from across Britain and Ireland, Pellew's new ship became more diverse, less a Cornish tribe afloat, yet he would still imbue her with the same qualities that defined *Nymphe* and *Arethusa*. Ultimately, in both sailing and fighting, the Indefatigables would prove among the finest frigate crews in history.

How a ship reached such a state is an intriguing question. How did a captain help to turn hundreds of tough, awkward individuals into an efficient and, therefore, happy company? There is, of course, no simple answer to this mystery and the general practices of good leadership did not necessarily do the trick. Ships were strange places – all-male societies, confined and isolated from the world, usually for months on end. In so volatile a space, it might be thought surprising that things did not go more spectacularly wrong more often. But it was certainly the case that the captain of a happy ship had to have his men's respect; and, which was more rare, he had to have respect for them.

Pellew's letters to the Admiralty at this time show two paramount concerns – that his ship should be fitted correctly, and his men treated properly.

Take one letter, for example, written at Spithead. Reading between the lines, we may see two hands, asking to see the captain and being brought aft to him: it was January, bitterly cold, and they were in tarred jackets, knitted caps clutched respectfully in hand; but their concern was money, because an error in the muster showed them to have been pressed, when actually they were volunteers, and they had been denied the bounty to which they were entitled. Pellew listened, asked questions and finding them 'two men of very good character' sent them away, reassured. Then he sat down to request the money on their behalf.[4]

A few weeks later, a senior officer wanted to conscript Indefatigables for extra duties at Spithead because of a fever outbreak on his own ship. Pellew could not demur but fired off a letter to the Admiralty, stating that his men were 'extremely fatigued' after a spell at sea, and insisting they be kept away from a source of infection. The order was rescinded. Within days he was writing again – first to obtain the wages due to one of his men from another ship, then requesting that a teacher be sent, at his own expense, 'to educate the ship's boys'.[5] Having run away from school himself, he insisted they should acquire learning while in his care.

John Gaze, the plain seaman who had become his follower and served in his ships as master, summed up his habit as, 'a kindness which allowed every safe indulgence'.

> No man ever knew better how to manage seamen. He was very attentive to their wants and habits. He personally directed them; and when the duty was over, he was a great promoter of dancing, and other sports, such as running aloft [and] heaving the lead, in which he was a great proficient.[6]

Perhaps, reading between the lines, we may discern something beyond mutual respect, that most unexpected of qualities to be found on a man of war – affection.

Of the thousands of plain hands to serve on Pellew's ship, only one recorded his experiences and these dated from between 1804 and 1808 when Pellew was a fleet commander in the Indies. Robert Hay's memoir is nevertheless revealing of his methods and how these endured even once he became an admiral. He was preparing to attack an admittedly feeble Dutch squadron in Java when, as Hay recalled, the company of his flagship, the 74-gun *Culloden*, obtained an illicit supply of liquor and she went aground. Beside himself with rage, Pellew swore that every drunken man would be flogged – but then instead removed his flag to a frigate, declaring as he went down the side, 'that since no trust could be placed on us, he would go and share the danger and honour of facing the enemy with those on whom he could depend'. Mortified, the men managed to refloat the *Culloden*, and the next morning Pellew came back on board 'to the joy of all hands'. The Dutch were swiftly dealt with and the company's delinquency was forgiven. Pellew, according to Hay, had 'the confidence, love and esteem of seamen'.[7]

Even enemy hands engaged his empathy. After the *Cleopatre* action, Pellew became angered by what he saw as neglect of the many French wounded brought to Portsmouth, and laid a complaint against the local agent for prisoners. When the case was examined and the fellow dismissed, *The Times* thundered its approval: 'Captain Pellew's humanity and gallantry must ever endear him to his country.'[8]

But, equally important, he could be tough as well. 'He studied the character of his men,' said Gaze, 'and could soon ascertain whether a man was likely to appreciate forgiveness or whether he could not be reclaimed without punishment.' Finding one of his old hands from the *Salisbury* was running a brothel on Portsmouth Point and had become 'a notorious crimp' – luring hands away to other ships for a fee – he requested permission 'to impress him as a very proper punishment'. In the event, the law caught up with James Welch before Pellew did, and put him on trial.

A captain who respected their rights as men – that helped to make a contented company. So was a clear disciplinary regime: he might have a particular phobia that made him reach for the cat, detestation of drunkenness, say, or of sloppiness; but that mattered less than consistency. Pellew flogged comparatively rarely and when he did it was usually for drunkenness. An easy-going captain, on the other hand, could soon find discipline turning lax and jeopardising efficiency. As for the modern notion of popularity, it had no place on a ship at all. A good captain might be loved, but he was trusted rather than liked, and for a simple reason: if the code of eighteenth-century seafaring was tough, so was the code of eighteenth-century society as a whole; and while this may be self-evident it bears repeating because the equation of naval service with misery is so entrenched. Para-doxically – given the range of offences for which the death sentence was imposed by the courts – the brothel-keeper James

Welch might well have been better off being pressed by Pellew than left to the mercies of the State.[9]

Tars were impetuous, improvident and short-lived. A good number of Pellew's first draft had died, been invalided out or died in action. Others had run or left the Navy. Even so, 133 of the 236 men who had entered in the *Nymphe* were following him into a third ship.[10]

They were all – captain and crew – blessed in one respect. Now with his own squadron, Pellew was employed in intense but relatively short cruises that would see the *Indefatigable* return every few weeks to Falmouth, and an anchorage that acquired for the hands as well as Pellew the qualities of a home. Here, too, he exercised a lenient regime, allowing a third of the men ashore at a time, with the result, Gaze noted, that 'very rarely a desertion took place'.[11]

A tumble of houses and inns sloping off hillsides to the estuary made up a cosy, egalitarian little society where officers and tars rubbed along in close proximity and where the 'taverns were numerous and, far from being thought disreputable, were the usual places of rendezvous in the evening for all classes'. Yet

Falmouth, base for the frigates of the Western Squadron, showing the return of Pellew and Sir John Warren with the prizes *Pomone*, *Engageante* and *Babette*.

this rustic haven had a stylish aspect too, for Falmouth had an importance quite disproportionate to its size: as well as evolving into a frigate base crucial for monitoring the French at Brest, its location between the Channel and the Atlantic made it the centre of the packet service, the Admiralty's means of transmitting orders to ships and squadrons in distant waters. In turn, fast-sailing packets brought letters and despatches from all corners of the world to Falmouth, thence to be taken by riders and coaches to London.

A boyhood friend of Pellew's sons, James Silk Buckingham, recalled Falmouth fondly as a place which 'sparkled with gold epaulets, gold lace hats and brilliant uniforms'.

> There was probably no spot in England on which on so limited a surface and among so small a number in the aggregate were to be seen so much of the gaiety and elegance of life as in this little village. Dinners, balls and evening parties were held at some or other of the Captains' houses every evening; and not a night passed in which there was not three or four dances at least in the more humble places for the sailors and their favourite lasses.[12]

A regular visitor to the Pellew home, Buckingham evoked a close-knit world involving play with Pownoll and Fleetwood and the benign indulgence of Sir Edward who 'often took me on board with him in his barge, which was sent from the *Indefatigable* every morning at ten'. Here he would meet officers, like the ship's new first lieutenant Richard Pellowe, a distant relation of the captain, and others whom he recognised as part of the network perpetuated in marriages and friendships ashore.[13]

With these ties came a duty. When the Pellews' friend and neighbour Captain William Kempthorne died in France after the capture of his *Antelope* packet, leaving a wife and six children 'greatly unprovided for', Edward and Susan came at once to the rescue. In a crisis so deeply redolent of Pellew's childhood after the death of his father, also a packet captain, Susan succoured the widow and her five girls while Edward took his friend's only son, William, under his wing and on the *Indefatigable* as a mid.[14]

Pellew had become almost as influential in this Cornish landscape as at sea, with a heroic profile and deep local roots, including a brother as Collector of Customs. He could be seen at the balls, dinners and evening parties he liked to host – an outgoing, generous creature, partial to madeira and with a seaman's love of activity on the dancefloor for which he was noted.[15] He was growing rich along with the dozen other frigate captains based in Falmouth and, with command of his own squadron – *Indefatigable* with the *Jason* and *Concorde*, soon to be supplemented by the *Revolutionnaire* and *Amazon* – both his status and prize earnings were bound to increase.

But currents of jealousy were also detectable in the egos strutting Falmouth's little society. Pellew's rise to fame, his victories and squadron command, had only hardened the animosity of two other influential frigate captains. Sir Sidney Smith was a colourful maverick who evoked mixed feelings – Nelson was not alone in thinking him a windbag – and whose record thus far was likewise mixed. Sir James Saumarez was more conventionally talented and had a recent frigate victory to his credit. Both came with connections but neither had Pellew's local éclat, and perhaps he flaunted it. When he held court for visiting dignitaries it may be assumed both Smith and Saumarez were conspicuous by their absence.

From the spring of 1795, a shift in Admiralty strategy gave Pellew's squadron a new role. The Channel Fleet was sent to blockade Brest, preventing the main French fleet there from escaping to launch an invasion of the British Isles. The Western Frigate Squadrons retained their independence as raiders, but were to act also as the fleet's eyes and claws. So began what would seem to Pellew interminable years in the treacherous Bay of Biscay, traversing the waters from north-west France to north-west Spain, between the island of Ushant and Cape Finisterre, monitoring the French bases – Lorient, Rochefort and Bordeaux as well as Brest. For the time being it was a highly active service which honed his skills – chasing and intercepting strange sail, capturing the French and questioning the neutrals, Americans or Scandinavians, for intelligence from enemy ports. In one early coup, he encountered a convoy with shipbuilding materials bound for Bordeaux, and took or destroyed fifteen sail.[16]

A few weeks later *Indefatigable* herself came near destruction. In pursuit of a strange sail three miles off Cape Finisterre on 7 May, she was flying along when she 'struck upon sunken rocks before which there was no appearance of rippling or discoloured water'.[17] The sea pouring in to the hold was soon five feet deep, and despite constant pumping and the efforts from carpenters from other ships she appeared in danger of foundering when Pellew stripped off and plunged over the side to inspect the damage.

He might have gone down with her, taking all hands with him, before giving her up; even with high standing at the Admiralty a captain who lost his ship might not expect another directly. But on the basis of what he found below the waterline, Pellew decided he could get her to Lisbon. He persisted when challenged by Rear-Admiral William Waldegrave, with whom the *Indefatigable* had fallen in. The admiral, it was recorded, 'wished [him] to abandon her, but Sir Edward undertook to take the ship to Lisbon if another ship were to accompany, to take out the crew if such became necessary'.[18] With officers and men 'working indiscriminately at the pumps' and favoured by fair weather, they came to anchor in the Tagus three days later.

A less creditable episode arose directly from this affair. The damage to *Indefatigable* was so severe she spent two months in Lisbon and prolonged inactivity may have affected morale; Pellew, as we have seen, thought 'dance and other sports' crucial to harmony, and this may have prompted his actions. Even so, to modern sensibilities what followed was outrageous.

One evening the captain and some of his officers were at the opera when a fiddler in the orchestra pit caught their eyes. In the words of Buckingham:

> They had long wanted for the frigate a good violin player to furnish music for the sailors' dancing in their evening leisure, a recreation highly favourable to the preservation of their good

spirits and contentment ... Sir Edward conceived the idea of impressing him.[19]

Later that night as the violinist left the theatre, he was met by a lieutenant and three hands who seized him and carried him off to the *Indefatigable*.

The kidnapping of Joseph Emidy – by no measure could the abduction of a foreigner in another land be called impressment – may be largely attributable to the fact that he was African. From the little known of his life, Emidy had been enslaved once already, being taken as a boy from Guinea to Brazil and coming under the care of a kindly Portuguese who brought him to Lisbon. Here his gifts were discovered and, after studying the violin, he began the musical career now interrupted by being taken forcibly aboard a British frigate. He was mustered as 'Joshua Emede ... Landsman' – the lowest grade of seaman.[20]

According to Buckingham, who later got to know him, Emidy saw himself as having been singled out for a new kind of slavery:

> ... required to descend from the higher regions of the music in which he delighted, Gluck, Haydn, Cimarosa and Mozart, to hornpipes, jigs and reels, which he loathed and detested; and being moreover the only negro on board, he had to mess by himself and was looked down upon as an inferior being – except when playing to the sailors when he was of course in high favour.[21]

This account – by an avowed Radical campaigner – does not quite square with what is known of Emidy's subsequent life. He willingly followed Pellew to his next ship, the *Impetueux*, on which he served, as a seaman rated able, until she was paid off in 1802.[22] Thereafter he settled in Falmouth where he created a new life as the leading musical figure in the West Country, making 'a handsome livelihood' as a performer, composer and teacher. One of his pupils was Buckingham, who performed with the Harmonic Society of Falmouth under the former slave's baton. Emidy, his pupil recalled, had 'charms enough to fascinate a young white woman of a respectable tradesman's family by whom he had a large family'. It seems fair to conclude, therefore, that the change in Emidy's life of being brought on to the *Indefatigable* did not turn out entirely to his disadvantage.

Whatever the truth about Pellew's treatment of Emidy, the British public was always more receptive to the virtues of its heroes than their flaws and a famous exploit soon after the *Indefatigable*'s return to Plymouth early in 1796 established Pellew as a champion of the age. More than a victorious captain, he became a hero of the people, one willing to risk his life for humble men, women and children. It helped that for once his swashbuckling derring-do took place in the public spotlight.

On 26 January, Sir Edward and Lady Pellew were in a coach bound to dine with the local vicar, Dr Robert Hawker, a renowned evangelical with whom Susan would doubtless have engaged in keen ecclesiastical debate, when they spotted crowds racing down towards the sea. Stepping down from the coach to join them, Pellew saw a dismasted ship aground in surf below the Citadel, her upper deck a seething mass of men.

The *Dutton,* with some 500 souls on board – troops and their families bound for the West Indies – and in the grip of a fever in which dozens of men had died, was in a miserable state even before going aground that morning. Forced by a gale to put in at Plymouth, she struck rocks while manoeuvring.

A witness, the brother of the artist James Northcote, described what followed:

> The ship was stuck on sunken rocks, somewhat inclining to one side, and without a mast standing; and her decks covered with the soldiers as thick as they could possibly stand by one another, with the sea breaking in a most horrible manner all around them; and what still added to the melancholy grandeur of the scene was the distress-guns which were fired now and then from the Citadel.[23]

At this point, the *Indefatigable*'s captain appeared, dressed for lunch 'with his uniform coat on and his sword at his side'.

Pellew was thirty-eight. He remained in magnificent physical shape, could still beat any of his men in a race to the tops and had recently impressed them with his prowess in the water. Since plunging over the *Indefatigable*'s side when she went aground, he had dived to the rescue of two more hands.[24]

He joined the crowd to hear cries of distress coming from the *Dutton*. The crisis called for someone to take the initiative – or so it was said at the time; the fact is, this particular stage was made for him and he took to it with relish. A story that he urged a boatman to join him in going to the rescue and on being refused said, 'Then I must go myself', has a distinctly apocryphal ring.

There was some mystery afterwards as to how he got aboard. Questioned on his deathbed, he told his son George that rigging from the *Dutton*'s mainmast had been washed ashore, providing a link to the wreck. He hauled himself out on a rope through a bitingly cold sea, repeatedly battered by heavy wooden flotsam swirling around.[25]

From the shore, Northcote observed:

> There was something grand and interesting in the thing: for as soon as they had pulled [Pellew] into the wreck, he was received with three vast shouts by the people on board; and these were immediately echoed by those who lined the shore, and garrison-walls and lower batteries.[26]

Pellew had come up the side to find soldiers of the 2nd Regiment, disorderly and terrified, milling about the deck. The crisis was ominously poised as some had resorted to the seamen's refuge in the presence of death, breaking into the drink store in pursuit of oblivion.

The cheers heard ashore came after Pellew mounted the quarterdeck and announced he was taking command. Order was not directly established, however. He had to draw his sword and go about threatening to run through anyone who disobeyed him. At least one drunkenly belligerent soldier was flattened. Still the peril had not passed. How, now, were hundreds of souls to be brought to safety?

At this point a small boat came alongside, handled by a drenched, brawny youth who shouted up to Pellew in a strong

Irish accent, inviting his orders. Jeremiah Coghlan, the mate
of a merchant vessel at anchor near by, had been inspired by
Pellew's example to row out and join him. 'Great God!' Coghlan
recalled years later, 'how strongly is the presence of that beloved
man before my imagination still . . . his mind directing and his
noble example urging others to exertion.'[27] It was Coghlan who
established the *Dutton*'s lifeline, taking ashore hawsers which
were then rigged with cradles for the able-bodied to be hauled
in one by one.

Other means of salvation had to be found for the more
vulnerable – women, children and dozens of sick men. Two more
boats came alongside while Pellew 'stood by with his drawn
sword to prevent too many rushing in'.[28]

Orderliness was crucial to the rescue. On shipwrecks it was
generally a case of every man for himself and devil take the
hindmost – including women and children. Slow and awkward
though the *Dutton* evacuation was, Pellew's coolness prevented
panic. One by one, while the waters swirled around, wide-eyed
youngsters and their mothers – some twenty of the soldiers'
families – were first to be lowered into a boat.

Pellew's own family, recalling his fondness as a father, liked
to tell how he took personal charge of a newborn baby, easing
it from its mother's care and then descending to deliver it to her
in the boat. Relating this episode to a friend many years later,
Pellew wrote:

> I felt more pleasure in giving to a mother's arms a dear little infant
> safe than I ever felt in my life. The struggle she had to entrust me
> with the bantling was a scene I cannot describe.[29]

The rescue went on well into the night as the able-bodied
– soldiers then seamen – were pulled to safety on hawsers.
Meanwhile boats continued to ferry the sick and injured ashore.

Pellew had not acted without help. As well as Coghlan's
critical intervention, two of the *Dutton*'s officers behaved 'with
the utmost coolness and rapidity' and stayed to the end. Pellew
left the ship himself when all but a few other men had reached

safety and when, with an insouciant, 'Well, mates, I think I can be of no further service. Farewell', he climbed on to a hawser and hauled himself ashore.[30]

Later that night the *Dutton* was battered to pieces. Pellew had taken quite a battering himself from wreckage in the water and spent a week in bed recovering. But everyone who had been alive on the ship when he reached her was brought safely off.

Tributes flowed in. Plymouth's mayor conferred the freedom of the borough on him and the Humane Society awarded him its annual medallion. *The Times*, while pointing out his humble origins (it noted that the society liked to reward 'the lower class'), celebrated an act of 'exalted philanthropy'.[31] The artist James Northcote was so impressed by his brother's description of the rescue that he painted Pellew's portrait against a backdrop of the sinking *Dutton*. Another local gentleman penned an epic – which he declaimed at a public entertainment to mark the occasion – of which the following stanzas are a relatively restrained example:

> While o'er the reeling wreck, the savage storm
> Poured all its lightnings, thunders, blasts and hail;
> And every horror in its wildest form
> Smote the firm heart – that never knew to fail.
>
> 'Twas thine, Pellew, sublimely great and good!
> For man, thy brother man, distress'd – to dare
> The deathful passage of the raging flood,
> And join the frantic children of despair.

The Palace went further. King George had always liked Pellew (in contrast to Nelson, of whom he had an abiding suspicion) and decided – 'as a public testimony of your general good conduct, as well as more particularly of the laudable Humanity and Spirit displayed by you on this occasion' – to make him a baronet.[32] Still lying abed, Pellew was so thrilled that 'my back was cured'.

Revealingly, the *Dutton* rescue was the feat on which Pellew reflected with the most pleasure in later years. When the old warrior might have recalled victories and the destruction of foes, he preferred an act of salvation. Succouring the helpless was bound up with his ideals of the knight-errant – ideals that smack today of quaint romanticism but chimed with Jane Austen's notion of a fraternity of Navy officers, described – in *Persuasion* – as having in 'their brotherliness, their openness, their uprightness . . . more worth and warmth than any other set of men'.[33]

As so often in his life, a crisis had also been the making of a deep bond. While still recovering from his injuries, Pellew sent for the young Irishman who had come to his assistance – Jeremiah Coghlan, three years in a merchant ship on the day he brought a boat alongside the *Dutton* – and invited him to join the *Indefatigable* as a hand rated able with the promise of early promotion. A wild boy of absurd bravery, Coghlan was nineteen and destined for great things thanks to Pellew's advocacy. This was not remarkable but for the fact that Coghlan, from Cork, was probably a Catholic, which normally sat ill with Pellew's religious and political prejudices. But on top of his warrior spirit, Coghlan was of simple birth. His captain came to love him as another son, seeing in him a reflection of his own youth.[34]

Not everyone was so pleased. William Hay, the *Dutton*'s second officer, had assisted in the rescue and resented the adulation heaped upon a Navy captain while his efforts were ignored. This led to a minor controversy many years later, for Pellew once carelessly asserted that the *Dutton*'s officers had come ashore before he went on board. In Hay's case this was unfair and on Pellew's death he wrote to *The Times* that it was absurd to say Sir Edward had taken command because the *Dutton*'s chief officer had never relinquished it – a fine point but rather lost in the circumstances.[35]

Sir Edward Pellew, now Baronet of Treverry, was soon back on the *Indefatigable* and off the French coast with his most challenging assignment yet. For all its perils and humanity, the *Dutton* affair had been essentially a *coup de théâtre*. What followed was more serious than life or death. A rising French general, Napoleon Bonaparte, was marching across Europe and by the end of 1796 Britain was isolated and in peril of invasion. When it came, Pellew was left by an incompetent commander to deal with it virtually alone. Nothing in his life caused him greater anxiety or dread – not of dying, but of disgrace.

6.

French Foe, French Friend, 1796–1797

A fateful year opened on a cheering note. Frank Cole joined Pellew's squadron with the *Revolutionnaire* early in 1796. There can be little doubt Pellew had asked for his boyhood friend to be attached to his congenial little empire at Falmouth. With friendship, however, went rivalry. Just as the two former mids had plenty to reminisce about as the jug circulated, chuckling at the memory of their banishment in disgrace from the *Alarm* twenty years earlier, as captains they would have had in mind that Cole had once been the senior partner. The orders Pellew received in March 1796 provided a new testing ground.

While the enemy fleet remained anchored in port, beyond the formidable chain of reefs and islands off Brest, there was nothing anyone could do about it. As an alternative, Pitt's strategists came up with a plan to foment internal unrest on the French mainland where pockets of resistance to the republican regime – royalist Catholics known as Chouans – endured. Pellew's squadron was drawn into a clandestine operation to assist them.

On an icy day in March, two heavily cloaked figures came on board the *Indefatigable* at Spithead and were brought aft to the captain's cabin. Their names were not stated, even in the letter marked 'Secret', which they handed gravely to Pellew, describing them as 'French gentlemen'. They also produced orders from Spencer at the Admiralty. The gentlemen were, in fact, royalist agents, and Pellew's orders were to drop them ashore in Brittany to contact Chouan leaders, depositing at the same time arms to sustain their struggle. Over and above duty, this was a cause close to the heart of an ardent monarchist.

The squadron sailing from Falmouth on 8 March consisted of

Indefatigable, four frigates including *Revolutionnaire*, a cutter, a lugger and three *chasse-marées* – small vessels for close-in work along the coast. They were returning to Pellew's former cruising ground, the notoriously stormy waters of the Bay of Biscay.

Setting ashore the agents was accomplished without incident and with the information they brought back Pellew made anchor at Houat, one of the islands off south-east Brittany. The next day he wrote in the log:

> 15 March. Moderate and foggy. Sent the cutter and lugger with the flat boats to land Arms etc. At 2am the cutter, lugger and boats returned. Made sail.[1]

As so often, the captain's log barely hints at complex events. The first challenge was avoiding French ships, the second finding sites still in Chouan hands where the arms could be landed. Pellew was more forthcoming in writing to Spencer of being 'surrounded on every side by enemies, and hourly expecting a superior squadron'. The operation, 'always carried out by night, and on the open coast', had been 'excessively difficult as well as dangerous'.[2] Several boats were lost and the frigate *Argo* was nearly wrecked. Twice *Indefatigable* exchanged fire with shore batteries and, all in all, it was testimony to a slick operation that between 15 March and 8 April they landed barrels of powder, muskets, carbines, sabres and money at four sites on the Brittany shore.

Although successful, Pellew recognised their efforts had been in vain. The Chouans were surrounded by superior republican forces and doomed. In a grim intelligence report, he described setbacks suffered by the rebels and offered a pithy summary: 'The Royalist parties in these provinces will be completely overturned in two months, if some powerful diversion is not made to draw off part of the troops which are now upon them.'[3] As it turned out, he was quite right, but by then he was desperately engaged with the enemy himself.

Brest, at the northern edge of the Bay of Biscay, was France's principal base with up to twenty ships of the line and a dozen frigates at anchor. It might be thought surprising that *Indefatigable* had not seen more action, but even at this point in the post-revolutionary era the French Navy – unlike the French Army – was inclined to avoid confrontation. A long-standing thesis that the Terror destroyed an efficient navy run by aristocrats has tended to obscure the fact that systemic problems existed before the Revolution. What can be said is that manning had become a critical issue for the French, with the desertion of thousands of seamen who were replaced by men seized on the streets; and, as so often, a revolutionary movement treated those it purported to serve – in this case conscripted peasants forced to the guns – with contempt, failing to feed or clothe them adequately. At the command level, purges had cost France many fine naval officers and, by introducing notions of ideological purity, corrupted morale.[4]

Pellew may have been denied action, but he became a fund of intelligence about events in Brest. Neutral ships leaving port would be intercepted and their captains invited aboard, to be wined, dined and pumped for information. At what point he sensed the French were up to something is not known, but he seems to have noted a quickening of activity in and around the port quite early in the year, long before it became the platform for an invasion of the British Isles.

The Indefatigables responded keenly. Between the lines of spare entries, the log crackles with a terse energy – whether in landing arms for the Chouans, pursuing strange sail or riding dreadful weather in a ferocious Biscay season. Captain, crew and ship had been sharpened to a pitch of pure, hard excellence. There is no precise means of quantifying this capability. It was organic and variable and, like any human endeavour, fallible. Among the error-prone elements was a new first lieutenant, James Thomson, one of Pellew's less successful protégés; Thomson had been a master's mate in the *Nymphe*, of whom he could write 'a more worthy man does not exist', even as his bumbling since being promoted threatened to 'drive me out of my senses'.[5] The ship herself remained imperfect: the Navy Board still refused his requests for her main and mizzen masts to be shifted to the next beam aft, with the result she was 'uncertain in stays' – handling clumsily when turned to windward and making the kind of close work in which she was engaged especially awkward.[6] Nor was she very fast, being by some way slower than Frank Cole's *Revolutionnaire*.

Even so, the *Indefatigable* now represented a more intangible but higher form of seafaring brilliance, in that no circumstance ever found her wanting and there was no challenge to which she did not rise. Discipline had attained a state where the men were virtually self-regulating: in 1795 there had been fourteen floggings out of a crew of 330, some of them repeat offenders and almost all for drunkenness; in 1796 there were ten.[7] (In the *Nymphe*, it may be recalled, there were six floggings over a similar period, but among 250 men.) It is time to lay to rest, once and for all, the assertion by Parkinson that Pellew was a strict if not severe disciplinarian.[8]

He had, moreover, the complete confidence of his men. One of them marvelled how it was as if 'in the hardest storms, he appeared to play among the elements'. Another mused: 'Blow high, blow low, he knows to the inch what the ship can do. He can almost make her speak.'[9]

As the squadron was cruising the Bay of Biscay on the evening of 12 April, a strange sail was sighted off Belle Île. The *Indefatigable* was not best positioned to give chase and Pellew signalled to Cole to cut her off in *Revolutionnaire* as he made sail himself. Into the dark they raced until, near midnight, Pellew 'saw several flashes bearing NNW which we took for the *Revolutionnaire* and Chase engaging'.[10]

Cole wrote that on coming up, he had identified a 40-gun French frigate and 'began the engagement which continued 45 minutes'.[11] When the guns fell silent nine French hands were dead and the surrendering captain identified his ship as *l'Unité* and himself as Citizen Durand Linois. The revolutionary appellation was a guise. From an aristocratic background, Linois would spend his career running with the prevailing wind and did so well enough to win the Indian Ocean command, even though in battle he could be limp and indecisive.[12]

Pellew was none the less full of praise for his friend Cole, ordering three cheers from *Indefatigable* as they came alongside and notifying the Admiralty of a victory by 'that attentive and zealous officer Captain Cole'. Possibly, just possibly, Cole may have been irked that his friend's tribute was not more generous still, for while Pellew noted his gunnery was 'close and well-directed', he added – referring to a French lack of appetite for a fight – that it had been 'but faintly returned'. And possibly, just possibly, Pellew was a bit peeved himself – at not being first up with *l'Unité*.

He made no such mistake when presented with his own chance a week later. On sighting another strange sail, he hailed *Revolutionnaire* and ordered Cole 'to take charge of the prize while he chased the ship in the offing'.[13]

She was another 40-gun frigate and as such was always likely to be overwhelmed in broadside-to-broadside action with a 44-gun razee, especially one with *Indefatigable*'s 42-pounder carronades. *Virginie*'s captain, however, was a mettlesome character. Although Jacques Bergeret saw he had to run for home, he was ready to put up a fight.

They started racing south in the early afternoon, from twelve miles off the Cornish coast towards France – masts straining and sea creaming at their bows, a harmony of creaking timber and thrumming rigging. Pellew, observing from the maintop, knew he had a worthy opponent within an hour, when he left the *Amazon* and *Concorde* trailing but failed to make any headway on the Frenchman. By nightfall she may even have started to edge ahead. Two factors kept *Indefatigable* in touch. The first was visibility: the moon illuminated a glittering night sea on which the *Virginie* swayed ahead. The second was a miscalculation by Bergeret, who pressed his ship so hard a topgallant yard was carried away, and she slowed. They had been in the chase for eleven hours and covered 115 miles when *Indefatigable* came up on her stern just before midnight.[14]

Indefatigable's action with the *Virginie* laid the unlikely basis
for a lifelong friendship with Jacques Bergeret. Granted parole,
the French captain was a guest in Pellew's home.

Bergeret wrote afterwards:

Our first Broadside did him a great deal of damage which however
did not prevent him coming yardarm to yardarm and there, by the
quickness of his fire, he did me the greatest damage.[15]

In these first minutes was seen the characteristic that above
all others separated the two navies – morale. Pellew noted as
they went into action, 'We hoisted English colours & gave 3
Cheers'.[16] And the Indefatigables, with the action hot around
them from fire that had shot away the gaff and mizzen top, stood
at their guns and replied, again and again.

On the *Virginie*, meanwhile, Bergeret was dismayed to see
men starting to abandon guns on the forecastle and quarterdeck
as a hail of metal and wood splinters exploded around them.
'Not without blows' could he get them to return; and, being now
barely able to return fire, he was compelled to get away from
those terrible carronades.

With smoke blotting out the moonlight, he bore up and
managed to slip some 700 yards off before Pellew 'got to rights

again and returned upon me with the greatest impetuosity'; and now Bergeret found there was no question of getting the hands back to the guns. 'My heart bleeds to tell you,' he wrote to his commander-in-chief, 'that I was forced to take Musquets to make use of them against the Top men and to send a Midshipman to strike them.' The *Indefatigable* raked her and *Virginie*'s mizzen came crashing down while Bergeret was still trying to manoeuvre her with the help of a few petty officers to come up by the razee's stern. Then with a crack like a thunderbolt the maintop fell.

From his quarterdeck Pellew observed this turmoil – and the gold-braided figure, hauling on ropes and hacking furiously with a hatchet at the wreckage while exhorting his men to fight on. In that instant he recognised not just a worthy foe but a kindred spirit. Just so, the basis of a friendship was laid.

Two hours into the action, the *Amazon* and *Concorde* finally came up and Bergeret – faced with not one enemy ship but three and 'in such a position as rendered it impossible to bring a single gun to bear' – struck his colours. He was surprised to find his casualties numbered no more than forty-three with thirteen dead and was concerned this 'might bespeak a weak resistance if the state in which the *Virginie* is did not prove the contrary'.[17]

Respect between enemies is not rare, nor innately virtuous. It may be seen as a form of mutual reassurance, in that worthy adversaries provide one another with the evidence of their own merit. It takes a different kind of temperament to treat a foe as a friend. When, three days later, *Indefatigable* moored in Falmouth with her prize, the two captains had spent time in one another's company and Pellew had resolved to help Bergeret in any way he could.

In the weeks that followed, the citizens of Plymouth were treated more than once to the extraordinary sight of the wife of a British captain being escorted around town by a French prisoner. It was pointed out that the officer with Lady Pellew always conducted himself 'with great politeness', yet tongues were bound to wag – especially when Lady Pellew allowed the fellow to accompany her on a visit to the gun wharf, a sensitive location where he might have observed naval hardware in the making. The affair created quite a stir and the local press went so far as to suggest that Captain Bergeret ought to be thrown into gaol. Susan, who had taken him along on a visit to the commissioner's wife in the certain knowledge that a man of honour would never take advantage of such a situation, was mortified by having thus imperilled her companion.[18]

Few would have ventured open criticism of Sir Edward himself, though it was noted he had been perfectly blithe in allowing his wife to be squired around by the Frenchman. Time was when this would not have been thought especially *outré*, for in the tradition of warfare between the two countries gentlemanly officers had occasionally extended a hand to a noble foe. 'I look forward to becoming your friend after I shall have learned to render myself [worthy] of that honour, by facing you as an enemy,' a French commander once wrote to Admiral George Rodney.[19] But the Terror had shocked all England and generated a virulent francophobia. While Pellew loathed bloodthirsty republicans as much as anyone, he honoured tradition, liked individual Frenchmen and had welcomed Bergeret as a guest. The enemy captain was on parole, living under the Pellews' roof, at the home they now kept in Plymouth.

Sir Edward's motives may not have been wholly altruistic. He had suggested to Lord Spencer that Bergeret be exchanged for Sir Sidney Smith, now being held in France – a ploy combining the neat notion of leaving a rival in his debt while obtaining freedom for his French friend. It might have come off too. Spencer thanked him 'for your anxiety about our friend Sir Sidney', and set the wheels for an exchange in motion.[20]

The month Bergeret spent in his captor's home shaped a family attachment that lasted their lifetimes. Bergeret once hinted he had fallen in love with Pellew's daughter 'your darling Emma', which was doubtless no more than French gallantry. More eloquent was the letter he wrote to Pellew just before being sent back to France which spelled out the basis of their camaraderie:

I am sensible of the good treatment by which you prevented me from feeling the weight of my captivity. Nothing could persuade me that I was among enemies. Not that I was by any means astonished by your behaviour. Such a generous one is always to be met with in the man who, like you, has given so many proofs of honour.

Believe me, for life, your devoted and grateful admirer.[21]

Bergeret left with a pledge of his parole which concluded that, should the French authorities decline to trade him for Smith, 'nothing will prevent my return but death'. He was as good as his word. On reaching France, he found the dashing Sir Sidney had contrived to escape, voiding the exchange and leaving Bergeret honour-bound to return to England. This time Pellew was unable to save him from Stapleton prison near Bristol. However, he did obtain an easing of Bergeret's conditions, and sent £100 for the nearby Bush tavern to provide him with food and drink. Later Emma brought food and clothing: 'Your darling Emma came at the prison gates,' Bergeret wrote. And: 'I had the comfort of seeing your charming Emma. I could not, I am sure, express enough how much lovely she is.'

Just before being returned to France in the summer of 1798, two years after their bloody action, Bergeret wrote to his erstwhile foe: 'I have experienced so much friendship and generosity from you.'[22]

Heartfelt warmth between the two warriors endured. They continued to write to one another and were to be emotionally reunited, a decade later and in a distant ocean, after Trafalgar. It was a curious friendship in that they never spent more than a few weeks together and their letters reflect mutual esteem rather than any common interest. In all likelihood Pellew's regard always went back to the first desperate hours of chase and battle; Bergeret was a phlegmatic, valiant officer in a French service that never had enough of such men.

At a time in his life when Pellew's character still speaks through his actions rather than his correspondence, this combination of intimacy and distance in one friendship casts some light on his dealings with others at the height of his success as a frigate captain.

He was not, to start with, a worldly man. That is not to say he was without cunning or ambition, but there were limits to both. In a service based on hierarchy, he accepted power as being absolute – although he also believed that, provided any challenge to it was made in a spirit of righteousness, divine order would somehow prevail. But being a public figure had exposed him to a more sophisticated world which, though he might observe it with suspicion, drew him on. Making occasional forays to London, he would start off at the Admiralty, where Spencer massaged his sense of self-worth by courtesy and attention. From there he would go on to Westminster, renewing his acquaintance with Pitt. The Prime Minister came to see him as an ally, though they had little in common politically, Pellew being a diehard Tory and Pitt a reformer who stood above narrow distinctions of Whig and Tory. They could have agreed that the defence of the realm was paramount (and therefore that Tom Paine's *Rights of Man*, a galvanising tract for the Radical movement, was seditious) but not much besides. Pitt's perception of him as a supporter was based partly on Pellew's association with his brother Lord Chatham; but it indicates, too, that Pellew had started to don camouflage in circles of power.

Like many sea captains, he was never very good at dissembling. Forthright methods and teamwork had raised the *Indefatigable* to excellence, and because he remained as gregarious and informal as circumstances permitted, he was less affected by the solitude of command than most. But he was forty and, apart from a three-year peace, had been at sea almost constantly since the age of thirteen. Gradually, with the passing of years on the quarterdeck and some inevitable distancing from his juniors, a sense of isolation grew. Increasingly, for confidences, for companionship, he looked to correspondence from home. With Susan's destruction of their letters, that side of him has been partly obscured. What remains are those in which he is found 'conversing with the friend of my heart who I have so long loved and respected' – Alex Broughton.

There are twenty-two of these letters among Pellew's papers, commencing at this time and continuing for fourteen years up to Broughton's death. Some were heavily crossed out in places by Broughton's family to withhold sensitive content, others may have been destroyed.[23] What still emerges is Pellew's state of mind at the time of writing, from the bright pride of his frigate command to the suspicions and anxieties of later years. To Broughton he was able to unburden himself as he could to no other male confidant – about family concerns, even ups and downs with Susan.

It was for Broughton's sake that he had taken on a new young follower – of whom the *Indefatigable* had a growing number, drawn from diverse backgrounds.

Jeremiah Coghlan, his protégé from the *Dutton* escapade, was in a category of his own – Irish, aged about twenty and entirely without influence. He had been advanced from able seamen to master's mate and being a 'tarpaulin' as well, rather than a gentleman, had a special bond with his captain.

But then Pellew always had a soft spot for 'a good boy', and William Kempthorne also had a claim on his attention, being the son of his late friend and neighbour, and having proved himself qualified for command 'from ability, sobriety and courage'.[24] Of a similar age to Coghlan, he came from a more officer-like background and was already a midshipman.

Another young man had caught Pellew's eye since he had taken command of the *Indefatigable*. George Bell had no special advantages of family either, but he did have a gift for navigation and, having first been made up to master, had been encouraged by Pellew to take the lieutenant's examination.

This trio, of Coghlan, Kempthorne and Bell, were Pellew's closest followers. He had also, however, taken under his wing a new group of would-be officers. These 'Volunteers of the First Class', prominent among them the Honourable George Cadogan, were distinguished by the potency of their patronage.

A real blueblood, a son of the 3rd Baron Cadogan, the fourteen-year-old had been placed on *Indefatigable* at Lord Spencer's – or at least Lady Spencer's – request, a flattering recognition of Pellew's eminent suitability for preparing the young Cadogan for greater things.[25]

Also listed in this class were two even younger boys and here, in the ship's muster, becomes clearly visible the Achilles heel that would repeatedly betray Pellew – the lengths to which he would go in furthering family interests. His eldest son, Pownoll, is among the first-class volunteers, listed as aged twenty. So is his second son, Fleetwood, aged fourteen, having joined *Indefatigable* officially in March 1797. Neither case is remarkable in itself. Senior officers constantly exploited influence to advance their sons including, among Pellew's close contemporaries, Sir Thomas Fremantle and Sir Thomas Troubridge. Nor would the doctoring of the ship's muster to credit both boys with extra years and experience have been thought especially heinous, even though Pownoll was not twenty, but eleven, and Fleetwood, far from having reached his teens, had just turned seven.[26] (This practice, known as 'false muster', was instrumental in the rise of Thomas Cochrane, a highly successful captain who was entered by his uncle Alexander at the age of five – thirteen years before he stepped on a ship.[27]) What made the case of Pellew and his boys so conspicuous, and ultimately damaging, was that there were two of them, that both remained under his protection for years, and that once exposed to the dispassionate scrutiny of others it became clear that Pownoll, for one, was not cut out for command.

For the time being they and their father could get away with it. But it was not just his own sons who were indulged. Initially Pellew regarded Richard Delves Broughton with a similarly indulgent eye as he came on board in a new hat and coat. Although declaring his friend Alex's young relative 'the most extravagant Dog in Cloathes you ever saw', he thought him another good boy, with 'the most enviable disposition'.[28]

Dick, as the boy was known, would spend years under his wing, despite repeated falls from grace and hints of scandal. Pellew's forbearance, combined with Alex's unknown relationship but keen interest in the boy, add to the mystery that surround him. He was born in 1781, after Alex's return from America yet before his marriage, and it is possible that he was an illegitimate son.[29]

The question that arises is how Pellew reconciled himself to the glaring paradox in all this – between, on the one hand, extracting the best from a crew he had raised to pure excellence while, on the other, tolerating favoured bunglers. For each dashing Coghlan he usually had a useless Pownoll or Dick. 'Interest' being the rule rather than the exception, this was not rare. Even so, Pellew took the practice to extremes, particularly as he became more susceptible to the influence of the powerful. He might have thought he could put the bunglers where they would do no harm, must have told himself that it would all redound eventually to the benefit of family and friends. Nevertheless, he was making a cat for his own back.

7.

'The Most Important Crisis of My Life', 1796–1797

At the end of 1796, Pellew's intuition that the French were up to something hardened into certainty. For weeks the *Indefatigable* had been thudding through heavy seas, blasted by easterly gales in the Bay of Biscay, her men chilled and soaked, when on 9 December she tacked and worked up the Iroise, the rocky western passage leading to Brest. As was his usual procedure, the captain went aloft to observe enemy activity – and saw a great fleet, not in the harbour, but in the outer roads. No fewer than eighteen ships of the line, plus frigates, were mustered, and from their state and position it appeared they were making ready to sail.[1]

Just what this activity signified Pellew could not be sure. For some time reports had filtered out of troops mustering ashore, yet had it been suggested the French ships were about to transport an army to invade the British Isles he might have remarked tartly that they seemed scarcely able to transport themselves. In one intelligence despatch back in June he reported: 'Whenever men are sent on board they immediately desert and so discontented are the officers from getting no pay that they connive at their escape.'[2]

He was not alone in scepticism. General Lazare Hoche was the French officer in charge of the invasion army about to embark. Hoche had confirmed Pellew's grim forecast for the Chouan rebellion by putting the royalists to the sword, and now had orders to land troops in south-west Ireland and ignite an uprising – for just as there were rebels in republican-ruled France, so there were in crown-ruled Ireland. Two factions, the Protestant-led United Irishmen and the Catholic-based Defenders, had begun the interminable struggle for Irish independence and needed foreign allies. Hoche, however, despaired of his naval partners:

> Our hateful Navy cannot and will not do anything . . . The commissioned officers chaotic and divided, organised indiscipline in a fighting service . . . arrogance, ignorance, vanity and folly.[3]

Despite Pellew's initial uncertainty about French intentions, his reports had been enough to bring a British squadron under Vice-Admiral John Colpoys to stand by off Ushant, while the main Channel Fleet under Lord Bridport was at Spithead – ready, in theory, to sail at a moment's notice. Firm evidence that a fuse was alight came on 11 December, when five more French ships of the line and three frigates arrived from Rochefort to join the Brest fleet. The next day four of them came out to chase off *Indefatigable*. This rare flexing of muscle was as clear a statement of French intent as anything. At dawn on 12 December, Pellew 'sent the *Amazon* for England & *Phoebe* for Admiral Colpoys'.[4] Anticipating that the French were about to show their hand, he was summoning both fleets.

Neither came to join him. Subsequently, their failure to respond was attributed to bad weather. It is true that haze and fog had fallen on the Bay of Biscay, to be blown away by ferocious gales. But there was more to it than that. Colpoys's squadron was no more than twenty-five miles away off Ushant. As for Bridport, the Commander-in-Chief of the Channel Fleet may have been more distant at Spithead, but he did not take his ships to sea until 3 January and then never so much as sighted the French.[5] Fog and gales became a screen to be drawn over their failings.

Pellew was now spending hours every day high on *Indefatigable*'s maintop, scanning the access to Brest's sheltered harbour. The sheer physical toughness of the forty-year-old Pellew amazed one young officer with him who recalled being 'so benumbed with the intense cold', he had to be helped down by the topmen, 'yet the captain was there six or seven hours at a time'.[6] He never flagged, intercepting anything that moved – including, finally, a fishing craft from which he learnt that thousands of troops had started to embark.

All this came finally into focus early on the afternoon of 16 December when Pellew was called back to the maintop and through the mist observed a great spectral host on the move. 'They loom like Beachy Head in a fog. By my soul, they are thumpers,' cried an officer presented on another occasion with such a sight.[7] Pellew's entry in the log was more prosaic:

> Counted 23 sail of ships coming out of Brest. They hauled their wind to the south.[8]

There were, in fact, seventeen ships of the line, thirteen frigates and a dozen transports, and they were carrying about 15,000 troops, along with horses and artillery.

With dark descending and only Cole in *Revolutionnaire* for support, Pellew's options were limited. He ordered Cole to sail for Ushant to tell Colpoys the French were out, while he set out to shadow the French flagship, the *Fraternité*. He may have hesitated before sending Cole off, for Colpoys had already been warned of the imminent sailing, but to this could now be added the fact that the enemy were bearing south-west, a course indicating they were bound for Lisbon and an invasion of Britain's royalist ally Portugal.

For some time Pellew had thought Lisbon the likely destination, and the French fleet's adoption of the awkward southern exit from Brest, the channel known as the Raz du Sein, only confirmed him in this view. However, it became difficult to monitor their movements as night fell. He set the *Indefatigable* ahead of the French fleet, firing guns and rockets to confuse their signals, which may have contributed to the loss of one French 74 at the mouth of the channel with almost 700 lives, before a general separation took place in the chaos of exploding lights and swirling fog. Having lost contact with the *Fraternité*, Pellew decided to join Colpoys so they might pursue the enemy together in daylight. That his conduct was, as he wrote to the Admiralty, 'actuated by every motive of honor and disinterested zeal', would never be in doubt.[9]

The next morning, 17 December, the *Indefatigable* reached the Ushant rendezvous where Colpoys had last been sighted. There was no sign of the fleet. The *Revolutionnaire* hove into view, only for Cole to report he had not been able to find the admiral either. Close at hand just two days earlier – so close, in fact, he was occasionally within sight from the masthead – the admiral and his ships had disappeared.

What had suddenly turned into 'perhaps the most important crisis of my life' cast Pellew into an agony of anxiety. He was at the heart of unfolding events, with neither orders nor support, left to deal with a French expedition that might change the course of the war. Error now would destroy him. From his cabin in the *Indefatigable*'s stern, he dashed off a frantic note to Spencer, warning that an invasion of some sort was obviously under way, although where he could not be sure. He would, he went on, spend a day seeking Colpoys,

> [but] . . . shall give the French fleet only 24 hours' start from last night and [then] shape my course for Cape Finisterre and so on to Lisbon to alarm that Court.
> God knows, my lord, if I shall be doing right, but left in a wilderness of conjecture I can only say that the sacrifice of my life would be easy if it served my gracious King and my country.[10]

Still plagued by doubts – had Colpoys already gone in chase of the French? – he spent the rest of the day vainly trawling for sight of the admiral. On top of bad weather and poor visibility, the wind came about to the south-west and quickly developed into one of the storms for which Biscay was feared. This at least would hamper the French, wherever they were bound. Pellew was already having second thoughts about sailing for Lisbon when, on the morning of 18 December, the *Amazon* hove in sight. She, it may be recalled, had been sent back to England six days earlier with his intelligence that a French expedition was imminent, and now, thanks to the news with which she returned, Pellew decided to sail for Falmouth.

The reason Colpoys had not been found off Ushant was that he had been well over a hundred miles to the north-east, up the Channel towards England.

Though he could hardly say so, Pellew had had his doubts about the admiral for some time, suspecting, rightly as it turned out, that this decent but nervy man had a horror of responsibility, and would sooner avert his eyes from a crisis than attempt to deal with it. Since arriving off Ushant in October with a dozen ships of the line Colpoys had shown little appetite for action. Shortly before the French sailed, Pellew had written to him and – rather flaunting his credentials as a fire-eater – offered to join the fleet so *Indefatigable* could 'take a place in the line between two three-deckers'. Colpoys demurred. The French had more ships and he thought it best to avoid confrontation. In a note, shown by Pellew to his friend John Gaze, the admiral replied 'he should have no occasion for [Pellew's] services in that way as a drawn battle might be fatal to England at that period of the war'.[11]

What Pellew hoped to find at Falmouth was further news of Colpoys or fresh orders from the Admiralty. Sensing something was terribly wrong, he wanted reassurance that his actions had met with approval and, perhaps more to the point, that he would not be held to account for any blunder or loss of nerve by a superior. The latter had by now struck him as a distinct possibility, as is clear from the fulminations of Gaze, who – reflecting on the crisis – wrote bluntly: 'How Colpoys could let [the French] escape, being so near, is inexplicable.' When the admiral claimed to have been blown eastwards, Gaze pointed out acidly: 'The wind, being from the east, was against him.'[12] This tough, taciturn man who spent his life at Pellew's shoulder, and marked his torment now, thought his captain's unflagging but largely unseen efforts over these months 'did Sir Edward as much credit as anything I know'.[13]

In the event, Pellew found no reassurance at Falmouth. The slowness of communication made the planning and coordination of strategy an extremely haphazard business. Although Falmouth was ideally placed to launch operations in the Bay of Biscay, it was far from the two main centres of naval operations – three days' journey to London by coach, two days from Spithead by packet.

Pellew's anxiety ought to have eased at this stage. Colpoys had received his report, knew the danger and the duty of response clearly lay with him. Pellew could have comforted himself with having done his duty. But here was one of those instances exemplifying the most ardent spirits in the age of sail. Mere duty was not enough for the officer convinced that with a single ship he might have the country's destiny in his hands.

Pellew did not linger at Falmouth, staying just long enough to take on fresh beef and beer before the *Indefatigable* and *Amazon* sailed again on 21 December. He was bound for Ushant again, hoping to discover what had become of the French fleet.

That same day, in fact, the French fleet was coming to off south-west Ireland.

Although mistaken in thinking they had been bound for Portugal, Pellew had rightly surmised the French had suffered separation on the foggy night they sailed from Brest. They followed a pre-arranged course – bearing north-west from the Raz du Sein for Ireland, battered by winds all the way. The flagship, *Fraternité*, never regained contact with her consorts, so although most of the French fleet had come to anchor in Bantry Bay on the Irish coast by 21 December, they were without the vessel carrying the Navy and Army commanders, Admiral Morard de Galles and General Hoche, with the result that no landing could be ordered. Next morning, a real tempest arrived from Ushant.

For a week the French tried to ride the storm. Morale was bad to start with and from what is known of relations between Navy and military, it is hard to imagine a more nightmarish state than was to be found on dozens of heeling, shuddering vessels loaded with thousands of seasick soldiers, terrified horses and tumbling artillery pieces. Some were driven out to sea, others ran aboard one another. At least three more were wrecked. No force was landed on Irish soil. Instead – singly and in twos and threes – the surviving ships started to make their way back to France.

Among them was the *Droits de l'Homme*, a new 74 in the best tradition of French innovative design – low-built and without a poop. She was approaching Brest on 13 January, near home and deliverance, when a lookout sighted a pair of frigates.

The *Indefatigable* and *Amazon* lay at anchor, carrying out repairs. The wind had ceased and it was a day of relative ease, 'the people variously employed', after the tempest visited on them. Scarcely had they sailed from Falmouth three weeks earlier before encountering furies that whistled through the rigging as shrill as a bosun's pipe and chased them all the way to Biscay. Pellew had been at sea for more than twenty years, had seen what the elements might do, but could still write: 'We have experienced a continued gale of wind for this fortnight past such as I have seldom met with.'[14] What they had experienced, in fact, was the same storm visited on the French off southern Ireland.

Pellew's men were still at their midday meal when a sail was sighted in the north-west. In the haze she could only be identified as 'a very large ship', but on her present bearing for Brest there could be little doubt she was French.

It was almost unthinkable that the 44-gun *Indefatigable* should have challenged a two-decker of 74 guns, even with the *Amazon* in support. The *Droits de l'Homme* had 36-pounders on her lower deck and might sink a frigate with a single broadside. But not only did Pellew scent battle when he signalled the *Amazon*: 'Make all sail in Chace', he saw vindication in the offing.

On the French ship, Captain Jean-Baptiste Raymond de Lacrosse had recognised the *Indefatigable* from her stalking of Brest and knew the reputation of her captain. In the normal course of events that should not have deterred a 74. But the *Droits de l'Homme* was handicapped – heavily loaded with about 560 troops, horses and military hardware, on top of her complement, and in all but the fairest conditions unable to run with her lower ports open. Restricted in his ability to bring her heavy guns into action, and wary of his formidable foe, Lacrosse opted to race for home.

The chase began about 170 miles south-west of Ushant, and as it did so the wind started to pick up once more. In the following hours it would rise again to storm force, blowing furiously from the west and driving them towards the treacherous coastline around Brest.

The *Droits de l'Homme* stood in the north-west, the frigates to the south-east, steering to intercept her before landfall. Such was the sailing pitch to which *Indefatigable* had been brought that within an hour she had left *Amazon* some three or four miles behind and at 3 p.m. found herself alone as she closed with the two-decker. Just before 4 p.m., Pellew beat to quarters, noting: 'The enemy steering very wild'.[15]

The *Indefatigable* was running rather wild too, for in Pellew's passionate chase she was careering along at fully 12 knots in a high wind and a great sea when the *Droits de l'Homme*'s fore and main topmasts were carried away. Directly Pellew 'reduc'd my sails to close reef'd topsails' to slow with her.[16] By 5.45, when the opening volleys thundered out, the *Amazon* had fallen eight miles astern.

Pellew had managed to bring the *Indefatigable* by the enemy's stern and fired a carronade broadside. Each of the 42-pound balls passing up the French ship left a trail of smashed bodies, splintered bulkheads and cartwheeling gun carriages before coming to rest, a smoking black lump. The *Indefatigable* then came up alongside, though constantly running ahead and having to wear, or come about.

Lacrosse was deprived of his most potent weapons, conditions making it impossible to open the lower gun ports, but he still had 26-pounders and hundreds of soldiers raking the British with musket fire each time they came up. He was a brave man – like Pellew's first antagonist, Mullon in the *Cleopatre*, he was of the *ancien régime* and had a spell in a revolutionary gaol behind him

Pellew was an early advocate of carronades, using these close-range guns to ferocious effect, particularly in *Indefatigable's* action with the *Droits de l'Homme*.

– and could not bear the thought of defeat. It is said he told a British prisoner that sooner than surrender to frigates, he would 'sink his ship with every soul on board'.[17] So he tried to ram his tormentor.

Pellew watched from the quarterdeck as the dark bulk of the 74 came about on his stern, looming above the *Indefatigable* by the height of a full deck and her bowsprit passing by the taffrail, close enough to hit the spanker boom. 'We unavoidably shot ahead,' he recalled.[18]

An hour into the action, *Amazon* came up – with such alacrity that after 'close fire for a little time' she too shot past the *Droits de l'Homme*.

Naval battles were confusing affairs, not dissimilar perhaps to the historical canvases of hulks looming large amid smoke and flames, masts cast down, yardarms askew, sails holed and draped over sides. In this case the disorder was all the greater for taking place at night, in a rising sea and while running repairs were being made to rigging. It took an hour before – in pitch darkness – the two British ships came up on either quarter of the 74.

Pellew wrote that the action 'often within Pistol shot was by both ships unremitted for above 5 hours'. The implications of this dry statement bear a little reflection. They were fighting while a gale shrieked through the tops and in heavy seas that surged over the sides, swamping men up to their waists. Yet the *Indefatigable* managed to use more than a hundred barrels of powder and ran out of wadding, so rope was cut up as a substitute.

Below lay mayhem. 'The ship was full of water, the cockpit half-leg deep, and the surgeon obliged to tie himself and patient to the stantions to perform an amputation.'[19]

The *Droits de l'Homme* had become a leviathan beset by sharks, terribly bloodied and flailing towards refuge at Brest. 'She never once altered course during the whole action,' wrote Gaze.[20] Her capacity to return cannon fire effectively was hampered by plunging decks and a constant need for repairs aloft. And yet:

> ... the enemy was fighting both sides with great vivacity by constant heavy fire of musquetry, his mizzen mast shot away, his fore and main yards flying about.[21]

Lacrosse thought that more than a hundred men on his ship were dead already. He was still standing, however, and his determination to 'sink his ship with every soul on board' sooner than yield had started to resound like a terrible prophecy. On and on they ran, eastwards towards France.

Reflecting on the situation at about 4 a.m., Pellew wrote:

> I believe 10 hours of more severe fatigue were scarcely ever experienced. The sea was high, the people on the maindeck were up to their middles in water; some guns broke their breechings four times over, some drew the ringbolts from the sides. All our masts were much wounded, the main topmast completely unrigged ...[22]

No one knew with any precision where the chase was taking them. Pellew was putting his faith in 'the confidence I felt in my own knowledge of the coast of France [which] forbade me to listen to any suggestion of danger there from'. The fact was, however, they were still hurtling towards Brest and, as he admitted, 'every creature was too earnestly and too hardly at work to attend exactly to the run of the ship'.[23]

At 4.20, with 'the moon opening out rather brighter than before', the *Indefatigable*'s youngest lieutenant, George Bell, came tearing aft, shouting that he had glimpsed land.[24] They were racing straight at the coast.

A battle for supremacy became in that moment a struggle for survival. 'Not an instant could be lost & every life depended upon the prompt execution of my orders,' Pellew wrote. Exhausted men 'with incredible alacrity haul'd the tacks on board & made sail southward' in order to escape the breakers now visibly creaming against an inky streak of coast. At the same time they sent up rockets to warn the *Amazon* and she tacked north, disappearing rapidly into the murk. It was the last they ever saw of her.

For almost an hour *Indefatigable* ran south-east – until foaming waves came again into sight dead ahead, forcing another change of course, to the north-west. Another hour, six bells and 7 a.m., and there it was again, 'the land ahead and on the weather bow and the Breakers close to leeward'. They had come to the state dreaded by every mariner: embayed and on a lee shore – in other words, trapped within the 30-mile crescent of Audierne Bay by a wind that was driving them towards the land.

Again the *Indefatigable* changed course, back to the south-east. Dawn was coming now and they could just make out the Penmark rocks approaching at the far end of the bay. Something else was visible too, within the bay – the *Droits de l'Homme* '. . . laying on her Broadside . . . the surf tremendous and beating quite over her'.[25]

Every available fragment of canvas had been raised to accelerate and bring the *Indefatigable*'s head about, away from the coast. Clear the rocks and she would be in open sea. Fail and she would share the fate of the *Droits de l'Homme*.

Men on deck peered through spray and spume. All they could do was to trust the canvas would hold, for if the sails started to tear and shred she would lose the momentum to carry them clear. One other dreadful possibility was that as they hurtled across the bay the *Indefatigable* would strike on some invisible reef – at which point the great masts would snap as if struck by a thunderbolt and come down in a havoc of wood, rope and sail, dragging them straight to their deaths. Rather than passing *over* the sea, she was going *through* it. In the distance could be seen 'a high and very steep point of rocky land, and the sea foaming with frightful violence against it'.[26]

For fully three hours the *Indefatigable*'s fate hung in the balance, yet such was the purpose she now embodied there was something almost predictable in the outcome. At 11 a.m., Pellew recorded, she 'passed close round the Penmark rocks'.

Everyone had played their part, including the bumbling Lieutenant Thomson who went aloft 'with extraordinary activity and coolness', to save the topmast when its loss would have doomed them. As for Bell, he had fully justified Pellew's faith in having him promoted from master to lieutenant. Astonishingly, there were just nineteen casualties. The *Indefatigable* was wounded herself – 'considerable damaged in the hull, mast and rigging & making a great deal of water' – yet able to set a course for home.

It was cloudy and a little breezy when she came to off Falmouth three days later.

The destruction of the *Droits de l'Homme* was as much an epic of seamanship as of battle. For all Pellew's improvements to the sailing qualities of his ship, some flaws in early razee design could not be ironed out and the *Indefatigable* always handled awkwardly close to the shore. One of her subsequent captains, Graham Moore, found her a real handful at such times.[27] That she was the sole survivor of the three ships to enter Audierne Bay was the ultimate testimonial to Pellew's seamanship, and to his finest command.

Inevitably, however, it was the battle that caught public attention. Lord Spencer wrote to congratulate him on 'having beaten an 80-gun ship with two frigates, an exploit which has not I believe ever before graced our naval annals'. The press quickly picked up the refrain.[28]

It helped that the Admiralty had a victory with which to obscure the shambles of the Navy's response – or lack of response – to the French threat. Confusion over quite what the threat had been also had some benefits. Gradually, the picture became clearer.

Pellew's first concern was for the *Amazon*. She, it turned out, had been wrecked not far from the *Droits de l'Homme*, although Captain Robert Reynolds and most of his men got safely off on rafts before being taken prisoner. Pellew immediately began to bombard the Admiralty with requests for an exchange 'to liberate my friend and his companions'.

The fate of the *Droits de l'Homme*, on the other hand, belongs to the canon of harrowing shipwreck narratives. The ship – named by some grim irony in honour of the rights of man – had survived the hell of the Irish expedition, with some 1,280 men trapped in a space meant for half that number, and had last been seen aground, broadside down, surf beating over her. At least a hundred men had been killed in the battle. Many more died of wounds while she lay there for four days, defying rescue efforts and being battered to pieces. How many drowned in trying to get off is disputed. A British prisoner on board put the toll at more than 900.[29] French sources maintained it was just over 300.[30] Both may be partisan.

Among those who did escape was the captain who had resisted to the end. Lacrosse joined that little French fraternity of Pellew admirers, writing a warm note to 'my dear and noble adversary' in anticipation of:

> that fortunate instant when both our countries will give, by their treaty of peace, general happiness to Europe . . . and then we will enjoy the reciprocal sentiments of an esteem acquired in the field of honour.[31]

The Ireland expedition was a debacle on both sides. But the real shock was for the British as it became clear that only the weather had prevented a French landing which, on such a scale, would probably have inspired an Irish uprising and civil war.[32] When it was followed a few weeks later by a short-lived landing on the British mainland near Fishguard, there was a run on the banks, precipitating a monetary crisis. To the fore in a highly-charged debate was one question: where on earth had the Navy been?

With the exception of Pellew's frigates, the Navy had not so much as sighted let alone come to blows with the French. Vice-Admiral Colpoys, as we have seen, left Ushant, blaming the weather, then made for Spithead. The man in overall charge, Admiral Lord Bridport, remained at Spithead until 3 January but even after being reinforced with Colpoys's squadron failed to intercept any of the returning French ships.

Pellew's pithy view of Bridport could be trusted only to Broughton: 'scarcely worth drowning, a more contemptible or more miserable animal does not exist'.[33] The real culprit of this particular piece, however, was Colpoys. As it became clear that a vast French fleet had reached Britain unopposed, then returned to Brest restrained only by the weather, prominent voices were raised against him. Criticism reached a point that Henry Dundas, Minister for War, had to mount a shrewd if devious action in Parliament against 'ill-founded misrepresentations' of Colpoys's conduct. He silenced the opposition benches by demanding:

> Has any man a doubt of Sir Edward Pellew's ability, inclination and zeal if possible to have given the intelligence to Admiral Colpoys that the enemy had put to sea? Or that Admiral Colpoys was not desirous to receive it?[34]

The question was nicely couched, although Pellew's lip may have curled at the way his name was invoked in Colpoys's defence. The admiral's absence was obscured – 'the state of the weather was such that it was impossible for [him] even to keep his own fleet under observation' – and his reluctance to engage dismissed with a lie: 'he could not be unwilling because he had a superior force to the enemy'.[35] In fact, he had been reluctant to engage precisely because of the French advantage.

Pellew had plenty to console him. Tributes included one from the Dowager Lady Spencer, mother of the First Lord and an influential Admiralty personage in her own right, who shared 'with the nation the wish . . . that your humanity and intrepidity had been crowned with the success they deserved by bringing your Prize into Port'.[36]

Perhaps the most treasured came from his old shipmate Alex Broughton:

> The Newspapers announced the noble exploit . . . and when I found my dear friend was well my Heart expanded at the account, and all the World shall record it, said I. So we quaffed Libations to your health and our brave Indefatigable defenders. But when, think you, did this good News arrive – just at the moment that my son was going to be baptized and blending your name and mine I called him Edward Alexander. Yes, my friend, he is my second son and though he made rather a forced march upon us having arrived a fortnight before he was expected . . . yet he is no unwelcome recruit, and you are his Godfather, and I cannot help thinking that my wife managed the matter on purpose, for somehow or other she is cruel fond of you, as they say in Devonshire.[37]

Whatever the trials he suffered at the hands of incompetent admirals, here was vindication enough – public acclaim, the admiration of the powerful, and the love of those he cherished. It could get no better.

Any summary of this, the high point in Pellew's career, invites a question. That he was among the greatest frigate captains of the age is obvious. But was he, indeed, *the* greatest?

Tidings of glamorous frigate battles were by now eagerly awaited by the public. They were also, however, comparatively rare. Throughout the Revolutionary Wars, a mere 5 per cent of frigate captains fought single-ship actions, and a total of just twenty-seven French frigates were captured or destroyed.[38] One of the most famous frigate captains, Sir Sidney Smith, never fought a successful single-ship action.

Since the start of the war Pellew had taken unaided two French frigates, *Cleopatre* and *Virginie*, and, in effect, defeated a third, *Pomone*. The destruction of a ship of the line, *Droits de l'Homme*, remained, in Spencer's words, an exploit unique in British naval annals. When old hands reminisced about noble actions against superior odds, Thomas Cochrane's capture of the Spanish frigate *Gamo* with the sloop *Speedy* was one with which it bore comparison, but there were few others. Among Pellew's most prominent peers, Sir John Warren captured numerous French privateers but no frigates. Sir James Saumarez took just the one, the 36-gun *Réunion* in 1793. Only two other British frigate captains were twice victorious in single-ship actions, Sir Robert Barlow and Sir Francis Laforey. Interestingly, neither received the same attention as Smith, Saumarez or Warren. None of them, however, could match Pellew's overall fighting record in frigates. As for seamanship, opinion was that only Sir Richard Keats, his friend in the Western Squadron, may have excelled him.

One other quality, stemming from seamanship, often escaped attention but was noted by John Gaze, the master on most of his ships. After the high casualties of his first victory, with all the anguish it caused him, Pellew had no more than three men killed under him in the trio of actions that proved so sanguinary on *Pomone*, *Virginie* and *Droits de l'Homme*. The high number of French deaths – about 160 just from cannon fire – were attributable to Pellew's specialisation in gunnery. His own low losses, Gaze said, were due to seamanship and shrewdness as 'he always evinced great judgment in the selection of his positions'.

Why then was there not more general admiration among his fellows for so consummate an officer? Where plain jealousy ended and something else began is hard to say. Maybe it was never more than envy. Then again, Pellew was able to annoy even a friendly fellow captain like Graham Moore. On reading Pellew's account of the *Droits de l'Homme* action, in which he wrote in regret at the fate of her 'brave but unhappy crew . . . perhaps more sincerely lamented by us from the expectation of sharing the same fate', Moore noted irritably: 'I doubt if a single man in the *Indefatigable* pitied them at the time, but if they did it was not for the reason given.'[39] It was a curious objection. Pellew may have expressed himself clumsily, but the sentiment was perfectly plausible. Somehow, he invited from his peers a kind of baffled antagonism – partly no doubt because of his ability, but also perhaps because they perceived in his blend of modesty and gallantry something disingenuous. Among those inclined to suspicion, Pellew seemed just too good to be true.

For now his detractors were few while the press declaimed his virtues all over again. Some measure of his status at this point can be seen in the frequency with which his name appeared in *The Times,* the most influential paper of the day. Between 1785 and 1795, Pellew's exploits had been recorded in its columns on thirty-two occasions. Over the same period, Nelson's name was mentioned just three times.[40]

It was right that Pellew should have savoured the moment, because it could not – did not – last. He was an ordinary hero, in that the public would appreciate him just as long as his last victory came to mind. That had ever been the case, and in all naval history there would be just one exception.

Two months after Colpoys's ignominious performance, another admiral redeemed the Navy with a victory over a superior Spanish fleet. He was Sir John Jervis, and it earned him the title which he adopted from the scene of his triumph. But the ultimate victor of the Battle of Cape St Vincent was a 39-year-old commodore who, it was said, saved the day by disobeying orders, led a boarding party in person and took the surrender of two enemy ships. The rise and transfiguration of Horatio Nelson had begun.

PART TWO

ECLIPSE

8.

A Protest Too Far, 1797–1799

———— ⚬⚬⚬ ————

Spring lit up the hills around Falmouth that year with bluebells and broom, dancing against the sea in a way that reflected the fortunes of Trefusis manor's new tenants. Sir Edward and Lady Pellew had reached a time when, blessed with family and fame, enriched by esteem and prize money, it seemed they could desire nothing more. The *Indefatigable* had required extensive repairs after her heroics off Brest and early in 1797 Pellew joined Susan and their youngsters at the manor, an ancient pile he had rented from the local lord. It stood on a headland opposite the town, proclaiming his eminence as he overlooked ships at anchor and south to the twin castles of Pendennis and St Mawes.

In twenty-seven years at sea, Pellew had won greater acclaim than any officer from so modest a background. He was more renowned at forty than either John Jervis or Cuthbert Collingwood, the two men often cited as having achieved most with the least advantage.[1] Although Pellew's visits to London's courtly circles were rare, they were still occasions when even the mighty Lord Spencer pampered him. The King was an admirer, the press loved him. In his native Cornwall, Pellew was little less than a monarch himself.

It was heady stuff and, perhaps as a result, he began to overplay his hand.

He had never been driven by any desire for high command. Prestige was one thing, and he loved it. Rank was another, and for a long time it seemed to make him wary. He may have recognised that, thanks to his background, he was not well suited to directing a certain class of officer. He was content in his situation – with an independent squadron, raking in a fortune and dispensing largesse: in his three frigates since the start of the war, Pellew had made about £10,300 for himself in prize money, equivalent to more than £3 million at present rates. This may be compared with the earnings of two other highly successful frigate captains – Sir John Borlase Warren (£8,930) and Sir Richard Strachan (£6,470).[2]

Yet, to judge from a letter to Spencer soon after the *Droits de l'Homme* affair, Pellew felt short-changed. Bemoaning that he had 'never for the whole war been permitted to run loose for a cruise', he asked to be 'placed in a situation where I might reasonably expect some emolument'. Now, it was true that easy pickings were to be had from French merchant ships, and captains junior to Pellew had profited by them; it was also the case, as he put it, that 'all I have made I have fought hard for'. But to conclude, as he did, 'Give me then my Lordship the first time in my life a chance of getting a prize', was coming it a bit high.[3] In reply Spencer pointed out gently that the naval service, 'in which you are employed with so much credit to yourself, is and always must be a lottery as to profit'. If Pellew had a growing reputation for cupidity it was perhaps not to be wondered at.

Perhaps because his wealth and reputation seemed assured, he turned to ensuring the future of his family. Reviving the fortunes of the clan had always been a powerful motivating force. As he entered his forties it became dominant, and it would be his undoing.

There were now five children, born over eight years. Susan and the family were used to his unpredictable returns from the sea – 'the true Sailor way' Jane Austen called it, the unannounced clatter of a carriage and a burst of the door, followed by a babble of children's voices and shining faces. Pellew was able to spend more time at home – among his 'cubs', as he called them – than was usual for captains, but it was not enough. 'I am longing to see them,' he could write to his friend Broughton after a few weeks away.[4] Loss of his own father as a boy made him all the more fond as a parent himself – and protective. It was partly to

Sir Edward Pellew at the height of his fame, aged forty,
just as the tide of fortune started to go out.
This engraving was based on a portrait by Thomas Lawrence.

have them close at hand, as well as from a desire to guide their
destinies, that he had brought the two older boys aboard the
Indefatigable.

Pownoll had, of course, first been entered on the *Nymphe* at
the absurdly young age of seven and his time genuinely on board

had not been an unqualified success. A bookish, introspective lad, he seems to have been daunted by the boisterous milieu and rank smells of the lower deck. He had nevertheless now spent part of four years on his father's ships.[5]

His younger, more physical and outgoing brother, Fleetwood, did at least show some appetite for the sea life. He had joined the *Indefatigable* when he, too, was seven, though said to be fourteen, and by this deceit was listed as a first-class volunteer. How much time either Pownoll or Fleetwood – 'Pow' and 'Fleet', as their parents called them – were actually on board is not clear. What is plain is that the practice of 'false muster' was used to the benefit of both. Familiar as he was with the corruption that existed at almost every level of naval life, from nepotism to fraud, it seems Pellew saw nothing very wrong with this, and it would have mattered less had he not been so transparent, or had the boys inherited more of his ability. Blinded by fondness, Pellew rarely doubted his sons' suitability or excellence in the profession he had chosen for them. From this time, his letters to Broughton constantly extolled their virtues: 'My dear Boys – they are really fine Boys, and will I trust do well.'[6]

His third son, George, was excluded from this masculine circle, having been disabled as a toddler in a domestic accident. The family had anxious years when it seemed he would never walk unaided until Pellew was able to write, just before the boy turned six, 'rejoycing that he is, thank God, obtaining the use of his Leg again'.[7] In adulthood, devout, scholarly George would be a more dutiful son than either of his elder brothers.

Of greater concern over this period, and the cause of many of Pellew's subsequent problems at the Admiralty, was his brother, Israel.

Edward had busied himself with Israel's affairs since their childhood, and the younger Pellew had given ample evidence that without his brother's help he would have foundered. Israel was given the 32-gun *Amphion* at Edward's insistence in 1795, but wanted something better. Again Edward lobbied Spencer – for Israel to have *Virginie*, Bergeret's old ship; and when the

First Lord demurred, Pellew wrote in 'mortification that you had actually given *Virginie* to Capt Hunt':

> We have all lived long enough My Lord to see the fruits of one Man's labor bestowed on Another, and that both the Credit and Reward of Actions have been frequently given to the Spectators . . . I have much to lament the impossibility I feel in acquiescing in Your Lordship's sentiments.[8]

The audacity of Pellew's assumption that a ship was within his gift because he had captured her, as much as his tone, revealed his detachment from Admiralty protocol. Israel, for his part, promptly confirmed suspicions about his abilities. He was on the *Amphion* in Plymouth in September 1796 when a fire started and she blew up, with huge loss of life. Israel himself escaped by leaping through the stern window and, despite evidence of negligence, was acquitted by a court martial. Edward barely paused before urging that he be given another ship. Still Spencer replied warmly: 'I hope very soon to have a frigate for your Brother and if I possibly can, it shall be a manned one in order that he may get into active life as soon as may be.'[9] Early in 1797, Israel was given the *Greyhound* and attached to Edward's squadron.

Pellew had meantime set off on another campaign at the Admiralty – to obtain the release of those captured when the *Amazon* was wrecked in Audierne Bay. Here was a proper cause, one altogether more worthy than promoting his brother, but his tone was clumsy. Captain Reynolds, he wrote to Spencer, should be exchanged at once and at any cost. When Spencer tried to fob him off, indicating tactfully that such matters had to take their course, Pellew replied in terms more challenging than acquiescent:

> I have to regret that my application to your Lordship should have proved so unfortunate and I shall not cease to lament the barrier which prevents the return of my valued friend to his disconsolate family . . . I must console myself therefore in the hope that some auspicious event may speedily operate to liberate my friend and his companions from Captivity.[10]

For the time being, Spencer continued to soothe his best frigate captain. In private, he may have started to think Pellew was getting above himself, and needed taking down a peg.

Her repairs complete, *Indefatigable* put to sea again in April and was quickly back in action on her old cruising ground off Ushant, capturing a French brig on 30 April and, two weeks later, a 16-gun privateer.[11] Bearing these fresh trophies, Pellew returned triumphantly to Falmouth on 22 May – and to a country in crisis.

The war was going badly. Bonaparte's victories in Italy and Austria had left Britain isolated – without allies in Europe and standing alone against France, Spain and Holland – when what naval historians call the Great Mutiny started at Spithead in the spring of 1797 with a demand by seamen for an increase in pay, unchanged for 145 years. It quickly acquired political and strategic dimensions. From the Channel Fleet it spread to the Nore, the major anchorage at the mouth of the Thames, then to the North Sea squadron at Yarmouth. Within weeks the mutineers numbered some 50,000, controlled almost 120 ships, and in negotiations showed a forthright ability to represent their grievances. As spring turned to summer, the great men-of-war at anchor became known as 'the Floating Republic'. With few exceptions, the mutineers behaved impeccably and at first had some wider support. Once trouble spread from Spithead to the Nore and Yarmouth, however, they were converted in the eyes of a panicky public into revolutionary Jacobins, agents of foreign subversion. A nation still in shock from the landing of French troops on its soil, and fearful of a new incursion by the Dutch, was traumatised.

Falmouth escaped the mutinies. Comparatively rich in prize money, hands on the independent frigates had more in common with their captains than with their fellows in fleet ships of the line. Pellew's squadron was detached to cruise energetically off Brest, in order to gull the French into believing the Navy was as active as ever. He succeeded well enough to have chased a larger enemy squadron into port, and then waited outside for two weeks, taunting them to come out.

Fatefully, however, two of his frigates were sent away for refitting – the *Argus* and the *Greyhound*, under Captain Israel Pellew. By the time they reached Plymouth, so had the mutiny. Soon after coming to anchor, the Greyhounds rose up and Israel was sent ashore, accused of tyrannical behaviour.

The facts of this affair are contested.[12] Israel insisted his men had presented no grievance to him and were simply following the mutinous example of other ships. But after he was sent ashore Sir Richard King, port admiral at Plymouth, told him to accept the complaint and stand down. Whether this was because he believed Israel really was a tyrant, or wanted to avoid confrontation, it amounted to a submission to the mutineers. Inevitably, Israel complained to his elder brother, and just as inevitably, Edward took it up with Spencer.

His timing was as atrocious as his judgment. The First Lord, beset by the greatest emergency in the Navy's history, could only have turned with foreboding to another letter from Pellew, on 31 May, about 'malicious and infamous' accusations against Israel. Pellew's crassness in bothering Spencer at such a time was again compounded by his tone. It verged on the hectoring. Of King's order that Israel should stand down, Pellew wrote:

> You my Lord cannot but see the impossibility of a Man of Honour signing his own sentence and stamping himself a Tyrant to the World. He assures me that he will suffer death before he puts his hand to such a letter. I most heartily approve his determination.[13]

Israel, he insisted, should be given another ship or another crew. Wearily, Spencer replied that he would find 'a situation for Capt Pellew on some other ship as soon as I can'.[14] He forbore to mention that ports were swarming with young captains, 'whom I am for want of ships [obliged] to keep in idleness'.[15]

It would have made no difference. Pellew was in full pursuit, a frigate after a ship of the line, and he could not restrain himself. Writing again to Spencer, he said vindication was as necessary for Israel's honour as it was for his own peace of mind. Then, in his zeal, he piled on too much canvas. It was not just his brother's prospects that were at stake, he concluded, 'but the steps I may be induced to pursue myself'.[16]

With this implicit threat to resign, Pellew fired his last broadside, and it went wide. He was ignored, and he never had the same influence with Spencer again.

In part, this was because he had finally got under the First Lord's skin. Pellew was seemingly oblivious to just how far he – a captain of plain origin addressing an aristocratic First Lord – had crossed an acceptable line. Blindness to wider realities, induced by isolation, was common among sea officers; a study could be made of what might be termed the psychology of the quarterdeck. In addition Pellew was suffering from an acute case of *amour propre*: having become used to attaining his objectives, he could not see when discretion was required. His wilfulness as well as rudeness offended the patrician Spencer.

While Pellew's fall from grace was neither public nor immediate, it coincided with Spencer's acquisition of a more refined and diplomatic protégé. They met that autumn, after Rear-Admiral Nelson lost his right arm in a landing at Tenerife and was invited to dine at the First Lord's home. Lady Spencer's first impression was of 'a most uncouth creature' who had the 'general appearance of an idiot'.[17] All the same, she thought Nelson 'a very delightful creature', and he and her husband got on famously. They were the same age and, whatever his failings, Nelson was not really uncouth at all. Within a year, his ascendancy was sealed at the Nile.

As for the Navy, revolution never did come. The mutinies petered out in June as the ringleaders became isolated and, ship by ship, loyalist seamen regained control. Death sentences were imposed on twenty-nine men, yet reverberations went on for years: seamen were more willing to express grievances; captains tended to become stricter or weaker.

Through it all, the *Indefatigable* remained unaffected. Over the summer, not one incident required unsheathing of the cat and Pellew was able to report that 'notwithstanding many temptations have been offered to disturb the harmony that has subsisted among us, the Conduct of the Ship's company has been perfectly good'.[18] However troublesome he might occasionally be, Pellew continued to show his immense worth to King and country. Never had he failed, never had he been found wanting. To interfere with this finely honed blend of ship, captain and crew would be folly. Yet that was precisely what Spencer now had in mind.

Pellew's first intimation of being brought to heel was being placed under a man he loathed. His memorable opinion of Lord Bridport – 'scarcely worth drowning, a more contemptible or more miserable animal does not exist' – was widely shared. While affecting the demeanour of a benign patriarch, Bridport was avaricious, arrogant and, at times, incompetent.[19] For months he had lobbied Spencer to have the frigate captains of the Western Squadron attached to his Channel Fleet – in part because, like other admirals, he resented their independence, but also because he wanted to cream off a third of their prize money. At the same time as wanting to pick Pellew's pocket, however, he disdained his simple roots. In short, the loathing was mutual.

Spencer's need was to balance priorities. The French expeditions had illustrated the need for good intelligence from Brest and consolidating the independent frigates with the Channel Fleet chimed with a strategic trend towards greater central control.[20] Sensing what was in the wind, Pellew had emphasised his desire to be kept out of Bridport's clutches and could reasonably point out that 'the French fleet owe not their escape to me'. For the time being Spencer stood by him. On confirming that the *Indefatigable*'s services were to be available to Bridport, he was at first reassuring: 'I think you will readily perceive you are not intended to be constantly under the Orders of the Channel Fleet Admiral.'[21]

Loss of the independence he had enjoyed for four years left Pellew 'very much down in the Dumps', as he wrote to Broughton.

On his joining the fleet, Bridport took a malicious pleasure in putting him to convoy duty. This was humiliating, for convoying was not among Pellew's strengths as a seafarer. Like many gifted people, he was impatient with those less accomplished than himself and in his keenness to be moving on was inclined to leave other captains in his wake.

He wrote in misery to Susan, who replied with one of their few surviving letters. Her response was to see the positive side of a duty that would keep him out of harm's way.

> My dear Edward's letter today from Torbay astonished me not a little. I feel for your mortification tho' I rejoice in your safety. I trust at least as there will be no prizes, so there will be no bloody bones. From Lord Spencer's letter there is no hope of your return speedily, so pray my dear Edward compose yourself and bear your Fate patiently. It is all, I have no doubt, for the best.[22]

Throughout his years at sea, their correspondence was exchanged by the Falmouth mail packets that carried despatches to the Admiralty and seamen's letters home. Susan would anxiously await the packets' arrival and, whether or not they brought tidings from her husband, would settle directly to her desk and launch herself on the page without address or preamble, as on another occasion, when Pellew was in the Mediterranean during an epidemic:

> Packet day, dearest Edward, is arrived – but no letters to answer. We hear the plague continues to rage, which makes us more uneasy at your silence. We pray for you incessantly – and bless his goodness in continuing us all well at home, excepting bad colds.
>
> George is learning the flute, which I encourage as an innocent and cheerful relaxation . . .[23]

There was always a good deal about family: Pellew's stepsister Frances had managed to scandalise Penzance by fleeing her marriage with a lover. But the pervasive sense of Susan's letters was one of reassurance from the domestic front. The pert bride had become an indomitable woman – a home manager, matriarch and confidante, as well as all-too-occasional lover, who yet retained with her spirit a sweet simplicity. For the titles and riches that came her way she cared nothing. Susan trusted to Providence, and usually managed to persuade her headstrong, intemperate man to do the same. She wrote to him constantly and her letters sustained him as the tide of fortune started to recede.

His spell of convoy penance done, Pellew went back to what he did best. Between October and January, the *Indefatigable* captured two large 22-gun French privateers, and Bridport – briefly appeased by the lion's share of this bounty – set him free to roam the Channel. Pellew promptly incurred his wrath again by taking a rich Dutch merchantman from Batavia to which Bridport had no entitlement at all while he – as he chortled gleefully – expected £6,000, the equivalent of almost £2 million, even though it would be shared around the squadron.[24] The mocking tone of his letters could only have aggravated Bridport further. On hearing that the admiral wanted him and Warren to be moved to ships of the line, so their frigates might be assigned to more compliant captains, Pellew wrote:

> I am much flattered by the Interest your Lordship takes in my welfare . . . but it has long been my determination, My Lord, to serve the War out in my present command.[25]

Antagonising admirals was never wise and Pellew soon paid for his impudence. Bridport insisted on having *Indefatigable* put fully at his disposal and Spencer was unwilling to confront the Commander-in-Chief, explaining to Pellew: 'I cannot possibly interfere with details of his Lordships' arrangements, and if I could I doubt whether it would do any good.'[26]

Further ill tidings were piling up. In the spring of 1798, Pellew suffered the first real loss of his adult life when his oldest friend, Frank Cole, left the *Revolutionnaire* a sick man and died within days. They had shared a boyhood in Cornwall as well as disgrace on the *Alarm*, and for the past two years had sailed together constantly. Pellew's letter to Frank's brother is a testament to twenty-six years of friendship, and as revealing of his tenderness as those to Spencer are of his capacity for boorishness.

My Dear John, Our loss is truly irreparable and time alone is the only recourse we have left to soften those painful sensations every hour brings to my remembrance. Never, never can I forget the tender blessing and last farewell of the dearest and most faithful friend ever man enjoyed. Painful in the extreme as that parting was, I would not now surrender the remembrance of it for a million lives – that inexpressibly tender sentence that 'I always loved you' is rooted in my heart.[27]

For the rest of the year Pellew had to suffer quibbles and petty rebukes from Bridport, even though the *Indefatigable* was enjoying a dazzling run off Ushant. One week in August, when the French Atlantic coast was thick with British ships of war posted to thwart another Ireland expedition, Pellew took a 16-gun privateer, followed three days later by a corvette, the *Vaillante* of 20 guns. Both of these fast, copper-sheathed vessels were bought into the Navy. Emboldened, Pellew wrote to Spencer, asking to be released from Bridport's control. The First Lord found himself unable to comply.

Pellew may have become used to having his appeals disregarded. But he still had no expectation of the chastising he was about to receive from Spencer.

He brought the *Indefatigable* to anchor in Plymouth on 25 January 1799. It was to be the last time. Three weeks later a letter arrived from Spencer, announcing that Pellew's seniority dictated he should no longer captain a frigate and he had been appointed to the *Impetueux*, a 74-gun ship of the line. On paper, it was a promotion. In reality, it was a punishment.

Pellew had never indicated he wanted a larger ship. Quite the reverse. He was a frigate captain, born and bred. The very qualities of seamanship and initiative that made him outstanding in independent command were wasted in a ship of the line, which meant being placed in a fleet under an admiral unlikely to encourage individuality. Plainly, too, the last thing Pellew desired was to give up his little empire at Falmouth with all that went with it.

His own wishes, it is true, were of no great relevance. It was quite usual for captains of his seniority to be moved to ships of the line, and it has been suggested Spencer had a deeper purpose – that he chose Pellew for the *Impetueux* because she was a troubled ship where the spirit of mutiny endured and his was the kind of presence that might bring order to her.[28] There is something in this. But then the First Lord ought to have considered that Pellew would need trusted followers with him: petty officers in key positions to help him to create a new order; and a good number of plain hands to dilute the mutinous mood. The real severity behind the appointment became clear in the way Spencer enforced it.

Pellew replied directly, and his tone is indicative of what he sensed in the wind. Gone was the injured protest. Instead he came close to pleading:

> I shall feel myself highly gratified if your Lordship will permit me to continue in my present situation, amidst Officers and Men who have served with me thro' the War and who look up to me for protection.[29]

Already though, he saw this was likely to be denied. And so he requested to be allowed to take at least some of his people. On both previous moves, almost his entire crew had gone with him.

Spencer's response was cold. There might be 'some opportunities' for taking his lieutenants and 'the Young Gentlemen'; but that was as far as he would go.[30]

Now deeply apprehensive, Pellew wrote that 'it goes to my heart to separate myself from the People who certainly for attachment have not been exceeded'. Still he hoped to take his oldest, most loyal hands, the Cornish contingent who had been with him since 1793.

> I enclose a list of Young Gentlemen and some few Men who from Neighbourhood and long Service with me I am very earnest to take.[31]

Spencer was implacable. He insisted Pellew could take only his 'Young Gentlemen' – spelling out that they must be 'bona fide' – including, naturally, the Hon. George Cadogan, his own protégé. For reasons known only to him, Spencer was determined to sever Pellew's connection with the tinners, fishermen and farm boys who had followed him from ship to ship.

It would not do to sentimentalise this bond. Harmony was a capricious element on any ship and there had been a four-month spell in 1798 when Pellew had sixteen men flogged, including two for 'mutinous expressions', before, as rapidly as it had appeared, the ship's dark mood passed.[32] But the union forged over six years ran deep. At a basic level it had been mutually beneficial, making the Indefatigables among the richest frigate crew in history. They had also shared peril and triumph, and even those hands whose waywardness brought out their captain's steely side respected him, trusted him and were reassured by the sight of his bulky form on the quarterdeck. And among them too were individuals in whom he had recognised particular qualities – notably his truest follower, Jeremiah Coghlan. Since joining him after the *Dutton* episode, the young Irishman had been made master's mate and Pellew had been hoping to see him promoted to lieutenant.

On a hazy, bleak February day, Pellew left his cabin in *Indefatigable*'s stern, turning his back on the quarters where he had planned and held court, had dispensed justice and celebratory claret, the gallery window overlooking the sea on which the sun had risen and set for the past four years. From the quarterdeck, he took his farewell of the Indefatigables. What he said is not known. The only record of that day is a prosaic entry in the log:

> Fresh breezes and hazy. Shifting the stores from the hulk. At work about the rigging. Recvd 573 lb fresh beef, wood, water and coal.[33]

And beneath it the scrawled signature, *Ed Pellew*. So ended his defining command, the happiest, most fulfilling and most accomplished service of his life.

He was more eloquent in his last letter to Spencer from *Indefatigable*, a passionate but finally dignified protest, written in the third person, at being sent to a ship 'amidst intire strangers'.

> It is fair then to presume Sir E. P. has no sensibility, no attachment, no feeling ... that he can part from faithful and attached Companions, grown from boys to manhood under him, without a sorrowful Countenance, or a Moistened Eye. He grants it may be thought so. But he begs to assert the Contrary. And he dares to say, to those who think thus of him, that language does not furnish words sufficiently strong to express his feelings upon such unmerited hard treatment; nor can time, however soothing, blot from his remembrance Circumstances so debasing to the reputation of an Officer. To your Lordship he leaves the regret for having occasioned them.[34]

He was not alone in believing himself hard served. His old mentor Chatham, the former First Lord, spoke for an older generation of senior officers when he wrote in sympathy: 'I should conceive there were few reasonable requests likely to be refused you, but the very moderate one of merely remaining as you were seems very singular indeed to be denied.'[35]

To add to his woes, one of the few who were permitted to accompany him, one of his 'Young Gentlemen', had become a burden. Early on, Pellew realised that Alex Broughton's young relative Dick did not have the makings of a sea officer, and from the boy's troubled behaviour it seems he would rather have been almost anywhere else himself. Explaining that to Alex would have been hard, especially if Dick was indeed his illegitimate son. While almost everything about the lad was a mystery, Pellew referred to 'your *éleve* Dick' and most of the passages censored from his letters by Alex's family relate to the boy. Where they are legible, Pellew's progress reports adopted a light but somewhat bemused tone: 'He is an odd boy and has slept on a Chest without Bed or Bedding this whole Cruize, having lost his Hammock.' Attempts to be reassuring sounded forced: 'He begins to attend to his books'; 'will one day make a good fellow'.[36] Whether Alex recognised it or not, the move to a new ship would either make or break Dick.

Pellew did pull off one last small but satisfying victory on the *Indefatigable*. Citing naval custom, he went behind Spencer's back to the port admiral, Sir Richard King, who gave approval for him to take 'the usual proportion of Persons granted as an indulgence to Captains going from their ships' – in this case twelve seamen and six petty officers. Spencer continued to be obstructive, but eventually ten men and three gunners followed Pellew to the *Impetueux*.[37] Among them was the wild Irish boy, Jeremiah Coghlan.

The move initiated a new phase in Pellew's service, in more ways than one. He felt the loss of his people and his ship profoundly, and it may not be taking matters too far to suggest that with them went some of his innocence. His zeal, flair and resolve, his sense of duty and love of country – these remained intact. But a brutal lesson had taught him that he could not presume to be aloof from Admiralty politics and made him, for the first time, susceptible to a certain cynicism. Faced in future with a countervailing wind he would not defy it, but run or tack.

9.

A Ship in Revolt, 1799–1801

The blue-coated figure who came up the *Impetueux*'s side in March of 1799 with an agility that belied his increasing girth presented a rare show of energy on that ship. For two months she had lain at Spithead, idling listlessly through the gloom of late winter and, deep in her bowels, seething; and so among the rows of men mustered on deck to hear Sir Edward Pellew's orders read that day were a significant number who sized up their new captain with sidelong truculence.

They took in a man in his early forties, his features worn by salt air, eyes narrowed from scanning the sea, a figure of imposing physique and reputation. But what they perceived was something else. The *Impetueux* had a bit of a reputation of her own, and what they saw was a threat to the status gained by seamen in their revolt two years earlier: Pellew was among the few commanders to have kept his ships aloof from mutiny; for that, and because he had clearly been sent to knock them into shape, he represented a challenge.[1]

What he saw was a ship in which slackness had become habitual, from loose canvas to untidy decks, from the tardiness of hands about their business to the hesitancy of officers to assert their authority. He had just come from Falmouth in what was likely to be a lengthy parting from Susan – neither yet knew that she had just fallen pregnant again – and although nothing daunted him, this bleak vision of his new command darkened his mood.

Pellew may have anticipated trouble, but he lacked first-hand experience of the turmoil that had been convulsing the Navy, and of the persistent culture of rebellion on its ships. He gained

Portsmouth and the nearby anchorage of Spithead – centre of
the Navy's operations.

his first insight a week after joining the *Impetueux* when he was
piped across to the *Gladiator,* joining other captains presiding at
a court martial.

Evidence given over the next two days, of events on the
Hermione, shook them all. A frigate in the West Indies, *Hermione*
had been captained by the kind of monster more familiar in
fiction than reality. Hugh Pigot ruled her with unpredictable
savagery – until, maddened by a particularly callous act of
cruelty, the hands rose up and cast him into the sea. Shouting
'Hughy's overboard' and 'Get the other buggers', they then
murdered several more officers before handing the ship over
to the Spanish. The *Hermione* mutiny was among the blackest
episodes in the Navy's history, and if the five accused in this trial
had been provoked beyond endurance there was never any doubt
about the fate of the guilty. It was some measure of naval justice
that three were acquitted while two ringleaders were hanged.[2]

Next day Pellew made ready to sail, and to confront demons
of his own.

The *Impetueux*'s troubles had not been born of brutality, but from something just as corrosive – feeble officers and lax discipline. Real power lay not with those ostensibly in authority but with an awkward squad of heavy-drinking belligerents among the hands. While claiming to represent the egalitarian principles of 'the Floating Republic', they had turned the *Impetueux* into a dangerous hulk, wallowing in drunkenness, indiscipline and factionalism.

As a 74-gun two-decker, she was a ship of the line – which is to say one that would normally take up a position in the line of battle for a fleet action. With a complement of 670 men, she had the male population of a small town, berthed on a single deck some 170 feet in length.[3] In such conditions, purpose and activity were essential to the making of an efficient, contented ship. Since being captured from the French in 1794, however, the *Impetueux* had been mainly deployed in the Brest blockade, where idleness distilled a profound misery. Disobedience was common. So was fighting. Remarkably, punishment was rare. In the year before Pellew took command, six men were beaten for insolence, while one especially bellicose hand, Stephen Walford, was flogged round the fleet.[4] Otherwise, officers trod warily around the men. One ineffectual captain was followed by another. The senior lieutenant was George Ross, said by the crew to be 'a father to the ship', but in reality intimidated by them.[5]

Pellew was not entirely without loyal hands. In addition to the 'Young Gentlemen', he had of course the old Indefatigables – ten men rated able and three gunners, who came on board on 21 March. Signs of trouble appeared directly, for just as a new captain represented a threat to the regime on *Impetueux*, so did his followers. Fighting broke out on the lower deck, followed by acts of defiance. On 26 March, three men received two dozen each for insolence.[6] It was the first time in ten years Pellew had punished anyone for that and the episode might have represented no more than a flexing of muscles – a testing of the new order. But on *Impetueux* it was just the start.

*

The Channel Fleet sailed in a mighty show on 1 April 1799 – like great cathedrals in steady, majestic progress: five three-deckers and twelve two-deckers, *Impetueux* among them. They were bound for Brest and, with a scent of battle on the sea air and a hum in the rigging above him once more, Pellew's spirits soared. 'We are ready for Citizen Bonaparte whenever he likes,' he wrote to Alex Broughton. 'We shall lick them Hellishly.' Under anyone besides Bridport, they might have done just that.

It was known that the French were again about to launch themselves from Brest with an army for an unknown destination. Bridport's orders as Channel Fleet commander were to contain them. He took up position off Ushant while frigates supposedly watched the port itself – ineffectually as it turned out. On 26 April a great enemy fleet, twenty-five ships of the line, slipped out unhindered.

Blame for this ghastly blunder was laid on Captain Percy Fraser of the *Nymphe*, who raised the alarm that the French were out, but once they disappeared in dense fog sent an ambiguous signal interpreted by Bridport as stating they had returned to anchor in port. Fraser was indeed partly responsible, and paid for it because he was never promoted again. But Bridport was too easily reassured – especially as (his own journal records) twenty minutes before he called off the chase he had received a signal from Pellew in *Impetueux* reporting eleven ships of the line under sail.[7] What the outcome would have been with Pellew rather than Fraser in the *Nymphe* – she, his first love – can only be conjectured.

Blunder was compounded by miscalculation. The French were bound for Egypt, where Bonaparte had been cut off since Nelson's victory at the Nile provided a turning point in the war. At this stage, however, it was feared the fleet was heading to Ireland, which preoccupied British strategists more than ever since the rebellion led by the United Irishmen the previous year, when about 1,000 French troops finally succeeded in landing in the north-west (too few and too late to affect the outcome).[8] Although Bridport was only following orders in sailing for Cork, he then spent weeks anchored off south-west Ireland, waiting for the French to arrive. Strains were soon showing within the fleet – nowhere more than on the *Impetueux*.

It may be recalled that in analysing Pellew's method, his follower John Gaze said:

> No man ever knew better how to manage seamen . . . He studied the character of his men and could soon ascertain whether a man was likely to appreciate forgiveness or whether he could not be reclaimed without punishment.

The problem was that the wretchedness of *Impetueux* went beyond individual troublemakers, or even of a cabal of hard cases. Other evidence was to be seen as she battled to make sail in good time, exposing clumsiness in the tops and negligence on deck. Men on the duty watch were constantly being found drunk and, on occasion, fell overboard, as occurred on 24 April, when John Smith was drowned.[9]

In three weeks off Ushant, Pellew had had six men beaten – for drunkenness, fighting and insolence; but it was off Ireland that matters got out of hand. Over four weeks of inactivity, no fewer than twenty-four men were flogged; the main offence remained drunkenness, but incidents of insolence were increasing. At such times even officers who disliked the cat felt compelled to employ it, and Pellew might have found himself echoing a friend, Captain Graham Moore: 'I am under the necessity of either winking at their licentiousness and disorderly conduct, to the ruin of discipline, or continually punishing them, which is equally revolting.'[10]

By the end of May it was plain that the French were not coming to Ireland. Bridport ordered a shift from the exposed observation point of Cape Clear in the extreme south-west to the shelter of Bearhaven, about 50 miles away. This amounted to an admission that he was in the wrong place, yet he still refused to leave. Among themselves his captains were openly critical. One who had already formed 'no very high idea' of Bridport's abilities complained in his journal: 'Our fleets are too often commanded by men of no talents.'[11]

On the *Impetueux*, meanwhile, the furies had been unleashed. Nine men were beaten in three days after anchoring in Bearhaven, four of them for disobedience or insolence.[12] So Pellew may have sensed what was in the wind – even before one of the old Indefatigables told him of a plot to remove him.[13]

At noon on 31 May, Pellew gave orders for the decks to be washed, then went to his cabin to dress. The officer of the watch, Lieutenant John Stokes, stayed on the quarterdeck, waiting for the hands to be turned up. While there he heard a sudden commotion, and men came swarming up a ladder in 'a vast crowd'.[14] Surprisingly, Lieutenant Ross was with them.

This invasion of the quarterdeck, a violation of the officers' sanctum, amounted to a threat in itself, and Stokes demanded to know what the men wanted. There was a murmuring before, as Stokes related, Ross 'reported to me they wanted to send a letter to Lord Bridport' complaining of 'cruel usage' by Pellew. Aghast, Stokes raced away to the cabin located at the rear of the quarterdeck to inform the captain.

When Pellew emerged, still in his dressing gown, it was to find 200 men milling about. At the sight of him they roared 'One and all! One and all! A boat! A boat!'[15] He later recalled:

> I asked what was the matter and was answered by Thomas Harrop and Samuel Sidney 'We complain of hard usage, floggings &' and muttered something about a letter to Lord Bridport. I repeatedly and vehemently asked for it, saying on my honour I should carry it myself, or send an officer with it, to which there was a constant cry of 'No, no, no! A boat of our own, a boat of our own!' The more I tried to pacify them, the louder the noise became.[16]

By now Captain Boys of the Marines was feeling for his sword, even as he observed Pellew's continued efforts to placate the men:

> Sir Edward asked again for the letter and assured them on his honor that he would take it to the Admiral . . . He intreated them for it, and not to forfeit their characters by such shameful conduct.[17]

Still the tumult continued. Calls by Lieutenant Stokes for silence were ignored. The hapless Lieutenant Ross, who had rashly associated himself with the men's grievance and then stood transfixed as mutiny unfolded before him, was brought to his senses by an order from Pellew to get the men to disperse; but when he tried, he too was disregarded.

The tipping point was reached when another hand, William Jones, shouted: 'We will have a boat. Damn me, we will take one!' Harrop then turned to the men, crying, 'We will take one ourselves.'[18] The chorus of agreement that greeted these declarations of revolt signalled the end of negotiation.

'You will, will you?' roared Pellew, and flew to his cabin for a sword. Recalling events on the *Hermione* and anticipating that he might be 'about to go overboard' himself, he had resolved 'to kill Sidney and Harrop'.

Captain Boys was ordering his Marines up on to the poop in preparation to open fire when Pellew re-emerged from the cabin – dressing gown flapping, sword in hand. Whether from this alarming sight, or the combination of officers advancing on them, the mutineers' nerve failed. Although Jones urged resistance, shouting, 'Don't be frightened. Stand to him,' Pellew drove them off the quarterdeck with the help of Boys.

The immediate threat had passed. But, having retreated to the gundeck below, some of the ringleaders tried to incite their fellows to return to the quarterdeck for an all-out attack, to kill Pellew and seize the ship. Harrop went round swearing: 'Damn and bugger a sword. Who cares for a sword? I would knock him down with a boarding pike.'[19]

Then, with a clatter of feet on the ladder, Pellew and the officers were among them in the dank gloom. Spotting Harrop by a gun carriage, Pellew seized him by the collar, 'drew a dirk, swore he had a good mind to rush it through him, and dragged him aft'.[20] Harrop's had been the loudest voice among the mutineers, and with his arrest resistance ended. Eight other men were quickly clapped in irons.

The letter that had been the ostensible point of the affair was found and brought to Pellew. Addressed to Bridport it ran:

The usage we have received since Sir Edward Pellew commanded us is such as we have never been used to this war ... It is unsupportable. Sir Edward has punished different people to the amount of forty-nine dozen and upwards for very frivolous Crimes ... We hope you will redress our Grievances with an other Captain and second lieutenant and fourth lieutenant. Our first lieutenant has ever been a father to the ship.[21]

The ringleaders had been secretly active for some time and, as the support of men admired on the lower deck was vital in any act of defiance, had recruited Samuel Sidney, a respected hand who could write – he drafted the letter – and had been a spokesman. Those behind him were known malcontents: Harrop, Jones, Stephen Walford and Michael Pennell. To raise a force sufficient to storm the quarterdeck, they had intimidated their fellows, threatening the reluctant with sticks to drive them aft.[22] This ugly echo of the hated practice of 'starting', the beating of men to their stations, cast the seemingly spontaneous protest by a significant portion of the company – roughly 200 out of 670 – in a quite different light.

Later reports had it that the mutiny was part of a wider plot intended to trigger revolt across the fleet. It was even suggested that the mutineers were a cabal of United Irishmen who intended to burn every ship and join the rebels on shore.[23] There was no evidence for either suggestion, and the latter was febrile nonsense. Yet the crisis on *Impetueux* was far from over.

That same day Bridport ordered the fleet to sail, having just learnt that the French were in the Mediterranean. When Pellew applied to him for a court martial of the mutineers, and an inquiry into their complaints, Bridport waved him away. Having dithered for weeks, he insisted that there was now not a moment to lose.

The race to the Mediterranean took almost two weeks, carrying them past the all-too-familiar seas off Ushant and those as-yet-unsung off Cape Trafalgar, through the straits to Gibraltar. There Pellew applied to another admiral, Sir Charles Cotton, for a court martial, again without success. When they reached the British base at Minorca he asked to see Lord St Vincent, the Commander-in-Chief. The answer came back that he was too unwell.

The Mediterranean Fleet that summer of 1799 was, in fact, in a state of utter disarray. St Vincent had come close to a breakdown, being, as he put it, deprived 'of all power both of body and mind'.[24] His right-hand man, Rear-Admiral Nelson, had been distracted since his triumph at the Nile – bewitched by Emma Hamilton in Naples. All the while Bonaparte was seemingly poised to launch himself on fresh conquests. The question was where – Malta, Minorca or Naples?

No wonder, perhaps, that the agony of a single ship was ignored. But the signal being relayed to the *Impetueux* was that Pellew did not have his admirals' backing. While there were no outright signs of another mutiny, the lower deck was still seething. Factional brawls erupted almost daily. The company were angry and wretched. Soon after they came in at Minorca, two young hands were forced to run a gauntlet 'for being caught in an indecent situation'.[25] Matters indeed had reached a point, Pellew wrote, that 'the services of this particular ship can no longer be made useful to the country'.[26] In desperation, he petitioned a senior captain, Sir George Grey, who had St Vincent's ear and convinced him that the crisis on *Impetueux* had to be dealt with. Pellew was always grateful to Grey for interceding with the cantankerous lord 'at considerable risk to yourself', and years later, as Grey was dying, wrote: 'To your goodness I was obliged for the opportunity of vindicating myself ... From that moment my heart was yours.'[27] (This letter was all the more thoughtful for being written when Pellew was a viscount and Grey had become lost to public view.)

The court martial opened on 19 June. Nine men, caps in hand, filed into the great cabin of the *Prince* where Rear-Admiral Cuthbert Collingwood and eleven captains were seated. With Pellew acting as prosecutor, ten witnesses gave almost identical accounts, including Lieutenant Ross, who cut a sorry figure as the officer whose efforts to ingratiate himself with the company had ended so disastrously.

Any doubts about the gravity of the case were dispelled in evidence. Acts of mutiny often consisted of no more than defying an order, say, to weigh anchor. On *Impetueux*, the mutineers had threatened the captain with explicit violence. When the time came for their defence, only Sidney dared to speak up, admitting to writing the letter, but 'with no bad intent'. He was the real victim – a respected hand who had been used by the ringleaders.

His captain tried to save him. The trial record shows that 'Sir Edward Pellew spoke much in favour of Sidney's character'.[28] His words failed to move the court martial captains, who sentenced Sidney, along with Harrop and Jones, to death. Pellew may have had more success with William McAdam, who, he testified, was 'very active, attentive to his duty and never drunk'. McAdam was ordered to receive a hundred lashes. Four others got a hundred, one received 200, and the ninth was acquitted.

The Mediterranean sky was bright the following morning when the three condemned men were brought up. At the last minute Pellew had petitioned St Vincent in the hope of saving Sidney; but that steely man had no truck with mercy and, as *Impetueux*'s log noted,

> At 9am Sam Sydney [*sic*] Will Jones & Thos Harrop were hanged at the yardarm. At 10 their bodies were committed to the deep. Read the Articles of War.[29]

The next day the remaining mutineers were flogged around the fleet before being dispersed into other ships with a few other dissidents. Lieutenant Ross went too, his career in ruins. So did the two landsmen William Sugate and John Fox – little more than lads at the ages of seventeen and twenty – who had been forced to run the gauntlet for sodomy.

'So ended our fight,' Pellew wrote to Broughton after this purge. 'Ever since we understand each other . . . An act of oblivion has passed and we are as quiet as lambs.'[30] And so they were, at least for a time. Contentment was another matter. Pellew strove to nurture those qualities that had distinguished his frigates: he went among the crew and got to know them, encouraging promise where he found it and organising activities, musical events and contests. He exercised them in sail and gun drills, but also protested successfully on their behalf to the Admiralty that poor caulking made the decks 'leak so much as to render it impossible for the people to sleep dry in their beds'.[31] They responded, to the point that this slovenly 74, far from being a ship whose services were 'useless to the country', was able to perform the directives of her exceptionally demanding captain. Still, he never succeeded in recreating the heady spirit of the *Indefatigable*, that special blend of flair and exuberance, amounting to a sort of ferocious élan. In the end, what made a happy or an unhappy ship could be an intangible thing. If the *Impetueux* had one discernible weakness, it was drink. Floggings became less frequent, but drunkenness and fighting persisted, as did cases of insolence and, in one instance, striking a superior officer. What is noticeable is that although these included capital offences, Pellew did not again seek recourse to a court martial – and, therefore, there were no more hangings.

He was not long in the Mediterranean. The French fleet remained elusive, then returned intact to Brest. Bonaparte went back to France as well, while Nelson sailed home to a mixture of adulation over the Nile and ribald mockery for his infatuation with Emma Hamilton. Meanwhile, Pellew found himself back with the Channel Fleet under Bridport and, which was almost as bad, once more blockading Brest.

Two welcome events awaited him at home. The first was finding Susan 'excessively large . . . round as a barrel'. Her pregnancy with their sixth and last child, Edward, overjoyed him and, anticipating Christmas cheer with family and friends after a grim year, he wrote to Broughton: 'Pray have you finished the repairs to your House and can you receive us into it this Winter as I expect Leave before Xmas day . . .'[32]

Before setting off for the Broughtons' fireside, and a week of feasting on roast game and captured French claret, he received a further piece of good news, one that could have been bettered only by an order to rejoin the *Indefatigable*: Bridport's ineptitude had finally exhausted the Admiralty's patience and he was being superseded. 'Heaven be praised,' Pellew exulted. 'Never was a man so universally despised by the whole Service. A mixture of ignorance, avarice and spleen.'[33]

Bridport's replacement was St Vincent. It was a fateful appointment in that Pellew's fortunes would rest with this man, and the signs were not promising for they had virtually no human qualities in common. And yet, outsiders by birth as they were fighting men by instinct, the former Sir John Jervis and Sir Edward Pellew were drawn together like two volatile elements. Inevitably, they were also fated to react furiously before spinning apart.

Lord St Vincent was one of the Navy's originals, an austere man of war with the imagination and tolerance of a Puritan fanatic. He pursued personal feuds as implacably as enemy fleets, fell out with his onetime protégé Nelson, refused to attend his funeral and described Emma as 'an infernal bitch'. To start with, he had no high expectations of Pellew either, thinking that, like most frigate captains, he would be fonder of prize money than battle.

Their first joint enterprise, in the summer of 1800, altered all that. It took Pellew back to the Brittany coast, which he now knew probably better than any British seafarer, again to assist French royalists. St Vincent, meeting his captains around a table in the great cabin, made a shrewd assessment of them and placed Pellew above far more senior officers in command of a squadron landing British troops in Quiberon Bay to bolster the rebels.

This operation, it has been said, showed Pellew at his brilliant best, for while it failed, his ability shone out in contrast to those with whom he served.[34] Certainly it gave the lie to a view that he had no gift for fleet command. His meticulous plan, involving six ships of the line, seven frigates and a dozen transports and smaller vessels, for landing a force of 4,000 troops on Belle Île, a large island in Quiberon Bay, won St Vincent's praise as 'the most masterly I ever saw'. Observing Pellew in these weeks, his new admiral saw other virtues in one who, if nothing else, shared his own simple origins, zeal and hardiness – and these warmed him as few things could his chilly soul. Captains who measured up to St Vincent's standards were rare, and most of those in the Channel Fleet he thought 'licentious, malingering and abominable'.[35] Nor had he a very high opinion of some of his rear-admirals, including Pellew's old rivals, Saumarez and Warren. To their chagrin, St Vincent came increasingly to prefer Pellew, explaining to Spencer:

> Although the naval command in Quiberon Bay may appear too important for a captain, I shall not divest Sir Edward of it unless I am ordered so to do, feeling a thorough conviction that no man in his Majesty's Navy, be his rank ever so high, will fit it so well.[36]

No testimonial Pellew ever received as a captain surpassed that.

All the same, being St Vincent's favourite could attract resentment. Giving a captain preference over an admiral was a violation of naval custom which could only offend senior officers. Saumarez, with whom he had not been on speaking terms for years, was livid.

The damage did not end there. Pellew's social distinctiveness had, as we have seen, attracted the wrong kind of attention to him before. Now, with the aristocracy and gentry more prominent than ever among a new generation of Navy officers, the hostility of some senior men gave younger captains licence to join in sneering gossip.[37] One incident involving Sir Henry Digby of the *Alcmene* was serious enough for Pellew to complain to St Vincent. Son of a royal chaplain, Digby was Pellew's junior by thirteen years, a star among the younger frigate captains, and one of two officers cited by St Vincent as treating Pellew with 'the most abominable disrespect'.[38] While threatened with a court martial if he did not make 'amende honourable', Digby was seemingly unrepentant. In the end St Vincent decided against the 'pestilential effect' of a trial.[39] As a result, however, nothing was done to scotch the snide insults. In an increasingly class-conscious age, Pellew gained a reputation in certain circles as a bumpkin. The jibe about his rise from obscurity – 'a man of mushroom extraction' – became established and took root. The poet Alaric Watts, a haughty literary type who never met him but was offended by his failure to reply to an unsolicited request, remarked that this would 'come as no surprise to anyone who knows anything of his origins'.

At the same time, Pellew's own ship had become a platform for promoting young gentlemen. Some of those on *Impetueux* were destined for higher things, including the young George Cadogan and Nicholas Pateshall, both of whom became admirals. Some were not, as had become clear in Dick Broughton's case. After four years, Alex Broughton's young relative was sent away to school by Pellew, who may have been hinting at some scandal in writing to his friend: 'I hope he will do well for his own sake and mine. I have never heard any more of the circumstances and conclude it has blown over.'[40] Either way, the pathetic figure of Dick faded into oblivion. Pellew wrote sadly: 'I can say with truth I have a fatherly affection for him.' Broughton's family blacked out the next four lines.[41]

Having St Vincent's ear did enable Pellew to launch the one youth he saw as being cast from his own mettle. Jeremiah Coghlan had been at his side for three years and was desperate for an opportunity. He got it when Pellew persuaded the admiral to give Coghlan the *Viper*, a 14-gun cutter, with the rank of acting lieutenant. Advised by Pellew to seize his moment with some eye-catching feat of derring-do, the Irish firebrand launched a night raid on a French gun-brig, *Cerbère*, near Quiberon Bay, and carried her with a handful of men. It is hard not to see Pellew's hand in this deed, which proved the making of his young Hornblower. His hand it certainly was that wrote to Spencer, requesting Coghlan's gallantry be brought to the King's attention so the regulations on length of service could be waived to enable his promotion.

Coghlan duly gained his commission and confirmation in the *Viper*. Sent to the West Indies, he would rejoin his benefactor again more than a decade later in the Mediterranean and remained properly grateful to 'the most generous and kindest of friends that ever lived – Dearly Beloved Man'.[42]

Coghlan's success helped to make up for a bitter disappointment. Weeks of planning and activity for the landing in Quiberon Bay came to nothing, thanks to bad weather and vacillation by Brigadier-General Thomas Maitland, who decided his force of 4,000 men was inadequate for taking an island defended by 7,000, even as he praised Pellew's assistance, declaring him 'as distinguished [in military operations] as he is for personal gallantry and professional knowledge'.[43] Pellew was left to take the rebel French leaders to England, describing them with earthy candour to Broughton as:

> Rascals who care not one Curse for all the Princes on Earth, and who provided Mass be sung care not a rush for who governs France. I am satisfied it can never come to anything. The Lower orders want only quiet and relief, the Priests their old gewgaws, the Chiefs to become great men . . . and all wish for John Bull to come over and play the first fiddle whilst they play Bass.[44]

William Pitt's administration, too, had realised the limitations of a proxy war and in the late summer of 1800 the strategic focus shifted to Spain, with a more ambitious plan – to land British troops at Ferrol dockyard to destroy ships at anchor and under construction. St Vincent again wanted Pellew in charge, but this time he did not get his way. Even though he continued to insist that Captain Pellew was far superior to Rear-Admiral Warren 'in seamanship and arrangement, and equal to him in enterprise', Spencer ruled the latter should have the fleet.

In the event, Pellew was lucky. As deputy to Warren he accomplished his task with panache, supervising the landing of 12,000 troops from flat boats, artillery and stores from launches, on a beach five miles from Ferrol on 26 August. Yet although they met no resistance, the Army commander, General James Pulteney, lost his nerve and that night ordered them to re-embark. Pellew was incandescent but saw that the real loser was Warren. Having 'bitterly lamented being deprived of the Command,' he wrote to his old mentor Lord Chatham, 'I have cause to be thankful.'[45] The contrast in fighting spirit between Army and Navy could hardly have been more striking. Small wonder, as the historian N. A. M. Rodger has noted, that it had become difficult to find British generals who inspired anything but contempt among sea officers.[46]

Pragmatism and age were perhaps starting to draw some of the fire from Pellew's own belly. Just past his forty-third birthday, he wrote to Broughton of his 'longing for peace, and that we may be near each other', going so far as to suggest that after a treaty the Pellew and Broughton households might remove together to France.

> We think of emigrating towards the South and looking for a Chateau under the Pyrenees – about Tarbes or Pau, a delightful part and fortunate enough to have been undisturbed by Jacobins.[47]

It was probably while *Impetueux* was being refitted at Plymouth early in 1801 that Pellew's one recorded meeting with Nelson took place. Little is known of the encounter beyond that they dined at the Fountain Inn and that Pellew was accompanied by young Coghlan, who was introduced, according to one of those present, as 'some sort of fire-eater'.[48] Nelson was the man of the moment, while Pellew must have been aware that his hour had passed. Nelson combined the capacity for greatness with the gift of luck. Pellew, for all his ability, lacked the Nelsonian ingredients of charm and grace, and his luck had run out. His efforts to promote Coghlan came to nothing either. Nelson was on the verge of an expedition against Denmark that brought him the spectacular victory of Copenhagen, but, as Pellew was to discover for himself, Nelson always made his own choice of protégés.

He was also finding that being regarded by St Vincent as 'my sheet anchor' had its drawbacks. With fears growing that

Bonaparte was mustering forces for an all-out invasion of England, the Channel Fleet commander tightened the blockade of the Brittany ports, doubling the number of ships from fifteen to thirty. Monitoring Brest was grim and exhausting work to start with. Under St Vincent's regime, constantly tacking close inshore against easterly winds, it was brutal. Many captains and some admirals – including Saumarez, who was overwhelmed by strain and had to be relieved – could not stand it.[49] St Vincent, who evidently relished their misery, grumbled: 'Seven-eighths of the captains of this fleet are practising every subterfuge to get into harbour.'[50] Praise for Pellew – 'No man regards and esteems you more truly than I' – meant only further arduous duty. An entire winter passed in the storm-tossed desolation of Biscay, of icy gales and salt provisions. Even Pellew was moved to a rare complaint: 'They do not let me rest much in Port. So we must go on but I believe they think me made of iron.'

Still, he had won a powerful new benefactor and when, early in 1801, the country was shaken by a political earthquake, his fortunes appeared about to turn. Pitt resigned after seventeen years as Prime Minister. With him went Spencer at the Admiralty. The new premier, Henry Addington, appointed St Vincent as First Lord.

Instead of early reward, however, Pellew was set for the most tedious cruise of his life. For eight months from March 1801, the *Impetueux* with a small squadron maintained a blockade of French ships twice their number in Rochefort. For week after week, as spring turned to summer and autumn, Pellew wrote in the log 'Observ'd the Enemy's Squadron in the same position as the last occasion.' The French never moved, while on *Impetueux* strains became evident again in fighting and drunkenness. But another constant log entry ran 'Served Lemon Juice as usual'. So although the drunks and belligerents were flogged, they remained healthy. Not one man died, nor were any invalided home in those eight months.[51]

With the approach of another winter their torture was starting to appear interminable when, on 21 October, one of Pellew's frigates ran aground off Rochefort and a French ship emerged under a flag of truce. Her beaming captain came on board to announce that Britain and France had signed a peace agreement three weeks earlier.

10.

St Vincent's Anchor, 1802–1805

Peace . . . it brought a longing for home and the prospect of release. Pellew had been at war for more than eight years. Had he still been engaged in action or any other pulse-quickening task he might have felt differently to see its end. As it was, by the time of the Amiens pact, frigate chases were distant memories, glory was gone and Pellew was thoroughly jaded. Under St Vincent's implacable regime, the captain he called 'my sheet anchor' had found the strength of his cable, and his spirit, tested to the limit.

He did at least quit Brittany with praise in his ears – even if it came from the enemy. Pellew's reputation stood almost as high among the French as it did at home, sustained by his grace towards old foes like Bergeret, with whom he maintained a warm correspondence. At the end of his nine-month blockade Admiral Jean-Baptiste Willaumez sent out a note from Rochefort 'on behalf of all the Frenchmen who can only be grateful for the treatment they have received at your hands' and regretting candidly that he had missed the opportunity of a lesson in sea warfare from a man of honour.[1] Attached was a little verse that reads better in the original than translation.

Au favori du dieu du mer	To the favourite of the sea god,
Au marin, Cher à la victoire	To the sailor favoured by victory
Qui n'eprouva aucun revers	Who did not know defeat.
À Ed Pellew salut et gloire	To Ed Pellew, salute and glory

The *Impetueux* too was, finally, at peace. In Cawsand Bay on 16 April the crew were paid off and Pellew watched them depart, solid hands and ferocious spirits alike, ragged figures with a few bundled possessions or chests hoisted on shoulders, bound for carousing, debauchery and uncertainty. Then he sat down to write to the Admiralty: 'It only remains for me to express my readiness for service whenever their Lordships may call on me.'[2]

The Treaty of Amiens was rapturously received by almost everyone besides a few politicians. 'Peace! Peace!' enthused Lord Spencer's sister Georgiana in a letter to their mother, while London crowds went wild and other cities celebrated with fireworks and bonfires. Nelson endorsed the terms and the Army concurred.

For Pellew there was just one problem with peace. He did not have the concerns of most sea captains about being sent ashore on half pay, for he had already been made a colonel of Marines, a salaried role, pending his overdue promotion to admiral. Even so, income was a worry. His earnings from *Indefatigable* had been severely eroded, partly by keeping a good table over two years in *Impetueux* when he had gone without prize money, and partly by acts of private charity. He rebuked one of his free-spending sons, Pownoll, by pointing out: 'You know the situation of your father and how many calls he has for money.' Moreover, while retaining the grand pile of Trefusis House at Falmouth as a family residence, he had no property of his own.

Fortunately, Susan was a simple soul and, he wrote to Broughton, they could 'rub along . . . Thank God that we are not ostentatious and can walk to church.'[3] His idea of rubbing along may have been relative, given an income of more than £1,000 a year – what a successful doctor might earn. Still, it was modest by comparison with Nelson's £4,000 a year in 1801, which helped him to lay out £9,000 for Merton Place, the grand home and estate in Surrey where he lived with Emma Hamilton after the peace.[4]

The fact is, though, it was neither his nor Susan's comforts that came to trouble Pellew, then to obsess him. Although he enjoyed prosperity and the power of benevolence it gave him, the supposed personal greed that would taint his name was largely a myth. Austerity was, after all, his oldest acquaintance. His real concern was preserving the family line he had established, by providing for his sons. He had raised the Pellews out of poverty and, in an age when wealth and influence were decidedly fragile, dreaded they might be cast back into it. With Pownoll and Fleetwood becalmed as naval officers that was a distinct possibility – especially as he, a seaman with no worldly experience, had few theatres in which to find an influential new role.

And so, at a loose end and anxious about the future, he went into politics. He did so with no partisan fervour, but rather under the flag of St Vincent.

William Pitt had not so much fallen from power as stepped aside for a respite after seventeen years, mainly as a war leader. He had made way for a government of novices and lightweights. The new Prime Minister, Henry Addington, was a diffident man and a mediocre leader who had never held Cabinet rank and was seen as little more than a stopgap. He did succeed in making connections among Navy officers, however, by appointing as First Lord one of their own. St Vincent, in turn, encouraged senior captains of his choice to stand for Parliament, and so, although he was a disaster in almost every respect in office, he did create an 'Admiralty interest' at Westminster that supported Addington.

Pellew had already considered a venture into politics. The public standing of Navy officers in general, and his own in particular, had brought an invitation a year earlier from the electors of Barnstaple, a port in Devon, to be their candidate. His naiveté is indicated by letters to Broughton, asking for his friend's view of the 'propriety' of becoming an MP. Was it, he wanted to know, an objective 'for an honest Officer' if it could be achieved 'at small expense'? What would the benefits be? There was a certain disingenuousness here, as there was in his claim to be 'rather puzzled' by the whole affair, before he owned up to what was compelling him:

> I think it may be useful in pushing the boys in Life and myself too – for I cannot rest where I am. I have begun my fortune but by no means finished it for a sit down.[5]

By the time of quitting *Impetueux* he had made up his mind, encouraged no doubt by St Vincent, who noted that he 'fills the eye of the public'. Pellew was under no illusions. In politics, just as at sea, his old admiral would expect absolute loyalty from followers. In return, he would confer favour. The gulf between Pellew's romantic youth and pragmatic maturity widened distinctly in his year ashore.

On returning to Trefusis House, he ran straight into a storm. Susan, loyal selfless Susan, was transformed – at least as far as her husband was concerned – into a vengeful cat. For the first time in twenty years of marriage, they found themselves in a state of war.

Susan's opposition to his political plans was visceral. Raised a county girl, content in Falmouth, she was hostile to domestic upheaval, particularly one involving removal to a city, and his blithe declaration that they would have to quit Cornwall for distant London, or, at a pinch, fashionable Bath, horrified her. This led to other divisions. Susan was a frugal soul who abhorred ostentation and in her eyes Edward had become, as she put it on a later occasion, 'too anxious for the things of this world'.[6] Whereas she had her simple faith, and a trust that all would work out for the best, he was full of fear over the transience of fortune, convinced that for their security he had to navigate his family as tightly as he did a ship. While appreciating the virtue of Susan's 'anxious endeavours to rear her family in the paths of Innocence and Virtue', Edward saw their salvation as lying rather in the realms of Influence and Money.[7]

This fundamental difference revealed a growing divergence between them in matters of principle. Susan seems to have worried, understandably, about her husband's suitability for dabbling in the dark arts of politics. Honourable in war, generous to friends, chivalrous to enemies, he was yet – like many seamen – quite unworldly. She sensed that his warm-hearted nature was in danger of being compromised – perhaps even feared for his soul. The rotten-borough politics of the era were distinctly rough and he would doubtless be required to hand out money to voters. And money was now a practical consideration. Years later Pellew would admit wryly that she reckoned his foray into public life as 'amongst my sins'.

Devout she was, stubborn she could be – and, it now emerged, capable of standing up for herself. From the outset Susan refused to fall in with his plans. If he wanted to move to London, so be it. He could take rooms there. She would stay on the hill at Trefusis House. Baffled and frustrated, Pellew wrote to Broughton that she 'detests this parliamentary plan and is indeed very angry and irreconcilable'.[8] One thing they continued to share – a desire that their children should 'become one day an honour to their country'.[9] To that end, as her handful of surviving letters to him show, Edward and Susan were always utterly devoted.*

For the most part they were reassured. The eldest, Emma, aged seventeen – and, naturally, 'all the heart of a father could wish' – was being courted by a Navy officer by whom she would go on to have eleven children. A second daughter, Julia, aged thirteen, would also marry a Navy captain with whom she seems to have been blissfully happy, while cherishing 'the beloved Father who must know that I love him dearly'.[10]

As to the boys, Fleetwood, aged twelve, had become – in his father's eyes – 'as fine, open, generous manly fellow as ever lived';[11] now at school, he was, of course, an excellent scholar too. George, eight, had recovered from his lameness and was pious and musical. Edward was not yet two before he was found to be a 'prodigious fine boy'. That left Pownoll.

Pownoll, or Pow, had been an enigma for some time and was now, at sixteen, a concern. Initially reluctant for the sea, he had dabbled in scholarship before returning to the comfort of his father's quarterdeck in a state of sulky resentment. As one who could rarely find fault in any of his children it is indicative of Pellew's concern that he no longer wrote of Pownoll as 'a really fine boy' but rather as 'clever and quick, but idle and

---

* Although Susan kept all his official papers, she destroyed his letters to her and only a few of hers to him avoided the fate that she ordained in one of the last: 'I hope you burn my letters – never omit it.'

unmanageable'. His statement, that Pownoll 'chose a Sailor's life ag'st my wishes', indicated too that he saw the lad was not cut out for it.[12] Having acted as protector for one inept relative, his brother Israel, he may have feared what the future might hold for his eldest son.

That rendered his understanding with St Vincent all the more valuable, and so, at the moment of decision, he persisted in defying Susan's wishes.

His first battle ashore found Pellew well out of his depth. Having been flattered by an invitation to stand 'upon popular grounds', and gulled into thinking he could win election at slight cost, he had written airily: 'I will not contest it at any greater expense than a few hundred. If I thought it would cost me a thousand I should be off.'[13] In fact, the landlubbers of Barnstaple proved adept at parting Captain Pellew from what remained of his prize money. Over the summer of 1802 the politics of alehouses and town hall, of parades and bungs, cost him dear – not least thanks to a grand climax in which he was 'conducted from the hustings to a barge upon wheels, ornamented with laurel, manned by prime seamen in white shirts with oars and steered by a lieutenant in uniform . . . the populace cheering their hero'.[14] He emerged victorious, but not before he had parted with some £2,000, including so-called travel expenses for individual voters, and survived a challenge from a rival who, in effect, accused him of bribery. Pellew was in all fairness probably the least shady of the four candidates, but the whole experience left him feeling bruised. It did not help that Susan's fears had proved well founded, as she was now determined to remind him. He moaned:

> I have really labor'd thro' a great deal of Mental Uneasiness and Vexation, the greater part arising from disquiets at home. Susan is still obstinately bent upon resistance to my wishes and I assure you has made me miserable. It is a great and lamentable misfortune she will not repose more confidence in me.[15]

His insistence that he had invested only 'odds and ends of prize money' did nothing to reconcile her, especially as it proved well wide of the mark. Their quarrels had become loud and bitter. 'It is terrible, with two Nice Girls at home, to hear domestic contention,' Pellew confided to Broughton. But while insisting his wife 'really ought not to be so foolish', he had become sceptical himself of the benefits, saying only, somewhat glumly, 'some good may arise to my family some day or other'.[16]

As it turned out, his entry to Westminster was belated. Though the Barnstaple vote was held in July 1802, his rival's challenge delayed confirmation of the result until February 1803 and, with the family in Falmouth, he spent part of the winter moored in a lonely London exile, living in rooms, eating in chop houses and doing his best to cultivate connections. It was an unhappy time and his new cynicism was becoming more evident. On meeting the Duke of Northumberland, a mighty grandee who somehow wielded political power in Cornwall, he had written to Broughton: 'I believe from my heart these sort of Gentry are incapable of friendship. However I am on my guard with him and will make as much use of him as I can.'[17]

And so, in due course, he did. As a landsman, Pellew became adroit at acquiring new patrons and influential supporters, the Duke among them. He did so not by fawning, although his letters did tend to the fulsome style of the day, but through the offer of mutual benefit. When he cultivated men of importance it was on the implicit understanding that he was not without influence himself, either as a captain, or – as he was soon to be – an admiral. Ambitious fathers were delighted to see their sons among Pellew's protégés, and for a long time he rarely turned one away, believing he could make officers of them all. In this he was mistaken; Dick Broughton would not be the only misfit to stand on his quarterdeck. As an admiral Pellew was too sanguine about accepting yet another 'good boy' when there were simply not enough officer vacancies to go round. And while this form of patronage was common enough, Pellew took it to such lengths that he compromised his own standards. All that can be said in his favour is he did it not to benefit himself but his sons. From this point his attitude was summed up by a letter to an Admiralty commissioner a few years later, written without a trace of self-consciousness and perhaps even a hint of threat:

> Do me all the kindness for my son [Fleetwood] you can. I may live to return it to one of yours, for you see the wheel goes round and round.[18]

Serving St Vincent did not help, for behind a mask of severe probity the First Lord's moral code was as ambiguous as his methods were questionable.

The Admiralty Board, as the government body responsible for the Navy was known, had passed from the distant era when it was headed by professional seamen to one of control by aristocratic civilians. In Pellew's time, first lords like Sandwich, Chatham, and Spencer, took advice from commissioners who were usually admirals, but they were not sea officers themselves; they held Cabinet rank and were susceptible to political pressure, notably in dispensing patronage and promotion. When St Vincent replaced Spencer as First Lord, he appeared a reversion to the Anson tradition, a great admiral known and respected across the Navy. He took office, moreover, with a self-declared mission – to reform and root out corruption in the dockyards and civil departments.

Those with first hand-experience of St Vincent's violent methods, the contradictions of his steeliness and indulgence, may have had an inkling of what lay ahead, but they were also those with the most to gain. Pellew was one, and to him St Vincent held out the prospect of a major command, the East Indies. Sir Thomas Troubridge was another. Troubridge had led the line in his fleet at the Battle of Cape St Vincent, was his real soul mate, and was now made one of his commissioners at the Admiralty. Arguably St Vincent served neither man well, and the spectacular falling out that would embroil all three of them was to be the death of Troubridge.

*

Lord St Vincent, a figure as dominant in the Navy in his way
as Nelson, and just as dangerous to his enemies.

After all the domestic upheaval and turmoil it had involved,
Pellew's dalliance with politics would have gone unrecorded
but for a single episode. Although entitled to take his place in
the Commons from early in 1803, he went back to sea almost
immediately and seems never to have attended Parliament at all
before making his first and last speech a year later.

Strains in the Amiens treaty had soon become apparent,
aggravated by French annexations in north Italy and occupation
of Switzerland, and the menacing posture of Bonaparte, now

First Consul for life. As levels of rhetoric rose, the Admiralty started assigning officers to ships, among them Pellew who, in March 1803, was given the 80-gun *Tonnant*. In May war was declared.

Taking leave of Susan after eleven months ashore, he reasoned philosophically that the break would do them both good. 'Time may soften down her feelings. She is a good Creature and the best of Wives.'[19] Even now, however, he realised they faced a far longer and wider separation. As he hinted to Broughton, he had been told by St Vincent that if all went well he would be awarded the East Indies command.

> If I go abroad, I go a great way. Your boys are too young I fear to receive my protection but you will always Command me – be perfectly silent in this for your Life. My love to Mrs B.[20]

Bonaparte had begun amassing an army of almost 165,000 men for an all-out invasion of England from Boulogne. Here, his theory went, the fleets at Toulon and Brest would muster to support the cross-Channel thrust at the decisive moment. In response two British fleets were sent to keep them bottled up: the first, under Nelson, went to Toulon; the second, under Vice-Admiral William Cornwallis, to Ushant. Cornwallis divided his ships into three squadrons to watch over Brest and Rochefort, and Ferrol in neutral Spain, which the French treated as a home port. Pellew was given charge of Ferrol.

The command lasted six months and was an all-too-grim reminder of his earlier blockade duties. Conditions over winter were utterly miserable as the *Tonnant* had not been caulked for years and leaked like an old bucket: 'We have not a dry hammock in the ship, and what is worse the Magazine becomes more damp every day.' Hopes were raised that they might be beset by the Toulon fleet on a break-out, and the squadron crackled with anticipation. When the challenge failed to materialise Pellew felt all the more enervated. 'These operations afford no profit or honour,' he grumbled as he prepared to sail for Plymouth. 'It is hard to always do Yr Duty for nothing.'[21]

His disgruntlement was natural enough. He was forty-five, had never served with less than distinction and was overdue for promotion to rear-admiral; yet still he was routinely assigned hard duty while far lesser captains gained flag rank. Time and opportunity were drawing away. He had grown stout and even his fabled agility in the tops was in decline. Homeward bound, he wrote to Broughton.

> I find, my dear Alex, that I am older than I was and can't get to the Mast Head so well as I used. I want to be an Admiral for I am tired of Squaring the Main Yard.[22]

Although he did not say so, he had already been presented with his chance. A recall to England had come, not on naval business but in order that Pellew might fulfil his political duties; and even if it was not fully spelt out, he knew what was expected of him, just as he was confident of what would follow.

The land to which he returned in March 1804 was in a febrile state – plagued by rumours of invasion, weakened by an unpopular administration and with a king gone mad once more. The Government was faltering, Addington fatally undermined by the opposition of Pitt, who had persuaded himself and a large section of the population that the country was in imminent danger of being overwhelmed. At the heart of a debate gripping Parliament was naval policy.

St Vincent's tenure as First Lord had been a disaster. Where Spencer was courteous and quietly efficient, St Vincent was violent, bigoted and messianic. His megalomania about purging what he saw as fraud among contractors led him into deeper waters – fanatical economic cuts which had made a terrible mess of the shipyards and curbed building just when the Navy was most in need of new ships.[23]

All this gave powder to Pitt's broadsides from the opposition benches: the Admiralty had neglected not only shipbuilding but recruitment, and as a result there were insufficient ships for the blockade. Pitt claimed that stopping the French would require a mass building programme of innovative craft known as gunboats.

To these charges St Vincent's riposte was a flat but ringing assertion: 'I do not say the French cannot come. I only say they cannot come by water.'[24]

The odd thing was, for all his administrative blundering, he was right. But matters had reached a point that the First Lord and his Admiralty colleagues were 'execrated by all parties'.[25] The public was close to panic.

It was in this situation that Pellew had been recalled, to support Addington – and St Vincent – in a Commons vote. Pitt was demanding an inquiry into Navy affairs, and the Government needed a credible advocate for the defence – ideally, an MP who was also a serving officer of note.

When a coach deposited Pellew in a wet and muddy square outside the Palace of Westminster on 16 March, his only experience of public speaking was from the quarterdeck. Yet that day from the floor he spoke pithily and with flair. In about five minutes on his feet he addressed the two issues on which he felt qualified to speak: the Navy's means for dealing with an invasion; and the opposition's advocacy of a force of gunboats as the first line of defence. He did not see, he said in his preamble, anything in Britain's naval defences 'to excite the apprehension even of the most timid'; on the contrary, he saw 'everything that may be expected from activity and perseverance to inspire us with confidence'. The whereabouts of the enemy was known – they were assembled at Boulogne in upwards of a thousand vessels, and although he would have wished to know when they intended to come out, 'I know this much, that they cannot all get out in one day, or in one night either.'[26]

The case for gunboats he dismissed with disdain – a 'mosquito fleet . . . the most contemptible force that can be employed' – before moving on to the real matter of substance:

> As to the possibility of the enemy being able, in a narrow sea, to pass through our blockading squadrons . . . I really, from anything that I have seen in the course of my professional experience, am

not much disposed to concur in it. I know, Sir, and can assert with confidence, that our navy was never better found, that it was never better supplied, and that our men were never better fed or clothed. Have we not all the enemy's ports blockaded from Toulon to Flushing? Are we not able to cope, anywhere, with any force the enemy dares to send out against us, and do we not even outnumber them at every one of those ports we have blockaded?

Concluding with some of his own experiences off Ferrol, Pellew sat down to cheers from the government benches and seething from the opposition. Some thought his intervention had been crucial – 'the gallant officer' won plaudits for his unexpected eloquence and Pitt's motion was defeated by seventy-one votes.

Politically, Pellew's speech made no difference. Beset on all sides, Addington resigned a month later, clearing the way for Pitt's return. To everyone's relief, St Vincent went back to sea, leaving the Admiralty in a mess which took years to sort out.

But for Pellew personally, the consequences were incalculable. True, he had his promotion to rear-admiral and the offer of the East Indies command confirmed before St Vincent left office; and he was used to jealous sniping, so jibes that he had 'lost his honour in gain of fortune' had little effect.[27] Where he suffered was in incurring the enmity of an individual far more powerful than any envious captain. Pitt had known him since his early frigate days and understandably regarded him as a supporter. Had not Pitt's brother, Lord Chatham, been his benefactor as First Lord? Had not Pellew been a public subscriber – to the tune of 5 guineas – to a statue in Pitt's honour?[28] In an age when politics revolved around personalities rather than parties, Pitt took Pellew's desertion to Addington as a betrayal. Once back in office, with his own man installed at the Admiralty – Lord Melville – he would ensure Pellew paid a heavy price.[29]

Pellew was defiant, writing to Broughton:

You will have heard me abused for daring to speak the Truth in the Great House but the Truth I did speak and am so perfectly independent of great Commissions and the support of any Great Man that I am determined I will speak the truth . . . I am quite sick of such Company. But I will not bore you on the subject of Politicks. We shall all soon have something else to do than talk if Boney makes attack.[30]

He protested too much. His claim to be 'independent . . . of any Great Man' was plainly nonsense. He was not the only Navy officer to have supported Addington; Nelson had as well, writing: 'Whenever it is necessary, I am <u>your</u> Admiral.'[31] But Pellew had become personally close enough to Addington – soon to be ennobled as Lord Sidmouth – for his son George later to marry the former Prime Minister's daughter. Pellew had also overstated his case in asserting: 'Our navy was never better found and never better supplied.' Although loyalty dictated that no serving officer would have said otherwise, to have stood up and done so in Parliament was unwise, as well as being untrue.

Where he did speak from the heart was in declaring the French would never, 'in a narrow sea, pass through our blockading squadrons'. Pitt was convinced to the contrary – and that his country was in the hour of its greatest peril; his anxieties were fed by a few naval supporters who believed too much confidence had been placed in St Vincent's intensified blockading system, and that 'should the fleet be shattered in a storm, or driven far to the westward', invasion was a distinct possibility. Pellew, for his part, had no doubt in the effectiveness of blockade. He could also draw on years of observing the French in battle (or, as had become the case, their reluctance to give battle) and his certainty that Britain had the ascendancy at sea would be vindicated.

His fervour to serve – to be engaged at the critical moment – was never in doubt, as he now demonstrated yet again. He had within his grasp the potentially lucrative Indies command. Were he to accept it, his fortune and the careers of his sons and followers would be assured. Yet, knowing the war was at a crisis point, he did something that showed, as nothing else could have, his greatest wish – to be there when 'Boney' made his attack. He wrote to Nelson in the Mediterranean, offering to serve under him.

Nelson, who was clear in desiring a 'band of brothers' rather than potential rivals, brushed him off, albeit gracefully.

Sir Edward Pellew by Thomas Lawrence. This portrait, from 1797, was thought the best likeness of the seven painted during his lifetime.

Fleetwood Pellew in action at Batavia – the 'flower of my flock' as his doting father called him, and his greatest sadness.

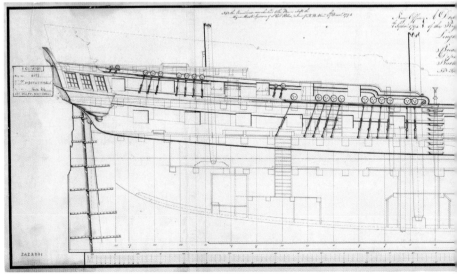

A plan of the *Indefatigable*. Pellew's favourite ship was a razee – a clumsy 44-gun super-frigate which he made a byword for sailing brilliance.

Pellew commissioned Thomas Luny to paint the wreck of the *Dutton*. Rescuing those on board was the exploit on which he reflected with the most pleasure.

'Sailors on a Cruise' by George Cruikshank records hands of Pellew's *Arethusa* celebrating a bountiful year for prize money in 1794.

Teignmouth, where Pellew made his last home ashore, painted by his neighbour Thomas Luny.

Destruction of the *Droits de l'Homme* by Ebenezer Colls.

Friend: Captain Sir Christopher
Cole by Margaret Sarah
Carpenter.

Foe: Rear-Admiral Sir Thomas
Troubridge by William Beechey.

The bombardment of Algiers by George Chinnery.

Vice-Admiral Sir Richard Keats
by John Jackson.

This copy of the Algiers map,
found among Exmouth's private
papers, seemingly acquired its
stains as he discussed tactics
around a table with his captains.

A late portrait: Viscount Exmouth, by Samuel Drummond, 1816.

I am truly sensible of the honor you do me in expressing a wish to serve under me, but you have always, my dear Sir Edward, proved yourself so equal to command a fleet that it would be a sin to place you in any other situation.[32]

Nelson's rejection was as fateful as it was deft. Pellew accepted the Indies command, but in the process removed himself from the climax of the war at sea. He would miss Trafalgar.

He took the *Tonnant* back to Ferrol, assured that promotion to Rear-Admiral of the White was imminent.[33] He knew, too, that his loyalty to St Vincent had benefited his sons: Lieutenant Pownoll Pellew was destined for the West Indies, where, his father prayed, he would 'do honor to the Service and his family' – even as his real anxieties were revealed in a notebook of advice for the boy, covering his every conceivable weakness, from health and hygiene to dress and duty (*see* Appendix). Of Fleetwood, now fourteen and 'an uncommon fine lad', he could say more confidently 'in two years he will be fit for a Lieut'.[34]

Pellew was departing from the grey waters of Ushant without regret. But he never quit any command without leaving on it some mark. During a spell of gales, he had made a valuable strategic discovery – that Betanzos, a bay near Ferrol thought by the Spaniards too perilous for use, contained within it a safe anchorage and that it provided a vantage point for monitoring the French fleet in harbour.

Another episode at Ferrol had personal consequences. Pellew kept on good terms with the Spaniards, who were neutral at this time, and despite the French naval presence was able to send ashore his secretary, Thomas Fitzgerald, to negotiate for the supply of fresh provisions; on one occasion Fitzgerald survived a French assassination attempt. From this escapade arose the longest battle of Pellew's life.

His successor was the Honourable Alexander Cochrane, the heir to an earldom and a man of violent, sometimes vicious, temper. They detested one another. Cochrane had coveted the East Indies command – and, because of his aristocratic connections, had been confident of getting it. His rage had disastrous results. First, he alienated Ferrol's governor, then incited an attack on Spanish treasure ships returning from South America, the effect of which was to bring Spain back into the war on France's side at the end of 1804.

Pellew was back at Portsmouth, fitting out for the voyage east, when a letter arrived from Cochrane 'full of charges of fraud and peculations' against Fitzgerald over his purchase of supplies at Ferrol.[35] As his secretary, Fitzgerald was to have accompanied Pellew to India but, a painfully honest man, he postponed his departure in order to clear his name. Pellew went up to the Admiralty and suggested that the clearest way of dealing with the charges was for Fitzgerald to return to Spain, where whatever evidence existed for a court martial could be found. Had this course been followed the affair would have been resolved; no proof was ever advanced for Cochrane's allegations, for none existed. As it was, lives were destroyed while, in Pellew's words, 'foul accusations, loosely advanced' lingered for decades, serving 'all the purposes the most malignant heart and bitterest enemy could have wished'.[36]

11.

Storm in the East, 1804–1806

———— ∞ ————

In thirty-three years there was little at sea Pellew had not seen. Yet virtually all that time had been in the Channel or North Atlantic. He had only crossed the Equator once, as a boy of thirteen, and never glimpsed either of the other two oceans, so his passage to India represented change in every way. Rounding the Cape of Good Hope and racing east with the Roaring Forties, he entered what might almost have been a new element. Gone were the chill grey bleakness of the Channel, the stormy cragginess of Biscay. In their place were the pink and gold of sunrise and sunset, the hurricanes of the Eastern Seas.

The Indian is the smallest ocean, but still covers almost 29 million square miles, from the Red Sea to Antarctica, from Africa to Terra Australis. This was now the domain of Rear-Admiral Sir Edward Pellew. Having ventured halfway across the world in his 74-gun flagship *Culloden*, he gained some insight into the vastness of this far-flung command by the hunt he had to undertake to find the man he was superseding. When he put in at Penang, expecting to find Vice-Admiral Peter Rainier, he had covered almost 15,000 miles. Of Rainier, however, there was no trace. So he sailed across the Bay of Bengal to Madras. Rainier was not there either. Only on returning to Penang, where Rainier put in a week later, did Pellew take command – in January 1805. He had covered a further 3,000 miles to locate the admiral and six months had passed since sailing from Spithead.

Pellew went to India 'in the hope of giving a blow to the inveterate and restless Enemies of Mankind'.[1] He had other objectives as Commander-in-Chief as well – launching his son Fleetwood and shaking the pagoda tree, as the local idiom had it for reaping the riches of the East. (Rainier had sailed off with some £250,000, worth about £75 million today.) But his greatest desire was to engage the foe.

In the event, his most inveterate enemies over the next four years were not French but British, and his biggest battle would be with a brother officer.

The agency of British dominance was the self-styled Grandest Society of Merchants in the Universe – more prosaically the East India Company, which had laid the basis for imperial rule with trade at three Indian presidencies, Madras, Bombay and Calcutta, and outposts at Penang and Canton. The Navy Commander-in-Chief was accountable not only to the Admiralty but, to some extent, the grandees and nabobs of the Company. His primary duty was protecting trade. With a fleet at Madras far more potent than the French and Dutch squadrons combined, that might have seemed no great challenge. However, the French had shown more enterprise here than in home waters; and the task of safeguarding the riches Britain derived from the Eastern Seas was bedevilled by the scope and nature of Company shipping as well as by the monsoon winds that defined sailing seasons.

The principal danger lay in the south. The French were established on two islands in mid-ocean from which men of war and privateers preyed on merchant ships in the Bay of Bengal – to devastating effect. Although so tiny they were mere specks on the map, Mauritius and Réunion had become a menace vastly disproportionate to their size. Among the first letters to greet Pellew was one from Lord Wellesley, the Governor-General at Calcutta (soon to be outshone by his younger brother, the future Duke of Wellington) lamenting 'the vexatious list of the Captures recently made by the French in these Seas, and carried into the Mauritius in the face of our Cruizers off that island'.

There was, despite its immense canvas, something oddly clubbish about the seafarers' world. The naval commander at Mauritius was Rear-Admiral Durand de Linois, whom Pellew had encountered in 1796 when he surrendered the frigate *l'Unité*. Linois was not a very dangerous opponent. He had missed out on an opportunity to deal Britain a spectacular blow the previous year, fleeing from a richly laden fleet of Indiamen in the mistaken belief that they were superior ships of war.

A potentially more formidable threat was posed by another old foe. Captain Jacques Bergeret remained a warm correspondent – during the peace Pellew had composed a testimonial, addressed to 'Officers of the British Navy', which concluded: 'I value [Bergeret] as my brother, am proud of him as my friend' – and had been posted to the Indies in the 32-gun frigate *Psyche*.[2] Within a month of Pellew's arrival, Bergeret took three rich prizes but before he could become a severe embarrassment to his friend, encountered the *San Fiorenzo*, a far heavier British frigate. The following four-hour battle was even bloodier than his action with Pellew in 1796. Fifty-seven of his men died and seventy were wounded among 240 before Bergeret surrendered 'out of humanity for the survivors'.[3]

It was a rare British success. Whatever its strength on paper, the Indies fleet was aging and ill-serviced – and even when ships were healthy, their crews were not. Fevers carried off almost 1,000 men in the years of Pellew's command, creating a need for hands that could be met only by impressment from Company ships. To these problems had to be added those of geography: Mauritius was seven weeks distant from Madras, so although Wellesley had urged Pellew's predecessor to establish a blockade, there were insufficient ships; no sooner did a squadron withdraw for provisions than French raiders emerged and sailed for Bengal.

In the spirit of high ideals that he brought to his first fleet command, Pellew persuaded Wellesley to release Bergeret, for having 'conducted himself in a very gracious manner towards our countrymen who have become his prisoners' – reasoning too that 'a spirit of amicable conciliation' towards the French might lead to a regular exchange with Mauritius, where British prisoners included the navigator Captain Matthew Flinders.[4] It was therefore probably more than coincidence that brought Pellew to Trincomalee in May – where he found 'lying here the *Thetis* cartel', bound for Mauritius with Bergeret.[5]

The two were reunited in an embrace on *Culloden*'s quarterdeck. Six years had passed since their last meeting and, as related by Pellew's secretary, Edward Locker, 'the manly tears shed found an honest welcome in every heart which witnessed the interview'.[6]

Among them was a young officer, introduced by his father to Bergeret with pride. Fleetwood Pellew certainly looked the part – a lithe, dark-haired youth of some beauty, he cut a striking figure in the lieutenant's uniform he had donned a month earlier. He was fifteen, which, privately, even the admiral admitted was indecently young while insisting he was 'full thirty in discretion, sense and manners'.[7] In applying for his confirmation, Pellew obscured the boy's age by claiming he had been 'six years afloat', although even that was questionable.[8]

On reaching Port Louis, Bergeret wrote as warmly as ever, sending 'regards to the young lieutenant' and urging Pellew to 'indulge a little less in that great exertion for which you were so remarkable in Europe but which cannot be used with safety in this climate'.[9]

By the same post Pellew had a letter from Matthew Flinders, relating his experiences as a captive at Mauritius. Thanks to Bergeret, 'whom your kindness and liberality have made the warm friend of every unfortunate Englishman', the mapmaker of Terra Australis had his conditions eased. But hopes for a regular prisoner exchange were disappointed and Flinders would spend five more years on the island.[10]

India came too late in life for Pellew to be beguiled by it. Wary of the miasmas believed to cause disease, he dosed himself with emetics, rationed his madeira intake and forbore to try curry. Even when the mercury fell below 90 °F he felt 'melting'. He also disliked the luxury and extravagance. 'Young men throw themselves on a sopha and dictate to a black clerk called Connicopaly – half a dozen sheets full of elegant Quotations from Shakespeare,' he growled. 'In short it is a climate of indolence and luxury – united with avarice and oppression of

Calcutta from Garden Reach by Thomas Daniell.
The appearance of tranquillity was deceptive.

which I am truly disgusted.' Remarkably, although radicalism of any sort was usually abhorrent to him, he thought the Company's treatment of the local populace tyrannical, likening it to Bonaparte's subjugation of Europe.[11]

By the start of what would be their lengthiest separation, he and Susan had put their troubles behind them. Five years would elapse before they saw one another again, during which she kept him informed of births (their first three grandchildren), deaths and marriages, and prayed for her distant menfolk while awaiting the mail packet. News of a fever outbreak filled her 'with terror for you and Fleetwood' and she fretted to hear he had cut down on wine:

> I do not approve of your water drinking system. Believe me dear, it will not do at your time of life – after having indulged liberally for so many years. The change will be too great. You must lessen your quantity by degrees and never take less than 2 or 3 glasses a day.[12]

Though Edward's letters did not survive her bonfire of their papers on his death, the flavour can be gathered from his tender references to her at this time, extolling 'my dearly beloved Susan ... & all her tender love for me', and 'the best of wives whose prudence, affection and upright character' he contrasted with his own 'vile passion of temper'.[13]

For all the simple strength of their love, it would not do to cast Pellew as unswervingly chaste. He was a robust man with robust appetites, certainly for food and drink, and although in home waters he could see Susan every few weeks, there is evidence that over the many years of separation he took physical comfort elsewhere. It would have been remarkable had he not. As an old nautical maxim put it, once past Gibraltar every man became a bachelor. Pellew liked women, and they liked him. In his fifties he conducted a fond correspondence with a young female for whom he conceived a paternal love. In India his activity on the dancefloor with Lady Barlow, the dissolute wife of the Governor of Madras, was remarked upon; he once wrote flattering her on 'your shapes', though there is no reason to suppose they were lovers.[14] Liaisons had to be discreet for one in his position, as the sole episode for which there is evidence (with a courtesan at Minorca years later) demonstrates.

At the start, Pellew had far too much on his plate for dalliance. Soon after arriving at Madras, in May 1805, he learnt that Linois had taken a heavily laden Indiaman, *Brunswick*, off Ceylon. A squadron was sent to hunt for the 74-gun French flagship *Marengo* and the frigate *Belle Poule*, but in these vast seas Linois had no difficulty in escaping. Wellesley's response in writing to Pellew was not to blame the Navy but to state explicitly what wiser heads at the India House were starting to recognise – that security of the Company's trade could not be ensured, 'while the Mauritius & the Cape remain in the hands of the Enemy'.[15]

Pellew had been at Madras for four months – absorbing the complexity of his new command and hosting dinners at his residence in Mount Road for local dignitaries – when the 74-gun *Blenheim* came in, flying the flag of a second admiral, and a real war started.

*

On a steamy August day, bearers jogged up to the Commander-in-Chief's house where they deposited a palanquin from which emerged a man wearing the uniform of a rear-admiral. Sir Thomas Troubridge was brought to Sir Edward Pellew. Both were extremely tall men, both growing stout. Troubridge, Rear-Admiral of the Blue, made the formal gestures appropriate to greeting a more senior officer, a Rear-Admiral of the White. The air was stiff and, amid the rising humidity of an approaching monsoon, both were perspiring heavily even before Troubridge proffered his papers and the door closed on them.

The Admiralty orders told Pellew that his command had been divided. Troubridge was to take over the seas east of the latitude of Point de Galle in Ceylon while Pellew retained those to the west. The Indies fleet of twenty-seven ships was to be shared.

Pellew could not believe his eyes. He was aware that intriguing against him had begun before his departure; Pitt's return as Prime Minister had brought to the Admiralty a regime hostile to St Vincent and all his works. For this reason, Pellew had delayed resigning as an MP until his last day in England when he had obtained a promise from Lord Melville, the new First Lord, that his command was secure.[16] Even after intelligence reached him by overland mail that Troubridge had sailed with orders for India, he was ignorant of the detail. He could not have imagined any prime minister – certainly not a passionate patriot like Pitt – putting a personal vendetta above the national interest, nor any First Lord being oblivious to what Pellew saw as the strategic imperatives.

To view matters from Melville's perspective, dividing the command was not in itself a bad idea. It had been considered before and, given the size of the Indian Ocean, had a certain logic. Melville had no personal antagonism for Pellew, even if his master Pitt did, but he had good reason for wanting the impetuous Troubridge, a member of St Vincent's board, as far away as possible. Melville did not mind ruffling the feathers of a few admirals. As part of his reorganisation, he had gone so far as to deprive Nelson of the most lucrative part of the Mediterranean command.[17]

What made the division of the Indian Ocean command so disastrous was the way in which Melville redrew the boundaries. While Pellew remained the senior man, responsible for protecting British possessions and dealing with the enemy at Mauritius, he was being sent to a station from which he could not adequately do either. As well as losing half his ships, he was to abandon Madras, traditionally the Navy's headquarters in the East and the only port in India with access to the entire ocean, and remove to Bombay, which was not merely isolated but – for four months of the year when the south-west monsoon blew – actually unsafe. Command at Madras and the main theatre of operations, the Bay of Bengal, went to Troubridge, though he was the junior man.

Stunned, Pellew's first response was to feign incomprehension of orders he saw jeopardised the war effort. He turned a blind eye to them. Troubridge wrote to the Admiralty:

> To my astonishment he gave me for answer that he did not understand by their Lordships commission to me or the instructions thereon, which I gave him to read, that I was authorised to take the command on the coast of Coromandel or the Bay of Bengal and that what he conceived to be their Lordships intent was the Coast due east from the South Line from Point de Galle . . . and consequently I am not allowed to consider Madras or Bengal within the limits of my station.[18]

Their first meeting ended in a shouting match from which Troubridge stormed out. Pellew's rage was directed mainly at two men in London. Pitt, he had no doubt, was the prime mover against him, but he held Melville – 'a poltroon' – the more accountable for having given his word of honour 'not to interfere with my Command'.[19] He could not contemplate open defiance, the most likely outcome of which would be recall and disgrace – even possibly court martial and execution. But the headstrong captain of earlier years had acquired subtlety and patience, and buried within the order he found the means to buy time – a clause that in a state of emergency, the senior admiral could take command of the entire fleet.

Pellew promptly claimed Linois had been sighted to the east where, it might be inferred, he intended to intercept the China convoy. (In fact, the French admiral was on the other side of the ocean.) Invoking 'the high responsibility with which I am invested', Pellew wrote with relish to Melville, declaring:

> I have judged it expedient to take the Rear-Admiral [Troubridge] under my orders until . . . the homeward convoy of Indiamen – in process of mustering at Penang – has been securely despatched.[20]

Three days later he sailed with the fleet for Penang, planning his next strategy.

The tragedy was that he and the man with whom he was now locked in mortal combat should have found themselves enemies at all, for they had much in common. Troubridge was the son of a baker who had served with Nelson when both were boys and fought his way up much as Pellew had done, winning St Vincent's wintry love on the way. An outstanding officer and seaman, Troubridge commanded *Culloden* at the Battle of Cape St Vincent where Jervis earned his title (and Nelson made his name) so even Pellew did not stand so high in the earl's opinion. Troubridge was 'capable of commanding the fleet of England', St Vincent said, 'and I scarce know another'.[21] He was not an easy man, a severe disciplinarian subject to savage moods and with far more of St Vincent's grim puritanism than Nelson's heroic charm. As a disciple of St Vincent's frenzied Admiralty reforms, Troubridge had actually fallen out with Nelson; but he had a formidable following and it was no fault of his to be the agent of Pitt's revenge. In confronting Troubridge as well as the Admiralty, Pellew engaged in a battle as fraught with danger as any in his life.

One thing was in his favour – his distance from their lordships in London. Whereas in his previous experiences mail packets to and from the Admiralty might be received within a matter of days, letters from India usually took five months to reach home and a reply as long, so he had time to weigh his response. As the *Culloden* swept east, Pellew drafted a letter pointing out the sheer madness of the division. Or, as he put it, 'the complicated circumstance requisite to carrying their Lordships' directions into effect':

> If I should offer opinions differing from those entertained by their Lordships I trust they will do me the justice to impute them to no disrespect of their authority – to no disobedience of their instructions – but I conceive their Lordships may not have been fully apprized of the local considerations which will operate against the proposed division of the command and if carried out it cannot fail to have prejudicial consequences.[22]

After this magisterial piece of humbug, he set out the case simply and cogently: he could not protect British territories while restricted in his theatre of operations; Bombay was unsafe or useless during the south-west monsoon; Madras was where the fleet had to assemble in an emergency and also the prime depot of naval stores.

He had decided, he went on in soothing vein again, 'to adhere to the precise letter of their Lordships' Instructions' – including dividing the fleet, though that rendered blockading Mauritius impossible – with one exception. He was retaining Madras, 'from a conviction of the necessity of making that the principal defensive station'. In conclusion, he was confident they would 'modify the plan' (passing judiciously over the fact that it was an order rather than a plan) but was 'ready to resign with cheerfulness', if they disagreed.

It was beautifully done, with the added benefit of being largely, if not entirely, true. He was not adhering to the letter of his orders at all; and, far from being cheerful, he was bitter as well as angry. He made no effort to hide this in writing to Addington – just ennobled as Lord Sidmouth – who also bore some responsibility because he had joined Pitt's Government and sought reward for Troubridge as a member of his Admiralty. To him Pellew pointed out reproachfully 'how severely the division of this Command . . . affects my reputation as an officer and as a man of honor':

Where a junior flag officer is sent to remove a senior from the most important part of which he possessed the whole, it is evident to every man of nice honor and discriminating powers that [he] must be held degraded in the opinion of the Public and his brother officers if he fails to contend for a revision of so unmerited and so hard a regulation.[23]

The two protagonists met again in Penang on 25 September, when Pellew announced breezily that as the French threat had not materialised, he would leave Troubridge to deal with despatching the China convoy. About the future of the command he seems to have been vague. Troubridge was still suspicious, writing 'the extraordinary measures you tell me you are to adopt are directly contrary to those ordered', but the mood seemed more conciliatory before their third meeting, on 27 September on *Culloden*.[24]

Pellew set out his proposals. He would hand over half the fleet for Troubridge to command the waters east of latitude 82.5°E – in effect keeping the Bay of Bengal and the Indian coast to himself. As for Madras, Troubridge might use it as 'a common rendezvous', but would have to make do with Penang for his base. Patronage and prizes would be shared.

The setting was unfortunate – the great cabin of the same ship Troubridge had commanded in his finest hour at the Battle of Cape St Vincent. But placed in such a situation, two fighting men were never going to agree. Another explosive exchange ended with Troubridge stamping out on his superior for a second time.

Troubridge wrote directly to Melville that he had been 'locked up' by Pellew at Penang. Too maddened to consider the compromise on offer, he went on: 'I believe such a bold defiance of Admiralty orders was never before exhibited.' Retribution must follow, as it would any other act of mutiny. 'Nothing can justify Sir Edward Pellew for not complying.'[25]

There is no saying how matters might have ended but for developments across the world. On 1 October, a coded message informed Pellew that a 'Considerable Force' was about to sail from France for India. Dated 7 May, it had taken five months to reach him by express overland mail. With a genuine emergency to deal with, he was exhilarated, dashing off a note to the Admiralty that he was taking the fleet to south India 'to await the arrival of the Enemy fleet'. He did not fail to point out that the crisis was 'strong corroboration of my opinion of retaining Madras'.[26]

He sailed from Penang on 4 October with every available ship. Troubridge was given the option of retaining the *Blenheim* if he convoyed the China trade but refused and was left flying his flag in an 18-gun sloop, the *Rattlesnake*.

For a man described by St Vincent as 'the best Bayard of the British Navy . . . with honour and courage as bright as his sword', the outcome was intolerable. Troubridge was left to brood at Penang, his bitterness swelling like a blister as months went by, awaiting a ruling, tormented by his helplessness. The *Blenheim* was duly returned to him, but once he had rejected Pellew's compromise, the offer was not repeated. For a year the two admirals glared at one another across the Bay of Bengal while events unfolded. But they never met again.

For Pellew the hope of a great and glorious fleet battle for the Eastern Seas persisted for months, even as confusion grew about where the French were bound. While still awaiting them he received fresh reports pointing to a 'Considerable Expedition directed against our possessions in the West Indies'. What he was actually hearing were echoes of the feints and diversions launched by Bonaparte prior to Trafalgar.

Pellew was in the Bay of Bengal when the defining naval battle of British history was fought off southern Spain. On that day, 21 October, *Culloden* was becalmed under hazy skies – a metaphor for all that had befallen him. In November he cruised between Cochin and Trincomalee, from December into January between Goa and Bombay. Still he remained unaware of the war's turning point. Not until 16 February did he receive news, and gave the order for 'a royal salute of 21 guns in consequence of a Victory obtained by Lord Nelson over the Combined Fleets off Cadiz'.[27] Even as he rejoiced, Pellew lamented his own missed opportunity – taunted too by the irony that the brother whose career he had saved had been there; Captain Israel Pellew in the 74-gun *Conqueror* had followed *Victory* in the van.

The Indies command had come to represent a new low, but though he did not yet realise it, the wind blowing through Whitehall had shifted in Pellew's favour. Melville was no longer First Lord, having been impeached on charges of malfeasance. Pitt was dead. Their successors had no axes to grind in a brawl between two admirals in seas that suddenly seemed less troubled, and good reason to back the senior man.

Admirals imbued their fleets with character, just as captains did their ships. Initially Pellew tried to bring to his command the same values of intimacy and loyalty he had employed as a captain. The results were mixed, and whether his objective was ever attainable across so large and diverse an organism as a fleet is questionable.

He was a natural commander, but he was not a natural admiral; at heart, he remained a plain seaman, happiest bracing himself in the tops with the wind in his face. At the age of fifty-one, just promoted Rear-Admiral of the Red, he was unable to restrain himself on an occasion when the *Culloden* lost her foretop in a storm and was among the first up the ratlines to clear the wreckage. He might have said, 'I can't get to the mast head so well as I used'; he could still get there faster than most.

This legacy of youth never entirely left him, even though, in a fleet admiral, it had its drawbacks. His friend and admirer, Sir Charles Penrose, offered a penetrating critical insight:

> He took everybody's duty too much upon himself . . . He could as often [have been] taken for the bosun or 1st Lt as the C in C . . . By occupying the duties they might have fulfilled he injured the proper system of labour . . . Work will never be so well done as when each person exerts himself in his proper station and the voice of a chief should be reserved for the occasion of moment.[28]

Captaincy of Pellew's flagship fell to a succession of followers. He had wanted Israel on *Culloden*, and when this was denied put forward Christopher Cole, a younger brother of his boyhood friend, Frank. The bond with Christopher, who had sailed with him almost twenty years earlier, was close but not without friction and after a quarrel Pellew remarked angrily that Cole was 'exceedingly high and always complained about being paid insufficient respect'.[29] Cole may have been given too much leeway; equally, he may just have wanted to be left to run the ship on his own.

Even now Pellew's instincts were for informality, creating a fellowship of the great cabin, a table around which tales and laughter circulated. He once described a junior officer as 'a great deal of fun' – evidence of a kind of levity rarely tolerated by admirals. But at times his rank and his manner combined uneasily. He may have been too congenial, so when his temper was inflamed the victim felt all the more injured. Arguably, Nelson's greatest gift was to inspire love while being emotionally detached. Pellew could inspire love: close followers like Coghlan worshipped him as a father; but he was incapable of detachment.[30]

As a commander-in-chief, he had come to India with lists of favoured officers from the likes of St Vincent and Spencer. (Spencer, their troubles set aside, remarked airily: 'If you could take George Cadogan out, you will confer an obligation on his father and on myself which would be sensibly acknowledged.'[31]) Balancing these interests required adroitness, particularly as he had quite enough protégés of his own – among them Edward Sneyd, Broughton's brother-in-law, and John Gee Smyth, the son of a friend of Susan's.[32] On a more pragmatic level, he had also accepted Lord Algernon Percy, the thirteen-year-old son of the Duke of Northumberland whom he had once scorned as a 'sort of Gentry incapable of friendship'.

As always, though, there was an inner circle who had gained entry to his heart. One was George Bell, the lieutenant whose ability and loyalty since *Indefatigable* days had earned him a promise of his own ship in India, and whose confirmation as captain of the sloop *Victor* was secured by a letter from Pellew commending 'his zealous service over a long period of years'.[33]

Another was William Kempthorne, whose quiet salvation by Pellew was a feat as distinguished in its way as any he performed at sea.

Kempthorne, it may be recalled, was the son of a friend so close that a door once connected their homes in Falmouth. William had joined the *Indefatigable* as a midshipman after his father's death and was promoted to lieutenant at Pellew's instigation, citing not only his ability but the family's distressed situation.[34] Then, in 1801, Kempthorne was brought to a court martial, accused by Captain Spicer of the *Renard* of treating him 'with the utmost insolence and contempt'. The evidence was unconvincing; it was still enough for Kempthorne to be dismissed the service.[35] And Pellew received a rebuke from the Admiralty Secretary, Evan Nepean, for his earlier support.

Far from apologising, Pellew offered a brisk return of fire:

> It was in the cause of humanity I pleaded, for a suffering and loyal family. The object of it I know to be deserving and I should be proud to call so good a young man my son. His cause is now hopeless and he must submit to it . . . but I shall not cease to regret that a loyal, virtuous and brave young man is lost to His Majesty's Service.[36]

Kempthorne's cause may have been hopeless but Pellew still stood by him and when, as a result, he was restored to the Navy as a mid, appointed him his signal officer. Before they sailed for India, he petitioned successfully for Kempthorne to be made up to lieutenant again, then urged the First Lord to confirm him so he might be given a ship: 'A more gallant, sober and exemplary young man I never knew.'[37] From destitution, Kempthorne was restored to honour, and his mother and sisters to respectability. In a 10-gun cutter, *Diana,* he went on to vindicate Pellew's faith, taking two Dutch warships off the Celebes. He, too, became part of that circle of young men who might be termed Pellew's own band of brothers.

Championing worthy outsiders like Kempthorne and Coghlan was a noble service that went unnoticed, far from the trumpeting that accompanied his feats in action. Unfortunately, it was also overshadowed by his public indulgence of two other young officers: Pellew always had a soft spot for 'a good boy', especially when it was one of his own.

Fleetwood was already with him; Pownoll had been in the West Indies for just nine months when he suffered disaster – losing his sloop, *Fly*, on a reef – and though he survived a court martial for negligence, it was a relief all round when his father asked that he be sent to India. Commander Pellew arrived in 1806. Henceforth, the admiral would have not one son under his personal care but two.

Fortunes of War, 1806–1809

In January 1806, Pellew wrote to the Company, proposing an invasion of Mauritius. After a year he had the measure of his command and a strategy to influence the war, for loss of the islands would drive the French from the East and safeguard the trade sustaining British power. No exertion, he informed the Bengal presidency, could prevent 'the ravages of the Enemy's Cruisers while they have it in their power to retreat to the Isles of France'.[1] Privately, to Sir George Barlow, the new Governor-General, he spelt out the real problem:

> The impracticability of blockading Port Louis effectually with the means I had even with an undivided command was obvious . . . I can do nothing more than keep frigates there as long as their supplies will last.[2]

Conditions for a landing were ideal. For the time being the French had only two frigates and ten privateers to defend the islands, and with India at peace Company forces were available and at hand. Pellew still had five ships of the line and could summon 'such frigates as may be necessary to transport the European troops'. Having made a successful combined operations landing at Ferrol, he was plainly suited to leading an expedition.

Had Wellesley still been in office as Governor-General he would almost certainly have seized the chance. But Barlow was finding his feet and had orders to cut spending. His reply to Pellew was that any attack should come from England. The truth was, the Company hoped the Government would seize the nettle first.[3]

The refusal was a blow from which Pellew's hopes for his

command never recovered. Engaging 'the inveterate and restless Enemies of Mankind' was always his greatest desire, and Mauritius was the one real threat within his grasp. Weeks later news of Trafalgar reached him. No naval strategy was quite the same after that, and when the Cape of Good Hope was captured from Bonaparte's Dutch allies early in 1806 the Admiralty decided that danger in the East had been contained. The cost of this miscalculation was to be severe.

Although Pellew would be vindicated, it is only right to add that he had good reason to draw attention to the Mauritius threat because it justified his retention of the fleet – while keeping Troubridge at Penang to guard against the lesser risk to the China convoys. For all his assurances that the fleet would be equally divided, it never was. He needed the lion's share to blockade Mauritius as best he could, even though it was never enough.[4] French frigates and privateers continued to carry out forays in the Bay of Bengal, and were soon to be joined by the swaggering figure of Robert Surcouf who, in an 18-gun sloop *Revenant*, proved the most successful of French privateers.

What made this all the more maddening was that British merchants conspired in their losses. Trade was shifted about the coast in so-called country ships that could be secured by convoying. Often, however, the merchants preferred to gamble, despatching ships alone to steal a march on rivals and gain the market first. That did not stop them complaining bitterly about the Navy's failure at protection when their vessels ran into trouble.

Over the first half of 1806 the two admirals held their respective stations, awaiting a ruling from London. The first signal came in July – a year after Troubridge's arrival – and merely acknowledged Pellew's proposals. Still, the fact that their lordships had not recalled him on the spot for insubordination indicated which way the wind was blowing.

But while the two admirals had ceased to shout at one another, they continued to shout about one another. Streams of invective poured from their pens and back to England, while local society buzzed with gossip.

Troubridge, the more isolated of the two, had no great threat to deal with in the South China Sea, where the Dutch at Java were a spent force. Although still at Penang 'shut up by Sir E Pellew', he declared, 'the heat does not effect [*sic*] me'. Yet he boiled, fists flailing at junior officers. And he brooded; the real reason Pellew would not hand over Madras, Troubridge concluded, was to conceal malpractice and corruption of the sort that he and St Vincent had been hell-bent on eradicating in British dockyards. In a barely legible note to a senior officer at home he wrote: 'Pellew has kept me out of command because I would not give him up the <u>Control</u> of the <u>Civil Department</u> which I thought <u>wanted much correction</u>.'[5] In fact, although victualling and naval stores had been subject to peculation in the 1780s, both areas had since undergone reform; just what Troubridge concluded needed correction, having spent barely two weeks in Madras, was never stated.

To an Army officer, Troubridge hinted darkly that he would one day demand satisfaction: 'His conduct to me has been infamous . . . he may be assured at a proper time I shall not <u>forget</u>.'[6]

Pellew affected to be above low tactics, but knew enough of what was in Troubridge's letters to write to Nepean at the Admiralty that his foe was:

> . . . more outrageous than ever . . . from a Public Correspondence full of invective and low insinuation, he has now commenced a private one of no less scurrility and abuse . . .
>
> I wish to God I was out of it. I would rather command a frigate with her bowsprit over the rocks of Ushant all my life than command here on such terms. For Heavens sake call one of us home.[7]

His private scratchings went deeper. In an eloquent and unusually introspective passage, he wrote to Broughton of the effect on him:

> I know not of one single estimable virtue that I ever had. I would at time wish to believe myself possessed of a good heart but, alas,

it is so hidden among rubbish and vile passion of temper, nursed by too much good fortune, that I am every day lamenting the opportunities power affords to the indulgence of Caprice. To say that I do not deliberately commit a bad action or do any Man injury is indeed but a very negative sort of virtue and I am obliged to seek Consolation in the recollection of the practice of others who I consider worse than myself.[8]

One he had in mind, naturally, was Troubridge, 'a Weak Man, entirely commanded by his passion . . . every week dishonouring himself by striking some of his Midshipmen or any body else who comes in his way'. Pretty rich for one of Pellew's own simple background was his dismissal of his foe as a baker's son – 'un garcon patisser from St Martin's Lane'.[9]

Redeeming qualities are hard to discern in this ugly and ultimately tragic business. The struggle was the more poignant, however, in that both men saw the future of their boys at stake. Troubridge had with him Lieutenant Edward Troubridge and admitted to 'the anxiety of a parent to see his son as high in the Service as it will admit'. He may have appeared the less indulgent; when Lieutenant Troubridge was engaged in taking a Dutch frigate and two rich cargo ships, his father declared: 'Had he done otherwise I would with great composure have put a pistol ball through his nob.'[10] But he still installed his son directly as post-captain in the frigate.

Pellew was even more blatant. The last time he had gone out on a limb for a relative was on Israel's behalf and it harmed his career. Providing for Pownoll and Fleetwood did lasting damage in another respect – to his reputation.

Commander Pownoll Pellew had barely reached Madras when his father promoted him to post-captain and gave him a 32-gun frigate, *Sir Francis Drake*. Any lingering belief in Pownoll's warlike qualities were promptly dispelled by the way he mooned over the daughters of local nabobs. 'He is always in love,' grumbled Pellew. Finally, he had to admit that his eldest son, though 'an open-hearted good Boy', was in need of 'a good Girl with either Money or Connections'.[11]

No such doubts were to be entertained about Fleetwood. Having assured Broughton 'I really cannot do him justice', Pellew did his best all the same:

> A more firm, manly decided young man of the mildest manners and civilest deportment there cannot be – the management of his ship is excellent, his officers and men love him – so just and so temperate, so regular and so minute upon all examinations of complaint.[12]

With so formidable a list of qualities it was only to be expected that Lieutenant Pellew would be found a ship of his own – a 12-gun sloop *Rattlesnake* which, as he was only sixteen, was outrageous enough; then, on the death of another captain, he was shifted to the 32-gun *Terpsichore*. Pellew's blustering tone in requesting the Admiralty to confirm Fleetwood as post-captain evinced some embarrassment:

> This is the only DD [Discharged Dead] vacancy I have had in my unhappy command, and the only reward I look to for all my anxieties is to get him confirmed. I would not go through my last year again to be Governor-General of India.[13]

Fortunately, Lord Howick, the new First Lord, had meanwhile acknowledged that Pellew had indeed been thoroughly ill-used. An order was at last on its way to India: Pellew was restored to sole command; Troubridge was to be dispatched to a new station – at the Cape of Good Hope.

While Pellew's presentation of the case had been persuasive, his saviour, it turned out, who had influenced the Admiralty in his favour, was the Duke of Northumberland, of whom he had once remarked: 'I will make as much use of him as I can.' But then the benefit was mutual. Among the young mids on the *Culloden*, it may be recalled, was Lord Algernon Percy, the Duke's son, who went on to become an admiral himself.

Victory over Troubridge enabled Pellew to show a generosity of spirit absent when they had been at war. He wrote to a fellow admiral:

I hope you will not believe me quite so bad as [Troubridge] will paint me. . . . We are both warm enough, God knows, but brothers could not agree as we were placed.[14]

Pellew evidently saw the affair would harm him. Troubridge was influential, a popular officer with potent political connections. He would indeed be in a position to blacken Pellew's name when he got to England. In the event, the outcome was worse than that.

Troubridge sailed for the Cape in a ship deemed unseaworthy by everyone who saw her, including her captain. Although she paused at Madras, Troubridge was in haste, desperate to avoid Pellew who was away to the south, and so would not listen to objections about the *Blenheim*'s leakiness. Humiliated and choleric, he fled Madras in the midst of the hurricane season. On 1 February 1807, the *Blenheim* was caught in a storm off Madagascar and foundered. The frigate *Java*, too, went down with all hands. For months rumours filtered back of castaways sighted on Madagascar, and Pellew sent Troubridge's son to investigate; but long before he sailed homeward himself it was clear their battle had ended in his enemy's death. Subsequently the ugly falsehood gained credence that he had conspired in this outcome by refusing Troubridge's request for another ship.

Perhaps nothing else in his lifetime did such harm to Pellew's 'character' – that hard-won accretion of dispatches in the *Naval Chronicle*, well-placed gossip and simple folklore that defined his standing among his fellows. Troubridge had considerable standing himself. Above all, though, he had the ironclad affection of St Vincent. The earl was a great hater, and when Pellew set himself against his favourite he invoked his undying enmity.

To start with, St Vincent had been appalled by Pellew's disobedience. 'Whether Lord Melville acted wisely in dividing the Indian Command is no affair of yours,' he fulminated. 'It is your indispensable duty to comply strictly with the Spirit of his intentions.'[15] When Pellew persisted, he turned malicious. Even back at sea St Vincent retained great influence and an ability to spread poison. One vague and casual slander – 'the whole

The Indian Ocean was notorious for hurricanes, and the point
off Africa near its confluence with the Atlantic was initially
known by mariners as the Cape of Storms.

race of the Pellews is bad in grain and some very bad traits of
the family have lately come to my knowledge' – was bound to
gain wide circulation.[16] St Vincent seemingly took his cue from
Troubridge's wild accusation about fraud in the civil department
at Madras and, because they had shared a mission to eradicate
dockyard corruption, took it at face value.[17] Between St Vincent's
toxic deposits and Troubridge's feverish visions, the effect was
pernicious.

Pellew did indeed have vices. But dishonesty was not among
them. Nor was meanness of spirit. Years after he had been cut
dead by St Vincent, when both were old and publicly revered,
Pellew (by then Lord Exmouth) asked one of his former captains,
Edmund Palmer, to act as a go-between. Palmer had family ties
to St Vincent but had to report:

> I cannot express to you how much and how deeply I lament the
> want of success in an object which I had set my heart upon, of
> becoming a means, tho' a humble one, of effecting a reconciliation
> ... Of this however I am quite persuaded, there can be but one
> motive ascribed to the advances which – will your Lordship permit
> me to say – you have had the true greatness of mind to offer.[18]

St Vincent remained characteristically implacable right up to his death. He never spoke again to the man he had once called 'my sheet anchor'.

Restored to full command, Pellew immediately alighted on a new peril. Actually, the Dutch at Batavia were no danger at all and the French were nowhere to be seen, but to remind the public at home of his existence – all the more necessary in the aftermath of Trafalgar – he conjured up the spectre of a link-up between Dutch and French fleets in the South China Sea. There is little doubt he saw, too, an opportunity to make a hero of another Pellew. The means was to be the destruction of the moribund Dutch squadron at Batavia.

That proved even easier than expected. When Captain Fleetwood Pellew in the *Terpsichore* led his father's squadron through the Sunda Straits and into Batavia in November 1806, the resistance consisted of a single Dutch frigate, four sloops and brigs, and a few small armed vessels. This was Fleetwood's moment – to lead in a boarding party, take the frigate and turn her guns on the rest. Pellew's account to Broughton of what followed, all bright-eyed pride, gives a touching flavour of a warrior father's love.

> I assure you, a prettier exploit I never saw. You will say, Aye Aye, here is the Father. I have therefore done – but I say not half what others say of him, and so let it rest; it is a great comfort to see that one has not reared a bevy of Pigeons. I assure you my Eyes ran over and my heart swelled when I heard a general shout on Culloden from the lookers on when the Dutch frigate opened her fire under British Colours – Well done, Fleetwood, well done, bravo – was the cry all around me. What Father could have kept his Eyes dry? I was obliged to wipe them before I could again look thro' the Glass – and that's true; but don't let Mrs B know it. I have not told my dear Susan because I know she will say it was cruel to expose the dear Boy, and upon my Soul every shot seem'd to go through me and made me quite forget that shells were dropping all round us.[19]

There is no reason to doubt the truth of this account. Fleetwood did possess ability and, for now, vindicated his father's faith. That did not justify the grotesque haste with which he was being advanced. Some years later, when his career foundered, it took Susan to point out, gently, to her husband that they had spoiled both their elder boys, Fleetwood especially. 'We have been disposed to think too highly of him – & he perhaps too highly of himself,' she wrote. 'Humility is the best school to learn useful knowledge in.'[20]

Whatever Susan had to say about favouritism, we may conclude that Fleetwood's fellow captains said very much more. Barely eighteen, he was made acting captain of the 74-gun *Powerful*. Pellew may have done this simply to embellish his record, and he was not confirmed in a post that would have made him among the youngest men ever to captain a Royal Navy ship of the line. But the resentment felt by officers of far great experience and years may be imagined. Still Pellew extolled Fleetwood's qualities: 'beyond comparison the finest youth of the Squadron, universally beloved' and 'the flower of my flock and the flower of my fleet'.[21] A Madras artist, George Chinnery, was commissioned to depict him leading the Batavia attack. Small wonder his head was turned.

Small wonder either that Pellew gained a reputation as a soft touch for personages with a relative to promote. He was besieged by successive chiefs at the Admiralty – where Howick had been replaced by Thomas Grenville and he by Lord Mulgrave – plying him with favourites, to the point that he grumbled that each First Lord had 'sent me out a list longer than his predecessor's'. His mail meanwhile became loaded with flattering notes from men and women of note, from Lady Nelson to the Duke of Kent, some of whom he had never met.[22] He shuffled the cards as best he could and always fulfilled obligations to particular followers like Kempthorne and Bell. The latter was made captain of *Culloden*, recognition for years of devotion, replacing Cole, who was moved to a frigate. At the same time, Pellew was unable to help some to whom he had made rash promises, including Broughton's brother-in-law, Lieutenant Edward Sneyd. Only gradually did he come to see he had allowed himself to become, as he put it, 'trammelled by weight of obligation'.[23]

A final year in the Indies offered little scope for enterprise. The Batavia raid was followed by a second expedition in which the rest of the Dutch squadron was destroyed near Surabaya in December 1807, but once more Pellew's request that Company forces join him in a combined operation – this time to seize Dutch settlements in Java – was rejected.

Meanwhile, British trade was plagued by the predatory brilliance of Robert Surcouf. The French privateer had returned to the Indian Ocean in mid-1807 in the *Revenant*, one of the fastest vessels afloat, and by year's end had taken twelve country ships. Pellew had not even the limited opportunity to bottle him up, the task of blockading Mauritius having passed to the Cape station. All he could do was deploy frigates to patrol for French raiders.[24] None of this reconciled the Calcutta traders to their losses, and shortly before quitting India he learnt they had laid a secret complaint against him at the Admiralty.[25]

The Calcutta memorial, as the affair was known, occupied much attention at the time, and caused Pellew deep disquiet. It can be summarised briefly because it had little substance and came to nothing. The charge was that, in attacking the Dutch, 'a prostrate foe', he had neglected to protect shipping in the Bay of Bengal. The point about the Dutch may have been valid but, as he pointed out, security could be guaranteed only if merchants agreed to convoying, which those at Calcutta declined. The Bombay traders, who accepted, suffered barely a loss and signed a testimonial that Pellew's system had cut their insurance premiums by half.[26] The new Governor-General, Lord Minto, also came to his defence, denouncing 'a most unmerited and most unfair attack from the underwriters of Calcutta'.[27]

They may have been seeking revenge. Pellew had been forced throughout his command to draw on Company ships to replace the Navy hands – almost 1,000 in total – who had died of fever and flux. Every fleet of Indiamen arriving from England would lose a proportion of its men, usually around 15 per cent, who were replaced by local Bengali seamen known as lascars. Pellew took them without enthusiasm and where officers in charge of impressment became over-zealous, leaving Company ships dangerously under-manned, he saw to it that hands were returned.[28] At the same time he stood his ground when necessary, as when challenged early on by the mighty Lord Wellesley, replying 'I regret there can be no easy adjustment to this unpleasant subject,' and winning his point.[29]

In the end, he had made the best of (and the most from) a bad job. The humiliation, pain and mistakes of his first command had cost Pellew in prestige and prominence; but he had gained materially. He brought to his dealings with prominent landsmen a geniality and spirit of collaboration alien to many naval officers. Minto was no lightweight, but a shrewd, regal eminence whose support had served Nelson well and who became an ally to Pellew, whom he described as 'a distinguished and meritorious person from whose prompt and cordial cooperation in every public service I have experienced important advantage'.[30] With Lord William Bentinck, Governor of Madras, he established a close working relationship that would be transferred to the Mediterranean and became a lasting friendship.

Most significant for their respective families was his bond with Sir George Barlow. Sir George was a brother of Sir Robert Barlow, whom Pellew had known when both were frigate captains, and with this common ground they were soon on familiar terms after Sir George moved from being Governor-General in Calcutta to succeed Bentinck at Madras. It happened that Barlow had a daughter, Eliza, and because Pellew still sought 'a good Girl with either Money or Connections' for Pownoll, he was delighted to find one who had both. Captain Pellew's marriage to Eliza Barlow at St Mary's Church was the Madras society event of 1808.

The attachment between the families was ill-fated. Pownoll and Eliza did not find happiness, he being as ineffectual a husband as he was an officer, she having inherited her wanton mother's wildness. Pellew's willingness to take another young Barlow under his wing ended in tragedy. Midshipman William Barlow had been previously noted for unruly behaviour when he fell to his death from the tops of Pellew's flagship in mysterious circumstances in 1811.[31] Pellew was mortified and felt responsible, having written to Lady Barlow: 'I entreat you to be at rest that I will take the utmost care of him.'[32]

For the time being, however, Pellew could conclude that his boys were launched and – because India remained a dependable source of riches – his fortune was made. With a share in prize money, freight charges and Dutch plunder, he had accumulated almost £100,000 (about £30 million today).[33] If that was less than half his predecessor's takings, he was still 'rich to my heart's content'.

Arguably the greatest achievements – largely unnoticed – of his command were two reforms of lasting benefit to British seamen.

Pellew had always ensured his men were properly fed and fairly treated. 'Be as kind as you can without suffering imposition on your good nature,' he told officers. In India he went further. To curb harsh discipline, he instituted a regime of punishment returns to be completed by all captains, so that with a check imposed on how often they brought out the cat, floggings declined. Pellew's system was adopted by the Admiralty in a step placing him among the leaders in a trend towards milder discipline.

A second reform arose from his confronting one of the Navy's most notoriously brutal captains. Robert Corbet of the frigate *Nereide* was attached to the Cape station, but put in at Bombay where the crew smuggled a petition to Pellew, describing mass floggings, the rubbing of salt into men's backs and frequent resort to the loathed practice of 'starting' – the beating of hands to their posts. Corbet sailed from Bombay before Pellew's orders for a court martial could be carried out, but was pursued by him to the Admiralty where an inquiry chastised Corbet and imposed an explicit ban on starting.[34]

Seamen appreciated such concern. The only known appraisal of Pellew from the lower deck dates from this time and was recorded by Robert Hay, a hand rated ordinary on the *Culloden*. Hay wrote that Pellew's qualities as a commander, and his efforts to keep his men contented and healthy – he would insist on their resting for three hours during the hottest part of the day – earned him 'the confidence, love and esteem of seamen'.[35] The most vivid aspect of Hay's portrait, however, arose from an incident prior to the second attack on Java, when hundreds of men, having obtained an illicit supply of liquor, were rendered unfit for duty and the *Culloden* went aground near Surabaya:

> The Admiral was highly exasperated, he stamped and raged in all the violence of passion. He swore he would never again hoist his flag in a ship manned with such a set of drunken scoundrels . . . He ordered his signalman to strike his flag and with it he repaired on board the *Caroline* frigate, telling us as he went down the side that since no trust could be placed on us, he would go and share the danger and honour of facing the enemy with those on whom he could depend.[36]

Stung with shame and remorse, the men sobered up and got the *Culloden* afloat. Pellew 'to the joy of all hands' came aboard again the next morning:

> Our Admiral who had forgot our bad conduct of the preceeding [*sic*] day now seemed in his element. His eye became more brightened, his countenance more animated, his voice more cheerful and his step more firm as we advanced. But though he would forget our faults, he never allowed himself to forget our comforts, and finding as we drew within a few miles of the town that it was past noon gave orders to pipe to dinner. 'Let the lads get their dinner smartly,' said he to the lieutenant, 'and their grog, for we will soon have other matters to mind.'

In the event, the Dutch offered no resistance. The tattered remnants of their fleet went up in flames and Pellew returned to Madras without suffering a single casualty.

But four years in the East had left their mark. His skin was a dark mahogany, the pock-marked face now also deeply creased, and he was, he admitted, 'grey as a badger and fat as a pig, running to belly'. His health, too, had suffered. 'My floor timbers are very shaky and I must very soon go into my Wife's dock for a thorough repair, or become hors de combat.'[37] It was time, he declared, to 'cheat Old Nick out of his prey, leaving bile and liver in this vile hot country'.

Before setting sail for home, Pellew wrote a last letter to Broughton, recalling their young days – 'knawing a tough beef stake at Charles Street, Westminster' – as being the happiest of his life. His longing for home, for reunion with Susan and his friend, was palpable:

> If my dear old fashioned Wife does but like it, I shall have a little snug House in Town, and as you and a certain Lady are but handkerchief size, we may hope to be able to stow you away for a Winter, and much joy would it give your old friend, who will meet you with his heart brim full of affection – for believe me, my dear Alex, neither distance, heat, fortune, nor success, can for a moment make me otherwise than you always knew me . . . I feel that our regard and friendship can but end with our lives.[38]

Broughton never read this last letter, having died three months earlier, the *Gentleman's Magazine* noted, on 1 March 1808, at his apartments in Worcester. No word from Pellew relates how he heard of his friend's death. That it grieved him more than any other loss in his life seems clear. The one to whom he could write as if 'conversing with the friend of my heart who I have so long loved and respected', was gone. He never found another, and that eloquent and endearing aspect of his own voice was silenced.

The voyage home provided an aptly turbulent farewell to the East. Pellew was in haste, having been delayed by the late arrival of his successor, Vice-Admiral William Drury, and anxious to reach home after a five-year separation from Susan. There seems to have been an element of guilt as well. She was loving, devout, he irascible and perhaps occasionally unfaithful. She was 'my dear good Susan', he 'a miserable sinner'. In one of his last letters to Broughton he had confessed: 'In shame I say it, I have been a wicked fellow . . . long have I repented, altho' I dare not look up with one atom of confidence but thro' the mediation of my blessed Saviour'.[39] His remorse may have sprung from prolonged reflection rather than any specific transgression; even so, this rarely expressed piety suggests a need for atonement.

The *Culloden* mustered with a fleet of Indiamen off Ceylon early in 1809. Pellew's final duty would be to escort them safely home. It was one he failed to accomplish.

The danger signs were there. The fifteen Indiamen were carrying saltpetre for the war and, under strategic pressure, some had been overloaded. Moreover, they were sailing when the seas around Mauritius were still liable to be assailed by hurricanes and after one captain had told Pellew that 'he dreaded the consequences should they experience any very bad weather'.[40] The *Culloden* nevertheless set a course that from the outset was shaped more towards the French islands than was usual.

After three weeks they became becalmed for a few days, and when a brisk breeze came up again Pellew persisted in a westerly course, with the French islands lying dead ahead, rather than the more prudent south-westerly one.

He never explained why. It was the most direct route and he was in a hurry; but it may well be that, leaving the sea of his disappointment, Pellew was hunting a trophy to carry home. He ran close to Mauritius in hope of a chance encounter with French warships.

On 14 March, after four days in rough, squally seas, the fleet reached latitude 23° 30'S, longitude 61°E, and lay within 200 miles east-by-south-east of Mauritius when, around dawn, they were struck by demented furies – or what the old hands called 'a perfect hurricane'.

The *Culloden* had her boats washed away, quarter galleries stoved in and mizzen toppled. With seas like moving mountains all around and shrieking demons in the air, the storm was the worst Pellew had ever seen and his old companion John Gaze was moved to suggest *Culloden*'s guns should be cast overboard to ease her. Pellew replied: 'She will do very well, and what would become of the convoy if we meet an enemy?'[41]

His resolve calmed those around him. The seaman Robert Hay recalled:

> All was dread, consternation and terror, but in looking at the Admiral's face all was confidence and safety. Dressed in a short jacket, a pair of trowsers, a small hunting cap and without shoes or stockings, he went about infusing courage and fortitude into all, but I verily believe that he himself, in his heart, thought all was over.[42]

The barefoot admiral was to be seen 'wherever anything of importance was going on'. The main topsail was still set and, with such a force of following wind, had become a threat to the ship. Pellew wanted it furled but was reluctant to order anyone to go up because the mast might fall and take them with it. When volunteers came forward 'he admired their bravery . . . [and] at last consented and a sufficient number of men were permitted to go aloft'. The loosened sail immediately shredded, 'pieces fluttering like so many pigeons in the air' while Pellew 'rejoiced that all the men reached the deck in safety'.

> We now scuded [*sic*] at the rate of 10 or 12 miles an hour under bare poles. The most steady and experienced hands were placed at the helm to prevent her if possible broaching too; the rest of the hands were seen clinging to the rigging, masts and spars, calmly awaiting their approaching fate.

It took three days for the hurricane to pass. Most of *Culloden*'s consorts survived with her, but four Indiamen, *Bengal*, *Calcutta*, *Jane Duchess of Gordon* and *Lady Jane Dundas*, were not seen again. About 500 seamen and a hundred passengers perished, including the Madras Army commander, Company officials, and many wives and children.[43]

The rest of the voyage passed without incident. On a bright morning in July 1809, exactly five years after hoisting his flag in *Culloden*, Pellew sighted the familiar foam-dashed rocks of Ushant and knew he was almost home. Some months passed before the missing Indiamen's fate became sufficiently clear to trouble the joy of his return.

13.

The Last Command, 1809–1815

By the time of Pellew's return home in 1809 the war against Bonaparte was being waged by Britain's soldiers rather than its sailors. It would be facile to say the war at sea was to all intents and purposes over. Yet Pellew's only contribution to 'bring down this Tyrant at last' would be as Wellington's usually forgotten ally in the Mediterranean. Of real action there was none, and for all the passion and ability he brought to supporting the Army, he suffered further disappointments. India had scarred him. He was haunted by personal demons, sure powerful enemies were plotting his downfall, brooding on resignation at perceived slights.

The Navy he found was much changed. He was not alone in discerning what one admiral called 'great Degeneracy and want of zeal throughout the classes of Officers'.[1] Every generation, of course, believes its institutions fall into decline, but it was the case that a heroic age had passed, and with it opportunities for glory. When naval officers looked back it was on the mesmerising figure of Nelson, embodiment of all that now seemed lacking. A charmed circle of officers, the Trafalgar brotherhood, could summon some of that magic, as well as cloaking themselves in its privilege. Pellew was not among them, and he carried a burden – as Troubridge's nemesis.

He made forays to London, cultivating old and new connections, at the Admiralty, in Parliament and at Court. (Once, near Kingston, highwaymen halted his post chaise, to which he responded by flinging open a door, brandishing his pistol. Fortunately they fled before discovering it was not loaded.[2]) These visits were important enough for Susan to quit their rural retreat and accompany him. He disliked the capital almost as much as she, writing enviously of Pownoll and Eliza 'feasting in the country upon strawberries and cherrys while poor Susan and I are visiting in London and choaked with dust'.[3]

What he found did not offer peace of mind. The contentious nature of public life, its plots and intrigues, was constantly brought home by doings at the India House, headquarters of the Company. He managed to see off the complaints against him by the Calcutta merchants, for which he received an apology, but he was unable to stop a far more unwarranted campaign that would bring down his new family ally, Sir George Barlow.[4]

Further anxiety stemmed from a whispering campaign about his handling of the civil department at Madras. This complex operation, covering victualling, stores and medical care, had been presumed to be a nest of vipers by Troubridge, whose allegations of corruption (made on the strength of his brief stay in Madras) were as indiscriminate as they were harmful. A handful of officials as well as Pellew were casually maligned in this way, including Thomas Hoseason, the naval agent, who returned to England in 1806. Given the expense of running the Navy's most distant fleet and the scope for fraud, it would be surprising if there had been no profiteering at all. However, since a cavalier era in the 1780s, costs had been cut and victualling at Madras had become comparatively efficient.[5] Any hint of scandal was still enough to horrify Pellew. Exactly what had occurred to explain a very strange letter from Hoseason is impossible to say. It came in reply to one from Pellew, who was obviously in a state of anxiety, although it may be concluded that Hoseason was the more worried of the two. The identity of the protagonist is unknown.

> What in God's name does he want of you – do keep yourself completely independent of him now that he has declared his intentions for I am really fearful that the assistance you propose giving him will in the eyes of your Enemys [sic] look ill altho God knows it proceeds from the kindest and best of Motives & from the liberality of your heart alone.
>
> You are too good in this case. Let him publish all he can, you need not fear. He has told me over and over again you were as

innocent as the child unborn and knew nothing of his transactions . . . For God's sake keep your mind at rest & do not let your self be imposed upon by any threats.[6]

Although something nefarious evidently lay at the bottom of this affair, nothing came of it. Hoseason had no further dealings with Pellew, although he did do business in the property line with another Madras worthy, Lord William Bentinck. All that can be said is that to judge from the letter's tone, Pellew appears to have been relatively blameless.

He was soon drawn into a real battle – this time one he saw as a matter of honour.

Pellew was deeply affected by the terrible fate that had befallen his former secretary, Thomas Fitzgerald, since being accused of fraud by Alexander Cochrane. Fitzgerald had been dismissed the Navy, his wife went mad with anxiety and died, leaving him with seven children to care for, 'one in a state of imbecility'. However, it was not only his servant's sufferings that moved Pellew to embark on the longest fight of his life, but the reflection on his own character. That, and his detestation of Cochrane.[7]

He started by taking the case to the Admiralty, pointing out that Cochrane had not offered any evidence for 'aspersions of the most repulsive and malignant nature'. Charles Yorke, the First Lord, was sympathetic; but as for appointing an inquiry into the victualling of Pellew's squadron in Spain – such matters ground exceeding slow. Pellew insisted on the need 'for redemption for [Fitzgerald's] family, reduced I am sorry to say to wretchedness'.[8]

To start with he prevailed on another of his new India friends, Lord William Bentinck, to find Fitzgerald a position.[9] The next step, clearing his name, took years. Pellew seethed at what he saw (rightly or wrongly) as Cochrane's influence at the Admiralty. Perceiving the hand of another member of the Cochrane family raised in the campaign against him, he wrote to a friend: 'Sir Arch'd C has on my acc't drunk the last bitter cup of Gall administered by a Board who should be gentlemen and whom I will put to shame yet.'

I have every day the knowledge of ill will and envy in the polite Neptunes* who of late have to my mind behaved with gross illiberality towards me ... and have absolutely carried their resentment so far as to punish that poor unfortunate friend of mine Fitzgerald for my offences.[10]

The precise truth of all this is hard to determine. Slander in darkened corridors was a potent weapon which had wounded Pellew all too often. Perhaps there was an element of paranoia too. Either way he stuck to his guns. His followers' afflictions always roused the fighter in him.

Three years later the Admiralty sent commissioners to Spain, who found Fitzgerald's accounts regular and the amounts paid reasonable.[11] After that he was able to return to the Navy, and was posted to the Mediterranean at Pellew's request, as an administrator. It did not rest there, however, because having gained his point Pellew insisted that Fitzgerald was due compensation. Finally, he took his battle to the Palace – in a petition to Prince William Henry, the future William IV, otherwise known as the 'Sailor King'.

My regard and esteem for this long injured man has never ceased ... He has fallen a sacrifice ... his peace of mind and his fortune equally ruined for upwards of twenty years. In recommending his hard and cruel fate to your Royal Highness, I do him but common justice, but much more would I do for him if it lay in my power.[12]

This last shot in the campaign was fired in 1827, twenty-two years after Cochrane's accusation. Pellew would have taken grim satisfaction from a postscript – a note stating that his arch-enemy finally accepted that 'led away by mistaken representations, he [had] been the innocent cause of the ruin of an innocent man'.[13]

A year passed in Devon. Susan, who handled the domestic ship as tightly as Sir Edward did a 74, had bought their first property – Hampton House, a substantial residence near Plymouth seafront. Her influence is also detectable in the path taken by

---

* An ironic term for the Lords of the Admiralty – i.e. sea gods.

Plymouth Sound was the scene of one of Pellew's most famous
exploits, the *Dutton* rescue, and for some years he and Susan
kept a house in town.

their two younger sons. Whereas Pownoll and Fleetwood had
gone to sea, George and Edward were destined for the Church.
Julia, the youngest girl, married a Navy captain. And another
young woman entered the household as a surrogate daughter.

Jane Smith was no waif. Pert and educated, she had wit and
wrote a vivid letter. Yet she needed support. The fact that her
late father had been a seaman suggests Edward's dutifulness and
Susan's devoutness combined once more to enfold a casualty of
fortune. Jane was ever grateful. 'What would have become of me
or where should I have been were it not for your dear family,'
she wrote to Pellew. She would address him as 'Dearest, dearest
Dad', adding, 'all my happiness is centred in living among you'.[14]
Once he was back at sea she became a regular correspondent,
enlivening his mail with gossip and warming his heart.

Fond distraction was one thing, inactivity another. Pellew
had been ashore for a year and was enervated by the summer of
1810, when he was given the North Sea command. What turned
into a ten-month blockade of the Scheldt offered little besides

frustration, while news of Mauritius being taken at last must have produced mixed feelings. Hopes for 'one kick at Bonaparte's flag before I dye' were receding. As for the ultimate dream, 'such a day as Trafalgar – how sweetly could I give up life in such a cause', that had surely gone.[15]

On returning to England in the spring of 1811 he received the last command of his life.

Commander-in-Chief of the Mediterranean was a jewel – the most distinguished post in foreign seas, deploying a fleet of seventy fighting ships to invest the southern flank of Bonaparte's empire in Europe.[16] It was also a monumental test. Recent incumbents had included Nelson and, another illustrious name, Cuthbert Collingwood. Both had died on duty. Who could match them? The last holder, Sir Charles Cotton, departed having barely tried.

Pellew's hopes, and his flag, were borne out of Spithead in June 1811 on the Navy's mightiest ship, the *Caledonia*, a 120-gun mountain of oak. Sharing his quarters in the gallery was Lord William Bentinck, bound for Sicily as envoy and Army commander. Pellew and Bentinck, by sea and land respectively, were to support Wellington's campaign in the Iberian Peninsula.

The *Caledonia* anchored on a blazing day at Minorca's Port Mahon, base for the fleet and one of the liveliest societies in the Mediterranean. Arriving ships 'were surrounded with boats, some laden with fruit, vegetables and all kinds of comestibles'.[17] Other boats brought guests, Mahon women renowned for their high hairstyles and beauty.

Pellew's message, distributed around the fleet, invoked all the proper passions:

> He looks forward with eagerness to that glorious day when in the presence of an inveterate enemy he may unite his efforts with Companions of approved bravery, zeal and loyalty in the noble cause for which Nelson bled and from which, under Providence, he anticipates the surest victory.[18]

As much as captains and men, Pellew was addressing admirals. He was always going to be compared with Nelson and was always bound to fall short. Barring, too, a major opportunity – the grand battle for which he thirsted – his role would be directing, organising. It would require diplomacy, even sensitivity, for the five admirals he commanded, notably Sir Richard Keats and Thomas Fremantle, had been part of the old Nelson brotherhood.

He was, at the outset, blessed in his deputy. He had known Keats for twenty years, since they were frigate captains in the Western Squadron. If ever he found a kindred spirit in a brother officer after Frank Cole's death it was in the warm-hearted warrior soul of Keats; and if ever he yielded to another in seamanship, it was the same man. Keats had been taken up by Nelson, in whose service he became the complete officer.[19] It is to the credit of Pellew and Keats, testimony to the Navy at its best, that they could become and remain the closest of friends. They made an odd pair: Pellew – big, gregarious; Keats – short, urbane; but they were as one in purpose. 'With such a man you have everything to expect and nothing to fear,' Pellew wrote.[20] Keats in his own generous way encouraged his new C-in-C even as he spelled out the challenge:

> Lord Nelson had the luckiest knack of hitting us off. Your Judgment and Self-Command will do much and your Champagne compleat the business.[21]

Fellowship was certainly part of the trick. Pellew always kept a good table and we may see his guests, ladies of Minorca among them, savouring madeira and hospitality in *Caledonia*'s grand stern gallery as they 'played at cards and then supped . . . everybody obliged to sing a song at supper, and all doing so good humouredly'.[22] After an all-day visit by a brother officer Pellew confessed: 'What with smoke, noise and drinking, my head is quite muzzy.'[23]

With Keats he hit it off naturally. At the same time he was at pains to get on good terms with another admiral. Thomas

Fremantle had been with Nelson from Tenerife to Trafalgar. He had also been a friend of Troubridge, and was sharp-tongued. Knowing he had the inclination to be awkward, Pellew set to work. After a meeting, he wrote to Fremantle:

> Sincere thanks for the good you have done my head and pleasure you have given my heart by your open and kind confidence . . . I know I have a hard task but you may also believe that I will not stay the week in Command when I lose the confidence of those I serve with . . . I do trust that you among many I esteem will not hide my faults from me.[24]

Reading between the lines – and he had developed a gift for allusion – it would seem Pellew realised that whatever faults he possessed would not be hidden by Fremantle.

Chief among Pellew's duties was monitoring Toulon where the French retained twenty-one ships of the line, including six of 120 guns. Pellew's strength was twenty-five ships of the line and twenty frigates, but they were scattered across the sea and he had no more than sixteen of the line to deal with Toulon. Now more than ever, however, the French Navy was desirous to avoid battle. For Pellew that brought to the fore combined operations with the military.

'It is my ardent desire to be well with the Army and its generals,' Pellew informed his admirals.[25] It was a role at which he had always excelled. During the Quiberon operation of 1800, one general declared him 'as distinguished [in] military operations as he is for personal gallantry and professional knowledge'.[26] This time he would be directing others rather than engaging himself, but it is hard to see how he could have done it better.

In 1811 the Peninsular War was on a knife-edge. While Wellington had a hold on Portugal and had won critical victories in western Spain with the help of local partisans, he was hugely outnumbered. Two factors were in his favour: Bonaparte's overweening ambition, which was about to set him on the road to Moscow and destruction; and naval power. The French lived off the land while, as Wellington put it: 'I have the sea to furnish whatever I want.' The Mediterranean Fleet had so far played a minor role – victualling, for example, came through Lisbon – but Pellew's arrival signalled a change, for among his orders was to assist Bentinck in opening up a new front on Spain's east coast.

With Wellington his dealings were formal, as was to be expected of that imperious man. Early on, however, Pellew won the Duke's gratitude by sending the 41st Regiment from Mahon to reinforce him, despite Fremantle's protests that their vital naval base would be left exposed to invasion from the French based at Tarragona.[27] Instead, the regiment contributed to the critical victory at Ciudad Rodrigo in 1812, and Wellington was duly appreciative.

With Bentinck at Palermo relations were more personal. Pellew genuinely liked Lord William – 'no intrigues' – although he proved an abler administrator than a general. In the summer of 1812 Wellington was awaiting a landing by British troops in Catalonia to which Pellew had assigned Rear-Admiral Benjamin Hallowell while encouraging Bentinck to proceed: 'You can be on the coast by the end of June. Glory and success will shower upon you.'[28] At the last minute Bentinck opted instead to focus his efforts on Italy.

Bentinck did not lack resolve, but two other generals, Frederick Maitland and Sir John Murray, were cautious to a fault. Maitland and some 6,500 men were brought to off Catalonia, at which point he declared the French force at Tarragona too strong and told Hallowell to take him to Alicante instead. Murray was worse. Having been put ashore by Hallowell with 16,000 men and besieged Tarragona, he panicked at reports of advancing French and re-embarked. Hallowell's fury – his 'strong expressions in regard to the conduct of General Murray' – was the subject of a mild talk in Pellew's cabin.[29]

For one of famed temper himself, Pellew showed real patience and tact. Of Maitland's reputation for dithering, he wrote, 'I have always rebutted the reports, as I ought.'[30] When the general proved his inadequacy, Pellew was cast down but kept his expressions private: 'My heart is too full of bitterness and regret to give vent to my feelings,' he wrote to Fremantle.[31] In Bentinck's case, he handled a delicate situation with sensitivity, passing on criticism by Wellington but offering his friend reassurance.[32]

> I am only anxious that you should feel more at ease in your mind and more confident that you have acted upon the purest of principles. I would not wish you a bed of Roses – you are equal to any exertion of Mind or Body.[33]

Fortunately, the campaign was led not by the Maitlands, Murrays nor even the Bentincks, but by a general who was reshaping the Army's image and reputation as he marched it across Spain. In August 1812 Wellington entered Madrid. Still more critical events were unfolding in Russia – as Pellew wrote perceptively to his admirals later that year: 'Altho' Moscow is gone, we are all in hope the French will suffer prodigiously in the winter.'[34]

Aged fifty-four when he went out, Pellew was old for a seagoing admiral. Nelson died at forty-seven, having written to Pellew a year earlier about his 'infirmities' as well as his intention to 'lay down the cudgels . . . after one last battle'.[35] Almost twenty years of war had left most others worn out, usually by their fifties, mainly by the seaman's curse – rheumatism – which they would suffer (as Pellew did) ever after. Among them was Keats, who sailed home in agony in 1812, aged fifty-five. A severe loss, he and Pellew remained close friends to their last days.

Pellew's level of activity, rare as it was for his age, demonstrated his determination to stay on until Bonaparte was defeated. Though it became apparent as the tide of war turned that the French fleet was *never* going to emerge, he still spent weeks on end with the Toulon blockade. Juggling squadrons, he kept up a blizzard of correspondence – with admirals, captains, local rulers and officials as well as the Admiralty. And he did it well. In an age when clarity on the page was essential for understanding between commanders across a large theatre, Pellew's letters stand as a model of expression. He was fortunate in having as his secretary the refined Edward Locker, who had been with him since Fitzgerald's resignation; but his own letters, in his awkward pointy scrawl, are pithy and sometimes eloquent.

He took great pains to explain himself when personal sensitivities were involved. On resolving, for example, to send Fremantle to the Adriatic, he wrote to Captain Josias Rowley, a highly accomplished commander, in terms that softened the blow of having his squadron passed to another officer, albeit an admiral, and brought an acknowledgment of 'the very handsome manner you have been pleased to express your approbation of my conduct'.[36]

With outstanding captains like Rowley his dealings were uncommonly warm. Another was Sir Edward Codrington, a Trafalgar veteran, who declared: 'I like Sir Edward Pellew ... He is a man of tried ability and courage.' Codrington also appreciated a commander who would go out on a limb for him. When he needed to go home in haste, Pellew did not hesitate to grant permission, although he was rebuked by the Admiralty for allowing Codrington to depart without a convoy.[37] Not all his captains matched up to their standards, and he could also be found writing to Keats in a temper: 'Captains of the Navy are very like spoiled children ... The subjects of discontent are infinite. Scarcely any do their duty from principle. Zeal is out of the question.'[38]

Informality had always been part of Pellew's system. As a captain, Codrington felt able to sign himself 'Your Faithful Friend'. Even this did not match the latitude given those closest to Pellew. The intimacy of that kinship is conveyed in a letter from George Bell, the last in a line of a protégés, in the summer of 1812 to 'My Dear Friend Sir Edward':

> I could not allow Coghlan to leave England for the Mediterranean
> without my most hearty wishes for your health and success ...
> I rejoice at your going to have Coghlan near you, for in him you
> will find a sincere Friend and a brave, honourable Man.

Adieu My dearest Friend and Believe me most gratefully, George Bell.[39]

Jeremiah Coghlan arrived in July and was installed as flag captain on *Caledonia*, the final seal on a bond forged in the *Dutton* rescue sixteen years earlier.

Personal warmth was sustained, with a few exceptions, across the command. One admiral, Francis Pickmore, crotchety and exhausted, was treated in the manner of an old retainer. 'You have by all your letters indelibly impressed on my heart the most gratifying sentiments,' Pickmore wrote. 'I will endeavour to merit your kindness . . . Such is the state of my frame I am irritably nervous.'[40] Towards this man, oppressed by the sufferings of a son in the fleet who went insane, Pellew showed real compassion.

Among his other admirals, he admired Hallowell for his efforts off Catalonia – 'full of Honor and Zeal, with a liberal heart'.[41] Sir Richard King was another matter, an unwilling subordinate whom Pellew dubbed 'Lawyer King' and 'Growler'.[42] With that vain maverick Sir Sidney Smith, who replaced Keats as his deputy, things were more awkward still. Old sparring partners and temperamentally chalk to cheese, they differed rather than detested one another. Pellew was exasperated by Smith's antics – 'as Gay and thoughtless as ever', he wrote.[43] And they disagreed over tactics: like most senior officers, Pellew saw the Toulon fleet as a threat to be contained and, if offered, destroyed in battle; Smith dreamed of spectaculars – night-time attacks with innovative weapons like rockets and mines. He was ahead of his time, but Pellew was right that the risk was too great when the war on the ground had turned. To Keats he wrote:

> You know a better head or finer disposition never existed. What a pity it shld be clouded with frivolity. But what can a man do with Rockets in his head and Diplomacy in his heart?[44]

There is a marked contrast between Pellew's handling of these men and another admiral. With them Pellew was indisputably in charge, blending some Nelsonian charm with some St Vincent-like ire. With Thomas Fremantle the relationship was more ambiguous. Fremantle could make Pellew appear distinctly vulnerable.

Pellew had cultivated Fremantle from the start because his reputation, his ambition and his standing in Nelson's old circle could have spelt trouble. His letters indicate a kind of courtship of a dangerous officer. In contrast, Fremantle's official letters to Pellew are terse, without personality.[45] But there were private letters too and while they have not survived some evidence points to a certain familiarity with the C-in-C.

Soon after assuming command, Pellew wrote to thank Fremantle for arranging a tryst with one of the ladies of Mahon.

> My Dear Fremantle will I am sure be satisfied that I feel my obligation for his care and kindness in the arrangement for this little personage . . . I have no doubt but I shall be highly pleased with such a friend and I trust she will have no cause to complain of the doubloons [sic] whatever else may be wanting. I would rather know her wishes than go wrong as it really is no object for me. Secrecy is all we both want. Can I know what house . . . Have it arranged as well as you can.[46]

That Pellew might have had the odd assignation ought to come as no great surprise. Nelson apart, sex in the lives of naval officers is a hazy area, but casual liaisons were natural and captains as well as admirals kept mistresses at Mahon. Fremantle, married to one of the most vivid of Navy wives, the diarist Betsey Wynne, appears to have had a lengthy affair himself and was plainly well connected with the local *demimonde*.[47] So there was nothing that ought to have given him a hold over Pellew. Yet his commander appears at a disadvantage, and not for the only time.

Fremantle flew high socially. Among the most dashing of Nelson's stars and married to an heiress, he moved easily in the best circles of Europe as well as England, with 'fiery black eyes', charm, intensity, a malicious tongue and, above all, ambition. When Nelson died, it seemed his greatest grief was the blow dealt to his prospects.[48]

Fremantle would indeed be a bad enemy. And – as another admiral who knew both men remarked – he had 'a most cordial dislike' of Pellew.[49]

Sir Charles Penrose believed that after Nelson's death Fremantle was unable to accept being a subordinate. For a golden age to return, as it were, the crown must pass to one of Nelson's intimates, namely himself. 'He could not brook the thoughts of a superior', Penrose noted, but became agitated, muttering 'I cannot play a second fiddle, I cannot play a second fiddle.' What made it worse, Penrose thought, was envy. He recognised in Pellew a better officer.[50]

Fremantle's rancour translated into snide asides, which doubtless got back to Pellew, reviving his social insecurities and renewing old fears and suspicions. Towards Fremantle he cooled, yet stood back from confrontation and the two became mutually wary, locked in a state from which the senior man had most to lose. Whatever he might have said in private, the closest Pellew came to criticising Fremantle directly was in a letter to Bentinck: 'No man can be more honourable and his greatest failing is that of over-straining and converting any transaction to his own ambition.'[51]

But by late 1812, still with no hint of action to occupy him, Pellew was troubled. An example is the anxiety that seized him when the second Lord Melville took over the Admiralty. The first Melville, his father, had used Troubridge to punish Pellew for political crimes, so in this instance at least suspicion was natural and it deepened when Melville ignored his letters. Pellew fired off letters to such friends as the Duke of Northumberland and Bentinck, railing against 'this mode of carrying on by a Raw Neptune' and threatening to resign. Now it became Bentinck's turn to soothe him. 'Your character is so entirely without equal no First Lord would dare not support you to the utmost.'[52] Finally, to Pellew's immense relief, Pownoll wrote to him of meeting Melville when the First Lord 'did nothing but talk of you and express his high opinion'. This caused Pellew to explode at a 'Dolt of mine for an elder son' who, had he passed this on earlier, 'would have removed a hundred suspicions from my mind'. Then the anxiety returned: 'Still, it is odd he has never acknowledged my letters.'[53]

Never could it be said Pellew shied from making a cat for his own back. He had managed to get brother Israel a senior post beside him with a letter to the Admiralty revealing his usual discomfiture when being audacious – a casual PS after expressing his gratitude for the command: 'Can I take my brother as captain of the fleet?' Israel's promotion to rear-admiral followed; the old spectre of nepotism was revived and soon gained in substance.

Captain Fleetwood Pellew joined his father in 1813. He was already under a cloud, having been transferred from the East Indies after censure by Pellew's successor for disobedience and neglect. William Drury did not hesitate to tell Pellew his son had been 'too much indulged' and had 'an entire misconception of the nature of orders' thanks to being 'given rank so early'.[54] Now, Drury may have been flaunting his power. He changed his tune soon enough when asking Pellew to help his nephew and, all of a sudden, Fleetwood was 'in high feather and gained all his ground with me'.[55] That did not make it any less galling to be rebuked for Fleetwood's failings.[56]

Sir Edward and Fleetwood Pellew were reunited at Mahon in February 1813. Aged twenty-three and growing into an ill-tempered profligate, Fleetwood was given the frigate *Resistance* and sailed for Sicily. On 13 May, off the island of Monte Cristo, the hands assembled forward and, when ordered up, cried 'No! No!'

The accepted explanation for the mutiny of the *Resistance* is that, in addition to his other faults, Fleetwood was a tartar. This is not borne out by the ship's log, nor by the trial of the seven men brought to court martial.[57] Rather than excessive flogging, their grievance was being treated as raw hands by a captain they saw as little more than a boy who made them exercise guns and sails long into the evening, though 'they were an old ship company and considered themselves to know their duty'. They had offered no violence, just wanted another captain.

The Articles of War made no fine distinctions, however. Four of the seven men were sentenced to hang, the others to receive up to 500 lashes.

What brought home to Pellew his own failings as a father and commander was that the mutineers were top hands of good character. For once, forced to choose between duty and family, he did not hesitate – appealing on their behalf for mercy. They were duly pardoned by the Prince Regent.[58] A week later, the *Resistance* was recalled. Fleetwood was sidelined, his Navy career over for now.

Fleetwood's shame appalled his family. Susan, a good barometer in such matters, made her astute observation that 'we have been inclined to think too highly of him – and he perhaps too highly of himself'. She was also honest enough to echo what many others had been saying – 'he was entrusted with Power too soon' – while trying to appease her husband's anger and distress:

> I do not, dearest, wish to add to your disapprobation of our child's conduct – I only mean to remind you of his youth.[59]

That Fleetwood's failings had been finally recognised by his father did not make any easier the parading of his own greatest weakness. Pellew might not have heard what others were saying. He could certainly imagine it. Susan was only half right in her attempts at comfort:

> How is it, dear, that you always think you have enemies projecting evil for you and yours? It is a sad alloy to your comfort and nine times out of ten ill founded.[60]

Such was his state of mind as the war neared its end. On 13 February 1814, one last opportunity for battle occurred when Pellew approached Toulon at daylight with fifteen ships of the line, to find six enemy standing out. A chase brought the *Caledonia* close enough to fire on the retreating French before they gained the harbour and Pellew had to haul his wind to escape the shore batteries.

And that, it appeared, was that. Two months later Napoleon abdicated and went into exile on Elba.

At home preparations were in hand for Pellew's return, and what Susan intended as a pastoral retirement blending Devon countryside and coast. Hampton House had been sold, or disposed of, to her old friend, the Reverend Robert Hawker, whose 'asylum for female penitents' had become too small, while the Pellews' former residence 'formed a more extensive settlement for these wretched women'.[61]

In its place she bought two properties. The first, West Cliffe House, was for herself and Edward and appropriately modest, its main virtue being that it overlooked the port of Teignmouth. Susan wrote in happy anticipation of his return, having acquired 'several little things to amuse you and improve the premises', but admonishing him not to bring home any of his usual 'wild bestiaries'. Pellew's fondness for souvenirs had deposited on her doorstep a leopard from India and marble from the Acropolis, part of the Elgin collection shipped from Constantinople. The latter she thought 'not very beautiful', and she wanted positively no repeat of 'your Jaguar ... for remember they are very expensive to keep, even had we room'.

> Nor do I think I can exist in the same house with monkeys, baboons or any of the animal act, so for pity's sake dispose of them. We have too many pretty grandchildren to want pets.[62]

What she did like was their horse, Boney – and the conservatory, 'a very complete thing of its kind and quite a <u>hobby house</u>', on which she received advice about growing lettuce and asparagus from 'a nice neighbour' in Exmouth – Lady Nelson, with whom she had become quite friendly. (The brutally discarded Frances Nelson appeared once to hold the holy aura of her late husband's name up to ridicule, introducing to Pellew one William Rolfe, 'in the hope that altho' "The Hero" is no more his only relation will find a friend in you.'[63])

Susan had also acquired a much larger and grander estate ten miles inland from West Cliffe House, at Canonteign, a

Canonteign House in Devon, built by Pellew for his eldest son
Pownoll, became the seat of the Exmouths.

spot abounding with woodcock and snipe. Here, in the hillside
mansion of Canonteign House, resided Pownoll and Eliza. The
eldest Pellew boy, having retired from the sea at the ripe old age
of twenty-three and at a loose end as usual, had become an MP
under the auspices of the Duke of Northumberland, maintaining
lines of mutual patronage. Susan feared Pownoll was 'too fond
of billiards and whist' and might 'be drawn into snares and
temptations' while in the sink of iniquity that was London. As
her letters to Pellew make clear, Susan had also observed that all
was not well with their eldest son's marriage.

A second female correspondent brightened packet days for
Pellew. Jane Smith, the young derelict taken in by Susan, kept
her 'Dearest, dearest Dad' abreast of more light-hearted matters
– visits to the opera at Covent Garden and theatre at Drury
Lane. She was not above exploiting her influence. Asking for
a midshipman to be promoted, she confessed: 'I wonder you
encourage me to write, for you know a letter from Jane Smith
and a politician are almost synonymous.'[64] Pellew would have
been content still. In Jane's letters he became again a figure he
valued in himself, a loving father.

The ending of the war brought recognition in a way that placed Sir Edward Pellew among the pantheon of giants. He was awarded the Order of the Bath and ennobled as Lord Exmouth of Canonteign.

All the family wrote in congratulation. Pownoll, in a sloppy scrawl, enquired as to the patronage behind it. Fleetwood's showy hand registered more interest in the financial reward involved. The two girls were genuinely loving and proud. But the most thoughtful came from the adopted Jane, who, recalling Pellew's action with the *Cleopatre* almost twenty-one years earlier, noted:

> You fired the first and last shots of the war . . .
>
> I now must take leave of the old Dear Name and congratulate you on your Title. I am sitting with Pownoll at his lodgings. We have just had a good laugh about dear Mother, supposing what she said at being Lady Exmouth. A Button for titles, she'll say. I heard from her yesterday. God bless you my dear, dear Father. I hope I must not drop that dear title for that of Lordship.[65]

Susan wrote with quiet pride. Her pugnacious, ill-educated husband had come a long way:

> My Lord sounds big and forbidding, but My Lady I have been so long accustomed to that I have nothing to regret but my change of name, which tho a pretty Title leaves me still to regret that of Pellew . . . May you live long and happily dearest to enjoy the Honors you have labour'd hard to acquire & which are so deservedly conferred on you . . .

Or again:

> I flatter myself we shall meet about the same time three years [since] we parted – neither of us I conclude much improved in appearance. Even Israel will allow that a man does not improve after three score, and a woman, I will boldly affirm, is going fast down the hill . . . God bless you, dearest, take care of yourself, endure to the end and praise God for his mercies. Love your poor Old Wife and though we have lived little together in this world, let us not be separated in that which is to come. Your Own Affectionate, S.P.[66]

Shortly before sailing home Pellew wrote wryly to Keats: 'I have no chance now of being shot and buried in a clean hammock in the pure Element of Salt Water but must be content to be thrust into a dirty hole with the frogs.'

But the truth was, he was tired of it all. 'I shall be heartily glad to throw off Harness.'[67]

PART THREE

EXIT

14.

White Knights, 1814–1816

———— ✺ ————

A grand cast of sovereigns and statesmen assembled in Europe's most cultured capital late in 1814 to recast the continent and dispose of Bonaparte's empire. Among those to be seen in carriages trundling about Vienna were the crowned heads of Prussia, Bavaria, Russia and Denmark, with those arch-intriguers Count Metternich, Prince Talleyrand and Viscount Castlereagh – followed by the Duke of Wellington – hard on their heels. Behind them came entourages of assorted counts, courtiers and courtesans, in a human parade that continued as autumn turned to winter, then spring to summer. Global boundaries were not easily redrawn after almost twenty-five years of war.

Lord Exmouth – formerly Sir Edward Pellew – followed these events through the columns of the *Exeter Flying Post,* looking out to sea from an upper-floor window of West Cliffe House in Devon, surrounded by his still-growing family and trying to interest himself in the orange trees he had brought home from the Mediterranean, his greenhouse grapes (never quite as sweet, he found, as those of Mahon) and Susan's asparagus beds. It is hard to imagine he was not distracted by the doings of the mercurial Sir Sidney Smith, now prominently engaged at Vienna. His former deputy had alighted on a new passion and, with characteristic vanity and vigour, was pursuing followers.

More than just national frontiers were at stake in Vienna. Grand issues were there for debate too, and of these few commanded attention quite like slavery. With the passing of the Slave Trade Act in 1807, Britain had launched a global mission and was pressing its European allies to renounce the trade as inconsistent with civilisation. Which was all very well – but, as other delegates insisted on pointing out, Britain had profited handsomely by slavery, and the trade was not confined to the Atlantic. It was alive and thriving in the Mediterranean. The moral high ground claimed by Britain, they suggested, was draped in hypocrisy.

A note kept by Lord Exmouth among his private papers put the case in a nutshell:

> Englishmen have been so engrossed with the wrongs inflicted by the inhabitants of Europe on oppressed Africans that they have entirely forgotten that there exists another species of slavery of which Africans are the cause.[1]

For quite personal reasons, Exmouth always had a close interest in Barbary slavery and had been appalled by evidence of its continuing impact while he was still in the Mediterranean. At Mahon in 1812 a petition was received on the *Caledonia* from eighteen foreign seamen, addressed to Sir Edward Pellew, 'the only person capable of redeeming us from slavery'. It related that they had been on a Spanish privateer wrongly accused of taking a Barbary vessel and were being held by the authorities at Minorca, pending being sent to appease the Dey of Algiers. 'To you we commit our liberty and our lives,' they wrote – seven Sicilians, five Turks, two Austrians, two Swedes, two Spaniards.[2]

Every human instinct cried out. 'I cannot aid or assist in sending to slavery these creatures of all nations who are innocent,' Pellew declared.[3] But preventing it was a delicate business. The Peninsular War had wrought an uncomfortable alliance between Britain and Barbary as Wellington's forces required a constant source of fresh provisions, and to supply them the nation leading the crusade for abolishing slavery had turned to those dependent on its survival – Algiers, Tunis and Tripoli. Of these, Algiers was by far the most formidable. While its seafaring power had passed a high-water mark, Algerine xebecs continued to prey on Mediterranean people, particularly fishermen from the smaller Italian states – Naples, Sicily and Sardinia. American seamen, too, were being enslaved, their ships and cargoes plundered.

Accounts of their treatment in the bagnios (or slave prisons), of 'being taken to the mountains to carry and break stones', recalled the Egyptian slavery of the Old Testament.[4]

Pellew's dilemma over the detained seamen was resolved on this occasion by a timely overture from the Prince Regent. Since 1811, he had been ruling in place of George III, his by now terminally deranged father, and wrote a Letter of Compliment to the Dey which brought the captives' release, along with the gift of a stallion to 'The Most Illustrious Admiral Pellew' as a mark of 'harmony and friendship between us'.[5]

No sooner had one thorn been removed from the path, however, than another appeared. Within weeks the Dey complained that the Navy's protection of neutral Sicilian and Greek ships was 'interfering with the affairs of Algiers and giving convoy to his enemies'.[6]

Pellew's problems were compounded by one of his admirals. Sir Thomas Fremantle, as testy as ever, was all for confronting the Algerines. 'We should resort to strong measures,' he urged. Fremantle liked to adopt the posture he would have expected from his idol. Back in 1799, Nelson fulminated: 'Terror is the only weapon to wield against these people.' But even Nelson had to negotiate with them: 'My blood boils that I cannot chastise these pirates.'[7] Since then the stakes had risen because, Pellew pointed out, 'as the prospect opens for our operations in Spain, the importance of getting supplies from Barbary increases'.[8]

This dispute with Fremantle brought them close to a real falling out. Yet Pellew still attempted to win over his junior, rather than order him flatly:

> I agree with you that it is a disgrace – not only to us but to Europe –
> to submit to these fellows, but the remedy is worse than the disease
> . . . If we fall out with the Dey now we throw away all the supplies
> of Tartus at a moment our harvests are failing in England.[9]

It happened that he was then about to send a squadron to deliver ransom for the freedom of hundreds of Spanish slaves at Algiers. Fremantle wanted to lead it, but Pellew feared his temper might get out of hand, so instead Captain Charles Adam of the *Invincible* sailed with 100,000 dollars raised at Cadiz by Wellington's brother, Lord Wellesley. A furious Fremantle was sent to the Adriatic.

Adam's report on his return highlighted other highly charged aspects of this moral maze. While at Algiers, he had observed a xebec frigate bring in a captive American brig, the *Edwin* of Salem, with her crew in chains. 'Among them was a man named John Clark, a native of Belfast,' Adam reported to Pellew. 'After examining him and being convinced he was a British subject, the consul and myself demanded that he should be given up according to treaty. But the Dey would not comply.'[10]

So long as the war in Spain continued, men like Clark were sacrificed for Britain's greater interests. The United States was under no such constraints and American anger at the treatment of its citizens by Britain as well as Barbary was rising. That same year of 1812, the USA responded to British violations of its maritime rights and impressment of American seamen by declaring war – and, in a series of frigate actions, inflicted the worst reversals suffered by the Navy in memory. At the same time, the US Navy began flexing itself for conflict with the Barbary powers, which continued to interfere with American shipping despite having received large payments in ransom and tribute.

Pellew had seemed to put these matters behind him when he left the Mediterranean. Honoured with a viscountcy, and with Bonaparte safely exiled on Elba, he could look forward to retirement on the Devon coast, the tending of his fruit and vegetables and rambles through the countryside shooting snipe. He had written a farewell letter to Fremantle which summed up, in its double-edged affability, their deeply ambivalent relationship:

> I thank you from my heart for your kind and friendly note and congratulations, and knowing the sincerity of your heart and your good disposition towards me I feel very much gratified by the handsome manner you have spoken of your chief since your return . . . I am going to taste the waters of Cheltenham in a few days. I shall hope to meet you in Town at all events in the winter.[11]

Since returning home as Lord Exmouth, he had followed the pursuits of another of his former admirals. No stage – not even the sea – was ever quite grand enough for Sir Sidney Smith and, seeking fresh laurels, he had moved to Paris and begun adopting causes. Sir Sidney wrote a crusading paper prior to the Congress of Vienna, in which he declared Barbary slavery was as desperately in need of abolition as the black slave trade, and founded a body known as the Knights Liberators of the Slaves in Africa. When Sir Sidney wrote to West Cliffe House, soliciting further help, Exmouth replied, 'I had read with much interest your address to the sovereigns of Europe', adding: 'I am greatly obliged to you, my dear Sir Sidney, for thinking of me among your knights. I shall give it all the support I can.'[12]

Lord Exmouth had been home for six months, and the Vienna delegates were still at their salons, when the world was turned upside down. His response to Bonaparte's escape from Elba in March 1815 was emphatic – merely exiling 'the Monster' had been folly: 'The evil of his <u>Living</u> is not to be calculated and I therefore vote heart and soul for his <u>Death</u>.'[13]

Exactly how he came to don uniform again is not clear. In a crisis, the Admiralty obviously wanted its most able commander back in the Mediterranean, but it is quite possible he made the first move, because he had plainly not yet adjusted to life as a landsman, writing to Fremantle: 'I am quite at a loss how to employ myself or what to do.'[14] Two days after Bonaparte reached Paris, Exmouth was reappointed Commander-in-Chief.

So, on 11 April, just a few days before turning fifty-eight and having recently insisted he was happy 'to throw off Harness', he came down to Spithead once more and resumed a life charted by the daily log of the 98-gun *Boyne*: 'Hoisted the flag of Lord Exmouth . . . Received 2,316lb of fresh beef . . . Weighed and made sail.'

Reaching Naples in May, he superseded Vice-Admiral Charles Penrose, who became his deputy. They worked well together. 'I heard from Lord Exmouth in his usual warm and friendly manner,' Penrose recalled. This modest, under-rated officer had a rare and impartial gift for analysing his contemporaries. 'The first seaman of the age', he called Exmouth, noting his abilities as an organiser, planner and communicator, his consideration for others – while making the telling observation that 'he took everybody's duty too much on himself'. Penrose was rare among senior naval men as much for his fair-mindedness as his candour.

The Hundred Days passed in an explosive whirl ashore without either admiral being greatly exercised at sea and in the aftermath of Waterloo, with Bonaparte secured once and for all, Penrose assumed his chief would depart, leaving him to resume command of the peace station. 'But the Admiralty seemed desirous of doing something,' he recalled. 'The surmise was easy, that something relative to the Barbary States was intended.'[15]

Christian slavery had come suddenly to the fore, for reasons less to do with Sir Sidney and his Knights Liberators than the US Navy. That summer an American squadron under Commodore Stephen Decatur had arrived in the Mediterranean to confront Barbary piracy. Decatur was a hero of the recent war with Britain, an imposing figure and 'a very pleasing, gentlemanlike man', according to Penrose.[16] He plainly impressed the Barbary rulers. The Dey of Algiers signed a treaty renouncing tributes and released a dozen enslaved Americans – albeit receiving hundreds of Algerine prisoners in return. Similar concessions were extracted at Tunis and Tripoli.

Small wonder the vulnerable states of southern Europe had become more insistent in petitioning their British allies. For where an American squadron could so readily secure the rights of its people, what might be achieved by the mighty Royal Navy? The fact that the Royal Navy had just been embarrassed by its American counterpart added edge to the question.

News that 'something relative to the Barbary States was intended' had meanwhile reached the chief Knight Liberator himself. Sir Sidney was desperately keen to lead a naval expedition but saw that, with Exmouth already in the Mediterranean, he needed to act swiftly. He was not without supporters: Smith,

Barbary slavery, an engraving from the seventeenth century
when the corsairs' power was at its height.

it could be argued, was a natural envoy – charming, a spy and
intriguer versed in Ottoman ways. Others suspected that if
matters should turn ugly, he might prove a disaster. Among them
was the Duke of Wellington who, on hearing Smith boast that
he knew Exmouth well, that he was 'a mere sailor . . . the most
unfit man in all other respects to command such an enterprise',

243

pronounced acidly that Sir Sidney was 'a mere vaporiser', adding: 'I cannot believe that a man so silly in all other affairs can be a good naval officer.'[17] Sir Sidney's bid to supplant his former commander failed.

Exmouth would certainly have brooked no rivals this time. He had resisted confronting Algiers before, but there was never any doubt about the intensity of his emotions when it came to slavery. Cornwall was the region of Britain most affected by Barbary corsairing, and when boys like Edward Pellew grew up they were familiar with tales of seamen's captivity; and though he may not have spoken of it, he would have been aware of his singular personal connection with one of those slaves, Thomas Pellow.

Thomas, it may be recalled, was a member of the same extended Cornish clan as Pellew, and another who had gone to sea as a boy. He was eleven when he sailed from Falmouth in his uncle John Pellew's ship in 1715 and, en route to Genoa with a cargo of pilchards, was captured and taken to Salé in Morocco. Most of Thomas's companions died, Captain Pellew among them, but he endured, converting to Islam (under torture by his own account) and serving in the sultan's army, thus obtaining sufficient freedom to marry and eventually escape – by camel across the Atlas mountains, before finding a ship to take him to Gibraltar. In 1738 he reached home in Penryn, twenty-three years after departing and just nineteen years before Edward's birth.[18]

If it is fanciful to see the last great endeavour of Pellew's life as some kind of personal reckoning, it is clear that he carried knowledge of these events, and this history, with him.

The *Boyne*'s log at anchor in Leghorn at the start of a new year gave little hint of momentous events: a light breeze barely stirred waters glittering in a winter sun; a pinnace was sent for provisions, returning with 1,864 pounds of fresh beef and 830 pounds of vegetables; caulkers sealed the lower deck and carpenters repaired the boats; and, with their fresh beef and pease, the men were refreshed by a pipe of wine and a puncheon of rum.

So fine was the Mediterranean winter, Exmouth had been able to sit on the stern gallery of the admiral's quarters while dealing with correspondence, when, early in 1816, he received a letter relating the Prince Regent's 'indignation at the unrestrained system of piracy and violence carried out under the pretext of war by the Barbary Powers against individual states'. The Prince, far more than his government, had been inspired to take up the cause of Christian slaves, being moved in particular by a plea from the King of Sardinia:

> It is the pleasure of the Prince Regent that Lord Exmouth may be directed to proceed off Algiers and also Tunis and Tripoli and endeavour to establish by treaty and satisfactory understanding that the flag and commerce of his Sardinian Majesty shall be hereafter respected by the Barbary powers equally with those of Great Britain.[19]

Had it been to represent just one nation, the mission that now started to unfold would have been straightforward. The complication arose from the desire of other vulnerable states – the Kingdom of the Two Sicilies, the Ionian Islands – to share in the protection of British treaties. And while some states were able to raise ransom money to free their enslaved peoples, others could not. In one case, the King of the Two Sicilies said he was willing to pay annual tribute to prevent future slave taking, which rather undermined his plea that British power be exercised on his behalf.

A further difficulty was that Exmouth had not received explicit orders from the Admiralty. The truth was that the Prince Regent's sudden compassion for Christian slaves was not fully embraced by his ministers. While they were all for 'increasing our Political Influence with those of our allies in the Mediterranean who have not maritime force to protect themselves', they were more concerned that this might 'considerably diminish our trade and injure our shipping interest – to the annoyance of the mercantile people'.[20]

The upshot was that Exmouth received an extraordinarily vague letter from Melville, marked 'Private and Confidential', in which the First Lord did not fail to point out that 'we have less reason than any other nation to complain of the Barbary States'. As to how far Exmouth should go in securing treaties, and by what means all these various strands were to be brought together – whether 'amicably or by force' – Melville concluded limply: 'Your Lordship will be the best judge of what steps you will take.'[21]

Exmouth replied that, as he understood it, his principal objective was to represent 'a general confederacy of opinion among all the great European Powers to bring the States of Barbary but particularly Algiers within reasonable and consistent bounds'. Some force might be used, but the key phrase was 'reasonable and consistent bounds', whatever those might be. So far as is known, he received no elucidation.[22]

Exmouth anticipated there might be trouble, as is clear from his despatching of Captain Charles Warde in the brig *Banterer* on a reconnaissance mission. Warde had meticulous instructions for surveying the formidable bastion of Algiers – particularly as to whether as large a ship as the 98-gun *Boyne* could be placed across the mouth of the harbour, and, if so, whether she could be raked by the shore batteries. Warde was to note the number of guns, their poundage and their positions, so too the location of the Dey's palace and whether it could be shelled from a ship in port. On no account was he to protect slaves coming on board, but should obtain all possible information about their numbers and circumstances.

There, as he scratched away, a youthful gleam perhaps came to Exmouth's eye as he went on:

> You may be able . . . to get a good view from your maintop by loosing sails and hiding yourself from view . . . You had better destroy this paper when you have read it. You are called by every duty of an officer to keep the most inviolable secrecy.[23]

The *Banterer* sailed from Leghorn on 28 January. Four weeks to the day, she was back with intelligence that spelt out the perils of confrontation.

At Mahon on 16 March, Penrose was brought aft on the *Boyne* for 'the pleasure of meeting Lord Exmouth again and hearing of all the grand deeds that were to be done'. Penrose was not alone among senior officers in sharing Exmouth's enthusiasm for the mission in hand and grateful that the C-in-C had gone out of his way to make him part of it, 'knowing how mortified I should be not to assist'.[24] Talking late into the night, they discovered they had both been mids in the squadron involved in the diplomatic spat at Algiers forty years earlier.

Their passion was not felt across the fleet. Peace had brought an expectation, even a longing, for home, and the mood of hands on most ships was unruly. 'Although no violence or mutiny took place,' Penrose wrote, 'discontent was so great officers were kept in a state of uneasy apprehension.'[25] This may have influenced a decision to send home a majority of the fleet. While retaining what he saw as sufficient ships to impress the Barbary rulers, Exmouth's primary task was securing treaties – and paying ransoms. On 21 March, fifteen boxes of silver specie worth 53,320 Spanish dollars were brought on board the *Boyne* before she weighed with four other ships of the line and six frigates and sloops.

Ten days later, at around noon, they shortened sail and came to anchor in the Bay of Algiers – a crescent fifteen miles across with, at its western edge, a white-walled city. Just offshore lay a crescent-shaped island guarding the approach. This fortified sliver of land, Alghezire (the island), gave its name to 'the Warlike City and Kingdom of Algiers'.[26]

'As discovered from the sea,' one visitor wrote, 'Algiers resembles in form and colour a ship's topsail spread out upon a green field . . . It rises in amphitheatre upon a very quick acclivity, surrounded by high walls with bastions and is entered by four gates.'[27] The formidable appearance of these fortifications was reinforced by Captain Warde's report: the batteries bristling from the walls surrounding the harbour, or mole, contained some 600 cannon – mainly 24- and 32-pounders; other estimates put the figure at a thousand.[28]

A boat soon came bobbing out from the mole carrying the British consul, Hugh McDonell, to be met by an 11-gun salute. An American by birth, the son of a Loyalist family who migrated to Canada where he served in the army, McDonell was level-headed and phlegmatic, and, after five years in Algiers, had no illusions about his bed of nails: 'A post of much trouble and still greater anxiety'.[29] What made it so was 'the ungovernable impatience' of the Dey, and – he had previously told Exmouth – 'the characteristic violence of this government'.[30]

> It is regarded here as an axiom that the well being of the State depends on being at War; and that its prosperity is proportional to the number of its enemies.[31]

The Barbary States had evolved from outlying satraps of the Ottoman Empire into near-autonomous and ruthless military regimes. Their cruelty may sometimes have been exaggerated, yet it was still the case that where a military corps – the dreaded janissaries – held power, it would be exercised with blood; and while the Dey was usually elected from their number, he did not long survive any shortcoming. A resident who saw four of them come and go wrote: 'A Dey of Algiers, while alive, is the most despotic and implicitly obeyed monarch on earth; but his reign is always precarious, and it is by *mere accident* if he dies a natural death.'[32] The previous year, two rulers had died within a month of one another, the first poisoned, the second strangled.[33] The new incumbent, Omar, a native of Mytilene on Lesbos, was thought an improvement by the consul, being 'endowed with good sense, intelligence and dignity' while capable of 'inexorable severity'.[34] However, his position had become precarious since agreeing the treaty with the United States; ratifying a pact with Portugal had been the death of his predecessor.

McDonell impressed on the admiral that, in order 'to preserve the confidence of his subjects, and not to fall in with the estimation of foreigners', the Dey was likely to make a show of studied superiority.[35] On receiving Exmouth's request for 'a private audience to conclude certain arrangements imparted by the Prince Regent', Omar duly declined at first, with the excuse 'that his uncle had shot himself the previous evening'. Exmouth riposted with a little display of his own. A messenger took the letter back, insisting on a reply within two hours, while out in the bay, *Boyne* and her consorts 'Exercis'd the great guns'.

At 9 o'clock the next morning, Exmouth came by boat to the mole. This was the harbour that had been created by linking the mainland and the island of Alghezire by a massive stone causeway that ran about 250 yards between the two. Alighting at the foot of the walls rising on slopes above them, the naval party passed by way of the harbour gate into a world blending the Mediterranean with the oriental – the fish market with the minaret. But what struck them was the darkness beneath the sun. Penrose found the atmosphere as forbidding as the fortifications, the ways narrow and few inhabitants to be seen, none of them women. The janissaries, in contrast, were a constant and sinister presence; to these guardians of military and political power, the foreigners represented a challenge and they were met with glowering looks and muttered insults. 'In truth, of all the places I ever visited,' Penrose wrote, 'Algiers was not one where it was safe to gratify curiosity.'

Entering the palace, they were brought before 'the terrible Omar', as the Dey was known, a man in his mid-forties 'of dark complexion, with a thick, shining black beard silvered with grey and fine expressive black eyes'.[36] His welcome was not encouraging:

> Seated on his cushions and enjoying his pipe, he allowed lords and admirals to stand before him as long as the business lasted and unlike any other Turkish consort, no coffee, sherbet or pipes were offered.[37]

As negotiations began, Exmouth found himself in the novel and disturbing role of bartering for human flesh. It was not something

at which he excelled. The Kingdom of the Two Sicilies had raised
250 Spanish dollars in ransom for each of its citizens.[38] The Dey's
bleak response was that he would accept no less than 1,000
dollars a head for Sicilians and Neapolitans. Then he offered
a chilly bargain for the Sardinians and Genoese – 500 dollars
a head. The gall of these terms was tempered by an immediate
agreement to sign peace treaties with the Two Sicilies, Sardinia
and the Ionian Islands – albeit at the cost of annual tributes.

Out in the bay, another sweetener was being applied. Each
ship of the line received a gift from the Dey – thirteen oxen,
seventeen sheep and sackloads of fresh fruit.

Hundreds of men emerged from bagnios over the next days,
to be loaded on boats and taken out to waiting transports. A
certain Valentino Cerigo was the first slave to be received on
board as a free man, one Bernardo Sifredi the last.

Exmouth could have had no delusions that the agreement
was a diplomatic triumph; but when the citadel and the *Boyne*
exchanged thunderous salutes on 6 April to mark the treaties'
signing, he had achieved his first objective. The transports
started back to Europe with 384 Neapolitans and Sicilians,
53 Sardinians and Genoese, and 23 former slaves of assorted
nations freed by the Dey as a gesture to his friend the Prince
Regent.[39] Another 714 Sicilians would follow when their
ransoms were received.[40]

The squadron sailed for Tunis that day, leaving in the bay
three American frigates which had just anchored.

At Tunis the mood ashore, rather than hostility, was something
closer to levity. Exmouth led his party on 12 April to the Bardo
palace where they found Princess Caroline, estranged wife of the
Prince Regent, staying as a guest of the Bey. The rotund figure
of the Princess had last crossed Exmouth's path in Naples where
she had cast herself at the feet of the gallant Prince Murat. Now
with a party of aristocratic companions, she was on a grand tour
bound for Athens and Constantinople, accompanied by a lover
named Bergami masquerading as a footman, whom, according

to Penrose, she appeared on the verge of discarding for 'the very handsome son of the Bey'.[41]

Exmouth was not keen to renew their acquaintance. The Princess had been a liability in Naples, commandeering ships 'to the inconvenience of the service' and exasperating their officers. She found a frigate inadequate to her needs, complained 'of being obliged to keep her own table' and, on installing herself in a ship of the line, wanted to retain it for the whole journey, trilling 'I am so very comfortable on board the *Leviathan*.'[42] The ship was aptly named for, Exmouth remarked acidly, the Princess had 'grown very large'.[43]

Penrose's description of the scene at the Bardo, where they were brought before the Bey and his sons – 'seated on a mound, their daggers glittering, turbans most beautiful' – placed on a vast divan and fed sherbet, might have come from Mozart's operatic farce, *Die Entführung aus dem Serail*:

> While we were enjoying this display of Turkish manners, the Princess of Wales was ushered with two of her attendants through the hall and into a side door to take her farewell of the Ladies of the Harem . . . The Bey, having complained of the gout, begged that the fleet physician be sent to him. The whole delight of the poor man was gluttony, and he never in his life was known to show any semblance of exertion, except one night when he got out of his bed to murder his brother.[44]

The negotiations went off smoothly. Exmouth, displaying some finesse in the diplomatic line, ordered the yards to be manned and fired a 19-gun salute to welcome a visit from the Bey's vizier. In addition to treaties being signed, 524 Neapolitan and Sicilian slaves were freed at half the ransom paid to Algiers, and 257 Sardinians and Genoese at no cost at all.

But the real breakthrough was spontaneous. Seemingly on the spur of the moment – for he had neither orders nor authority for such a manoeuvre – Exmouth urged his host to cease enslaving Christians. The Bey hesitated briefly, then assented. Exmouth left with a signed agreement that in future any captives not already covered by treaty would be treated not as slaves but as 'prisoners of war, conformably to the usages of Europe'.

Two weeks later at Tripoli an identical agreement was struck under which 414 Neapolitans and Sicilians, and 154 Sardinians, Genoese and others were freed. Tripoli, too, renounced the practice of Christian slavery.

At this point, Exmouth set back towards Algiers. He had just received orders from London for an official protest to be made to the Dey on the grounds that the treaty obtained by the Americans 'might affect the interest of Great Britain' because it rendered the United States exempt from tributes; Britain's allies, on the other hand, would still have to make annual payments.

But Exmouth saw a return to Algiers as an opportunity for more than expressing diplomatic indignation. Haggling for slaves had left a foul taste in his mouth, sharpened by the personal appeals which had found their way to him: a 'Petition of 20 slaves at Algiers'; a 'Petition of some men in Captivity at Algiers' ... There were fifteen of these in all. One came from the seamen of three Neapolitan poleacres taken as long ago as 1803. Another, from a Spanish hostage named Antonio Higuero, described 'the entire pillage of my house' and 'the frightful captivity of being put into Irons of eighty pounds weight and taken to the mountains to carry stones'; Higuero was certain he would have died, 'had not God reserved me as a monument of Christian liberty'.[45]

On 5 May, off Tunis, the *Boyne* paused while Exmouth scribbled a note to his old political leader, Henry Addington, now Lord Sidmouth. Having gained some insight into Barbary negotiating tactics, he was going back to urge Algiers to follow Tunis and Tripoli in abandoning Christian slavery. 'More heartily glad should I have been to have put down for ever all these States, had policy so recommended it to our rulers.' As it was, 'I sincerely hope we have finally smoked the horrors of Christian slavery. We have released 2,500 poor Creatures and left the Dungeons empty – I hope for ever.'[46]

As so often, he was too sanguine. The dungeons were far from empty.

15.

Massacre at Bona, May–July 1816

On the morning of 15 May 1816 William Shaler, the American consul in Algiers, arose and looked out as he did every day from the terrace of the consulate, high above the bay. The naval squadron at anchor below could mean only one thing. Lord Exmouth had returned. As the American envoy at the Dey's court, Shaler's business was to acquaint himself with such matters, and because he invariably found 'a veil of mystery is thrown over British affairs here', he decided to go down with the Danish consul later that day 'and pay our respects to the Admiral', to discover what was in the wind.[1]

Shaler, consul for the past year, had observed Britain's efforts so far on behalf of its European allies with scorn. He was proud of the treaty he had helped Decatur to secure for the United States and had become convinced Algerine power was 'nothing but a phantom'. Britain, he thought, 'might with a single vibration of her Trident annihilate the pretensions of these barbarians, force them to abandon their abominable practices and seek their living in honest industry'; and its failure to do so could only be 'to encourage the insolence of the Algerines towards other nations'.[2] The consul had a tendency to deride or condemn the actions of a hostile Crown, but this particular conviction contained more than a grain of truth. While Britain might no longer derive vital war provisions from Barbary, it still suited its commercial interests to tolerate the corsairs' interference with the trade of others.

Exmouth had returned with six ships. With Penrose having gone to Malta, his brother, Vice-Admiral Israel Pellew became his deputy. These resources hardly amounted to a trident, and

Exmouth was still uncertain as to how far he might wield it. But he left the *Boyne* that morning intending to state his case forcefully.

Once again he was accompanied by McDonell, the British consul, walking up from the marine gate along narrow, darkened alleys. And once again there was an edge in the air as they were brought to the pipe-smoking figure of Omar, reclining on a pile of cushions.

A formal protest in the Prince Regent's name against the American treaty terms was duly presented. Ah, replied the Dey with a dismissive wave of his hand ... that treaty had been annulled. It had been imposed on him unfairly and he was reverting to the pact of 1796 under which the United States paid tribute. The American squadron at Algiers during Exmouth's last visit had been told to obtain a positive response in three months, or he would declare war.[3]

Exmouth moved on to Christian slavery. European nations were united in resistance and indignation against the system of piracy and enslavement, he said. Tunis and Tripoli had sworn to renounce it and unless Algiers followed suit, the Dey 'would have the world in arms against him'. Surely he could see it was preferable to follow their example voluntarily, rather than be compelled to do so by force. In three hours, McDonell related, Exmouth pressed his case 'with all the ardour and zeal which such a cause of humanity is capable of inspiring' – and with some apparent success.

> The Dey appeared to yield to His Lordship's forcible representations and said he would submit his proposals to a divan which was alone competent to pronounce on so momentous a question.[4]

In retrospect, McDonell may have seen that the divan – a council of senior janissaries – was always going to be loath to abolish a cornerstone of the Algerine economy and, being composed of ruthless individuals who intrigued constantly for power, would turn without pity on any sign of compromise or weakness. When Exmouth returned at 7.30 on the morning of

17 May, change was immediately apparent. Robed figures hung menacingly around the room and the Dey was truculent. 'In an altered tone, he retracted everything favourable to the cause he had said the day before,' Exmouth noted. 'Warm and long discussions followed in which much difference of opinion was excited.'[5]

Warm discussion turned into a blazing row when the Dey said he could do nothing without consulting the Grand Porte at Constantinople, and that would take six months. This mention of a supreme Ottoman authority that no longer prevailed in Barbary was an obvious stalling tactic – to which, McDonell reported,

> His Lordship was induced to observe that from the present temper of Europe the consequences of so unsatisfactory an answer might be war.[6]

The Dey looked bland. Rising, Exmouth announced that as a gesture of displeasure he was withdrawing McDonell and would take him back to the ship. This was 'peremptorily opposed' by the Dey, who said the consul had outstanding debts and would be prevented from leaving until they were paid. Exmouth was astonished. He admitted later: 'I could not believe an attempt so contrary to common sense and existing treaties would be made.'[7]

As the naval party with McDonell made their way back to the harbour, a messenger overtook them saying the Dey wanted to know Exmouth's intentions. 'I will let him know once I am on board,' he retorted.

By now there were men milling around them, raising voices and showing enough hostility for Exmouth to link arms with McDonell as they walked on. But at the marine gate they were confronted by guards with pistols who manhandled the consul, separating them. The crowd had become a mob and there was some talk of detaining Exmouth himself: 'Much agitation was created by a numerous party who I understood debated on stopping me also.'

Unimaginable though it would have seemed that morning, the Navy's Commander-in-Chief was being forced to withdraw by a ragtag of banditti. Explaining this did not come easily. 'The consul would inevitably have fallen a sacrifice on the first shot being fired,' Exmouth wrote. 'Finding further remonstrance would only lead to violence, I proceeded to my boat.'[8] McDonell, having been parted from the admiral, had to return to his home near by.

Soon afterwards, the American and Danish consuls approached the harbour with the intention of calling on the admiral when Shaler was 'surprised to find everything in motion and parties of armed men moving in different directions'. At the marine gate they too were molested before an officer of the guard recognised them and apologised, explaining that 'we had been mistaken for English officers'.[9]

Back at the palace, the Dey had been seized with a passion and, perhaps goaded by the janissaries, was barking orders for the arrest of every British subject in the land. The full, catastrophic consequences of this action would become clear only in the weeks to come.

Exmouth had left the *Boyne* at 7.30 and was back at 9.00, when he signalled the squadron to clear for action.[10] Blinded by anger, his impulse was to bombard the city. Or so his actions are usually interpreted. In his official report, he said he intended 'to assume a position in which I could act should [the Dey] commit any open hostility'.[11] Either way, it was sheer good fortune that a strong breeze came up in the west as they weighed and swept them across the bay, out of range of the harbour's heavy cannon. For some hours they worked to windward, tacking in a futile attempt to regain the western side, until at 4 p.m. they shortened sail and anchored.[12] Here news reached Exmouth of other diplomatic outrages.

Oblivious to the turmoil in town, Captains Warde and Riddell had been out riding at McDonell's country home in the morning when they were surrounded, dragged from their horses and robbed. They were then brought, dishevelled and bruised, to the Dey who looked astonished and, perhaps starting to comprehend the forces he had unleashed, apologised and had their property restored to them.

Meanwhile, McDonell decided to leave town while passions cooled and proceeded to his country residence. That same day soldiers came to the house and ordered him, his family and staff to stay there, and placed a guard outside. In effect, the consul had been put under house arrest. The British flag was lowered.

Shaler's report of these events makes striking reading. Scarcely a year since the end of their war, Britain and America remained antagonistic and the consul, who never really lost his hostility for the old colonial power, could see no merit in its conduct. The British ships' manoeuvrings struck him as 'struggling and disorderly'; indeed, 'had the spirit and enterprise of the Algerines been equal to their pretensions, Lord Exmouth's squadron might have been crippled'. Shaler went so far as to take the Dey's part in the dispute, describing Exmouth's demand for an end to Christian slavery as 'justly regarded as inconsistent and extraordinary'.

> The Dey rejected his proposition totally, expressing doubts of his acting on legal authority and reproaching him for his dishonourable and puerile conduct in terms of biting severity.[13]

The representation of Omar as stern and forthright in the face of deceit does not bear much scrutiny. McDonell thought what distinguished him, apart from his courage, were 'great cruelty, deep cunning and dissimulation'.[14] Right now though, he was vulnerable. He had been elected by fellow janissaries after winning distinction in local wars. But as an outsider – a former Greek mercenary – he had become isolated. And although Algiers' fortifications might still be seen as virtually impregnable, the Algerine fleet had lost any offensive capability against an enemy navy. McDonell saw that, without slaves, Algiers 'could not put its squadron in a proper state for going to sea'.[15] There were voices within the divan pointing out that in releasing more than a thousand Christians, Omar had surrendered a strategic as well as an economic resource. Another mistake, and he might not survive it.

On the evening of this stormy day, Exmouth sent Captain James Dundas ashore under a flag of truce.[16] Omar received his demand that the consul and his family be released pending settlement of outstanding debts, with evident relief. Now the crisis had passed, would the admiral care to come to the palace again to discuss their differences? The admiral thought it best not to chance his temper again. Instead, he sent his brother.

Sir Israel Pellew went ashore on 18 May. Though the Dey may not have been quite as contrite as a report of 'his ample public concessions' suggests, he was still keen to soothe his guest, apologising 'for the violent measures he had pursued' and promising 'exemplary punishment' for those who had assaulted the captains.[17]

At the end of the meeting, Omar mentioned casually that in his fury he had sent orders to the outlying towns of Oran and Bona (modern Annaba) for 'English ships and property to be detained'. He regretted this mistake, naturally, and in Sir Israel's presence, despatched messengers to both places, rescinding the order.

On 20 May, in what appeared a final reconciliation, Exmouth returned to the palace accompanied by McDonell. The Dey opened the conversation by saying:

> There had been a fire between him and me which had heated us both and that he regretted exceedingly his warmth of temper had led him to adopt such violent measures.[18]

On the crucial issue of abolishing slavery, the Dey said he expected a reply from the Porte in six months. Exmouth demurred. To obtain an answer in two months, he offered a frigate to take an Algerine envoy to Constantinople, to which Omar agreed. They parted with an exchange of gifts – a sword for the Dey, a stallion for the admiral.

Omar's talent for confounding an adversary may be glimpsed right to the end. When the frigate *Tagus* sailed for Constantinople, she took gifts to the Grand Porte of brocade, parrots, lions, leopards – and 200 black slaves; the Dey had contrived to use a Royal Navy ship to cock a snook at the Abolition Act.[19]

Exmouth discarded his diplomatic guise with immense relief. He had made plain to the Admiralty his frustration at being unable 'to proceed to extremities' without clear orders. What he needed to negotiate was the authority to counter bluff and deceit with fire. As McDonell observed drolly in one of his official dispatches: 'Nothing is more versatile than the opinions of the Algerines.'[20]

Thanks to McDonell, diplomats if not their skills had risen in Exmouth's estimation. Just before sailing, he wrote thanking the consul for his efforts and praising, 'the manly firmness you have displayed throughout all the violence and embarrassments of the late discussions'.[21] They had established a bond and, whatever Exmouth's failings in the subtle arts, McDonell honoured his humanity. 'No task is too arduous for His Lordship,' he wrote. 'The character and honour of a great nation could not be confided to a commander of greater determination and ability.'[22]

Five weeks later, on 26 June, after passing up a lushly coated Sussex shoreline, Exmouth sighted the church spires of Portsmouth and made ready to go ashore. By sunset, when he struck his flag, a carriage was waiting to speed him overnight to London. Those who had shared the events of the past year watched him go, knowing not when, or even if, he would return.

Something had been done. But had it been enough? Exmouth thought so, at least in view of the exceptionally hazy brief he had been given. On the other hand, in pressing for the abolition of Christian slavery he had actually exceeded his orders, and come close to starting a war. A letter to his brother Samuel, written on his way home, indicates anxiety about the reception that awaited him:

> I intreat you to observe the utmost silence on this point, as it may lead me into an awkward situation. For I have acted solely on my own responsibility, and without orders. The causes and reasoning on which, upon general principles, may be defensible, but as applying to our own Country may not be borne out, the old mercantile interest being against it.[23]

The old mercantile interest . . . that was the rub: Shaler had been right in perceiving a potent lobby as responsible for the blind eye to Barbary corsairing when it involved Britain's trade rivals. But much had altered in the year of Exmouth's absence. Political leaders, responding to a new global landscape, were hastily trying to dispel what Castlereagh, the Foreign Secretary, termed 'this canard . . . that we cherish'd piracy as a commercial ally'.[24] A trenchant debate had begun and Westminster was starting to consider strong measures against Algiers.

Something else was about to transform British policy. By the time he landed, Exmouth seems to have heard rumours of the disastrous aftermath to his row with the Dey. Certainly by the time he reached the Admiralty, so too had reports of events at Bona.

Captains Warde and Riddell had been the first to suffer the Dey's command that British subjects be arrested. That same day, 16 May, riders also set out up the coast. On 18 May, Omar issued his rescinding order, but it came too late to the port of Bona, about 250 miles to the east.

At 5 a.m. on 23 May, the honorary British vice-consul, a trader named Escudero, was roused by armed guards 'who seized upon my person, my brother and my family' and, after robbing their house, took them to town.

Hours later, about 800 coral fishermen – Sicilians protected by treaty and so honorary British subjects – moored their boats, as they had done for some weeks, and came ashore intending to mark the Feast of the Ascension. Attempts to confine them turned, in Escudero's words, into a tumult. From his confinement he heard guns open fire as they tried to flee.

> On the first movement a fire with grape shot was opened from the fortress & of musketry from the troops. Few effected their escape, many were killed and the remainder without regard to the condition of those wounded were conducted to prison; and their boats, fishing nets and effects were left to the mercy of the Moors.[25]

When the Dey's belated order arrived the next day, the terrified survivors were freed, but even though their boats were unfit to sail, having been plundered of rigging, 'no entreaties could dissuade them from going to sea, such was the horror of beholding the dead bodies of their brothers and friends, still scattered in every direction on the beach'. Escudero arranged burials for the dead which he counted initially at about 100 with a similar number of wounded. Later he concluded there were more. 'The slaughter was great but the number cannot be known as [some] bodies were thrown into the sea and river.'

Reporting the massacre to McDonell, he said he suspected that the local governor 'in extenuation of these enormities and evils, will claim he was driven to use force' when in fact 'the victims were a disarmed and pacific people'.

McDonell received this first dispatch a week after Exmouth's squadron had sailed and went straight to the Dey who, as predicted, responded that the Christians had opened fire first. McDonell warned him 'that ample reparations would be expected for these unheard-of excesses'. Omar said the consul seemed to be trying to provoke a misunderstanding when he and Exmouth had agreed there should be 'perfect oblivion of all their differences and the consequences'. McDonell departed, noting dryly that 'Lord Exmouth certainly did not mean to subscribe to a forgetfulness of outrage against the interests and dignity of his nation.'[26]

Although some appalling incident had occurred, McDonell suspected at first that the vice-consul's horror at what he had witnessed might have led him to exaggerate. This idea was dispelled once Escudero reached Algiers, when McDonell questioned him and concluded that if anything, 'he had suppressed mentioning many acts of wanton cruelty'.

The Dey, confronted with an eyewitness account, still evinced no sign of remorse. He was 'pleased to say he disapproves of the proceedings . . . [but] observes that it was not to be expected so great a number of Christians could be arrested without several lives being lost'. McDonell had four years' experience at Algiers yet was still taken aback by that.

I mention this to say that the Dey is unconscious of the horror and disgust with which all of Europe will hear the late melancholy events. He thinks of them with cold indifference if not, perhaps, satisfaction. No person has been called to account.[27]

The actual toll of the massacre at Bona was never established, although it was probably closer to 200 than 100. In political terms, however, the outcome would have been the same, for Europe did indeed react with horror and disgust.

The criticism had begun even before Exmouth's return. Much of it ought not to have ruffled even so thin-skinned a creature as he, for criticism from the opposition press was only to be expected. 'Our admiral,' lamented the *Independent Whig*, 'has been honoured with a mission to the Prince of Ruffians at Algiers, and has patched up a something, which is called a Treaty, as if the ringleader of a banditti of Corsairs would adhere to any treaty . . . It is quite a farce to talk of a treaty with this rascal.'[28] Insults from radical pamphleteers were just as predictable; William Cobbett delighted in sharpening his pen on establishment figures and his judgment in the *Political Register*, that 'able seaman as his Lordship is, he is a much more able courtier', was comparatively mild.

But any impugning of his honour troubled Exmouth, and the fact that questions had also been raised in Parliament added to his edginess. Already the implications of paying ransoms to secure treaties had given rise to objections, especially as it became clear that this would only encourage the corsairs to seek Christian hostages elsewhere. Reports to this effect were starting to arrive from Tuscany and Genoa. It was also being said that even those states that had been given protection by the treaties now thought 'the benefit small and temporary, and the expense burthensome and lasting'.[29]

None of this could be blamed on Exmouth, who had carried out every point of his orders and, off his own bat, won the agreement of Tunis and Tripoli to give up slavery. Having come home under the apprehension that he might be condemned for going too far, he was first bewildered and then angered to find his mission disparaged for not going far enough. His temper was not improved when press reports from America, crediting the success at Tunis to Princess Caroline rather than himself, appeared in some British papers.[30] Rightly or wrongly, he came to see the hand of old foes at work.

As he alighted from his carriage in London on 27 June, a real storm was breaking.

Three days earlier, in the first report on the killings, *The Times* had published a brief extract from the French press to the effect that the English vice-consul at Bona had been assassinated and 'the foreigners employed in the fishery there massacred' – as a result of 'discontent occasioned by the treaties concluded by Lord Exmouth'.[31]

Details of what had happened took weeks to emerge. It was plain from this point, however, that an outrage had occurred and a response was called for. On 1 July *The Times* reported: 'Lord Exmouth, who only arrived in town on Wednesday from the Mediterranean, has been every day for several hours with the Board of Admiralty.' An editorial in the paper caught the public mood while reflecting the Government's economic priorities:

> Vigorous measures, it is said, are to be immediately carried into effect against the Barbary powers. We have said if the British flag has been insulted or British honour compromised, there can be no hesitation in chastizing the barbarians; but we repeat that the country's finances are not in a state to permit our lavishing money on the defence of powers from whom we have little gratitude to expect.[32]

Events were moving at pace. Just four days after coming ashore, and even as coffee-house readers were still debating how best the barbarians might be chastised, Exmouth returned to Portsmouth.

He would have been loath to admit it, but a massacre of innocents had given him the kind of opportunity for which he had waited years – a high-minded cause with the prospect of

Lord Exmouth at Algiers.
Strands of faith and redemption are evident
in this engraving from his later years, showing
decorations showered on him by European states.

real action. A punitive expedition against Algiers offered heady possibilities – of retribution and rescue, mercy and glory. When Exmouth left the Admiralty it was with the agreement that he should be allowed to finish what he had started. While he went to prepare his ships for war, the Cabinet drafted an ultimatum to the Dey.

All hands were mustered when the admiral came up the *Boyne*'s side again on 1 July. He addressed them from the quarterdeck and without being explicit about the 'particular service' on which he was embarking said it concerned unfinished business in Algiers and he wished 'to invite them to return thither'.[33]

It might seem curious that they should be invited rather than ordered, but at the end of a war all hands were entitled to a discharge. As it was, hostilities had ceased more than a year earlier at Waterloo and even back in March Penrose had remarked on discontent in the fleet. Now men were not just desperate to go home, they were insistent on having their pay. A bare dozen hands and a few Marines volunteered. Appeals to the men of the *Ajax*, *Bombay* and *Leviathan* fell similarly flat and all four ships were paid off.[34]

Raising a new squadron from scratch, manning and equipping it, all within a matter of weeks, posed a substantial challenge. Impressment had been abolished, the nation was at peace, and when Exmouth shifted his flag to the 100-gun *Queen Charlotte* on 6 July, he was appalled by the state of her crew. She was 200 men short of her fighting complement of 837, and 60 of the existing company were found 'from infirmity, age and wounds quite unfit for service'. Described variously as 'dumb', 'cripple' and 'lame', they were discharged.[35]

He set to work. Captain James Brisbane joined him from the *Boyne* with a few trusted lieutenants and petty officers who were sent around the taverns and grog shops, urging the more profligate jacks who had just been paid off to sign on again. Their efforts were sustained by the appearance in town of leaflets announcing that volunteers would receive an additional two months' pay, in advance. By 18 July it required ten clerks to take sufficient coin on board the *Queen Charlotte* to pay them all. Other routines of ship life were falling into place: that day 775 gallons of rum and 517 gallons of brandy were also brought up the side.

With still more men required for the rest of the squadron, messages were sent around coastal towns – with some novel results. About fifty smugglers at three naval prisons were found fit for duty and sent to join the squadron. So were half a dozen poachers who had never been to sea in their lives.[36]

More ships were coming to anchor – the *Albion* and *Minden*, both 74s, *Prometheus*, a 16-gun sloop, and *Hecla*, one of an innovative class of vessel known as a bomb. The plan taking shape in Exmouth's mind called for five ships of the line, five frigates, five sloops and four bombs. It also called for an early departure, and Spithead resounded with the hammering of carpenters, the bawling of officers and the chants of men hauling in unison.

One figure stood out – a red-faced giant, his silvery hair lank with sweat, who wore a calico shirt with nankeen trousers and a scarf around his waist, and was as loud in his exhortations as any of his officers. Exmouth's familiarity, even his tendency to take too much upon himself, worked to the greater benefit at such times. Towards the end, he wrote to Sir Byam Martin, the Comptroller, thanking him for the speed with which the squadron had been equipped; but his own efforts were crucial.

One aspect about Exmouth's preparations for his return to Algiers stands out – his awareness that conflict was likely and would cost many lives; and a strong sense that his might be among them.

For a start he refused to accept for service those closest to him, notably his brother Israel. Once before when they had shared a dangerous quarterdeck, the younger Pellew had been banished with the words, 'Israel you have no business here. We are too many of us.' His request to accompany the squadron again was rejected.[37] Other old followers, Coghlan and Bell, were also forbidden. Of the two exceptions, one was John Gaze, who had been at Exmouth's side for the past twenty-three years, had served as master on virtually his every ship in that time and was not going to leave him now. The other was William Kempthorne, son of his Falmouth neighbour, boyhood friend of his sons. Kempthorne had never entirely escaped the taint of his court martial fifteen years earlier, was still a lieutenant at the age of thirty and, having recently returned from an uneventful service in Newfoundland, swore he would rather die than be denied the last chance for promotion he would ever get. Exmouth gave him *Beelzebub*, one of the bombs that would be closely engaged in any action.

That Exmouth contemplated his own mortality is plain from a letter written just before departing, entrusted to Keats, his closest friend, to be delivered in the event of his death. It was addressed to his heir. Pownoll had never escaped the shadow of his brother Fleetwood; an unhappy boy had grown into an undistinguished man, an MP thanks purely to his family's ties with the Duke of Northumberland, a failure even as a husband – for it was clear by now that his marriage to Eliza had brought them both misery.[38] Still his father loved him, and would not depart without attempting to heal old wounds.

My Very Dear Pownoll,

When this reaches you the Father who loves you will be no more. I depart with the sweet reflection that my life has been useful to my children. Respect my Memory and above all respect and honour the best of Mothers.

Be a protector to your family and may God's blessing attend you. I trust you will all be united in the closest bonds of love and friendship, united you will all be invulnerable, divided ruined . . . Stick by your profession, you are not trammelled as I was by weight of obligation. Loyal you must ever be.

I assure you My Dear Pownoll you are all alike dear to me. Your Mother will do all she can for you and I hope you will enjoy her confidence and assist her affairs. She will be able to do much for you and you know how deeply she feels for you all.

I believe I have been <u>basely & vilely belied</u> but Truth will at last prevail for I am innocent.

God bless you, My Dear Pownoll, be virtuous and you will be happy, so prays

Your Affectionate Father[39]

The shift of tone is jarring: 'I believe I have been <u>basely & vilely belied</u>'. Even now he was prone to demons, haunted by what others might be saying behind his back. Parting shots from the press, of the kind in *Bell's Messenger*, loftily expressing a hope 'that Lord Exmouth will accomplish his errand more effectually than before', only confirmed his suspicions.[40]

In the end it came down to honour, and hope of redemption. Nelson had had his foibles. They were forgotten, his reputation shone bright. Exmouth envied his fate. 'Such a day as Trafalgar,' he had written in a despairing moment, 'how sweetly could I give up life in such a cause.' Yet his true inspiration was not Nelson, but another fallen officer. Philemon Pownoll had shaped his character and died at his side – had embodied for him the chivalry and humanity of another age. These were what mattered to Exmouth, and they account for the deep, seemingly disproportionate injury inflicted by the barbs to which, like any public figure, he was exposed.

Still, he had no mawkish desire for martyrdom. He had his cause, his opportunity and a moment when he alone would be accountable for the outcome. He seems to have been content. His final actions were related by John Wilson Croker, the Admiralty Secretary, and not a man normally noted for his warmth, who recalled:

the singular magnanimity with which on sailing for Algiers he left behind as his last act a letter in which he took upon himself all the responsibility & exonerated the ministers who, he declared, had done all that he asked or desired for the success of the attempt, so that if he should fail, the fault would be his not theirs. This was proof of a moral courage and political integrity of which I, at least, know no other example.[41]

He was to have five ships of the line, five frigates, five sloops, four bombs and two transports. Should it come to a battle, they would be engaging a far superior weight and number of heavy cannon, concealed in emplacements and protected by stone walls. Yet he went 'strong in the cause of our suffering fellow creatures' and trusting 'the Wooden Walls of old England will be found a match for all the Walls of Algiers'.[42]

16.

'Wooden Walls Against Stone', July–August 1816

———∞∞∞———

He sailed from Spithead for the very last time at 8 a.m. on 24 July 1816, forty-five years after his first departure from the great anchorage as a boy of fourteen. Moderate breezes on a cloudy day quickly gave way to an unseasonably strong south-westerly, and he had to fight all the way to a rendezvous with his remaining ships at Plymouth three days later. This had the unforeseen but happy consequence of driving the tacking ships close to Teignmouth where a crowd of local citizens, including Lady Pellew and other members of the admiral's family, came out on a cliff south of town, to cheer and wave handkerchiefs.[1]

Unlike an army on the march, a fleet on the move was able to prepare, to train and to innovate, and so although his ships' companies had been brought together from grog shops and prison cells, from smacks and 74s, Exmouth knew he had perhaps four weeks to instil a sense of teamwork. A general order was issued directly they sailed and thereafter not a day passed that the logs did not record a brisk regime of exercises concentrated on the admiral's old speciality – gunnery. On a typical day, rounding Cape Finisterre on 3 August, those hands not engaged in exercising the great guns were employed in making wads for them. Exmouth had managed to obtain an unusually plentiful supply of powder and ball and, using a target device invented by a young lieutenant named George Crichton and attached to the fore yard, was able to set gun crews to compete enthusiastically with one another for accuracy and rate of fire from an 18-pounder on the quarterdeck. Marines also used targets to sharpen musket fire; accuracy would be critical if it came to picking off gun crews in the embrasures of Algiers.[2]

By the time they reached Gibraltar, Exmouth was satisfied:

> Altho' hastily gathered together, I have found in good will and good heart ample means to produce in our Young Recruits all the knowledge of their arms and duties I can wish. And I shall enter in our task with more real satisfaction than I should have with the old and trained People who preferred their congee to the honor of embracing the Cause of their suffering fellow Creatures.[3]

The spirit may have been good. Strength and numbers were still a concern. Nelson had once been asked what force he thought would be required to attack Algiers from the sea and, on the basis of his victory at Copenhagen, replied ten ships of the line. Exmouth had five.

There is some question over whether he had wanted a larger fleet or opted for the smaller number for purposes of manoeuvrability in a limited space. The former seems the more likely. Of Algiers' defences he had said: 'If we threaten we should also perform – and must open 200 guns against 200 guns.'[4] When he set out to attempt the most ambitious attack of its kind since Copenhagen with five line of battle ships, five frigates, five sloops and four bombs – roughly half of Nelson's force – he did so because those were the resources available.[*] Plainly there was more to the respective challenges of Algiers and Copenhagen than ship numbers; but having said he ought to have parity, Exmouth was preparing to engage an estimated 600 guns with 300 – because half of his would be pointing in the wrong direction, out to sea. He did have one other card up his sleeve, yet would still have the disadvantages of firing from rolling decks and casting his wooden walls against stone battlements.

A Dutch frigate squadron he found at Gibraltar provided some further firepower. Holland, too, had suffered from Barbary

---

[*] Nelson's fleet at Copenhagen consisted of ten ships of the line, nine frigates and nine bombs.

piracy and had sent Vice-Admiral Frederick van Capellan to patrol the Mediterranean where he had met Exmouth after his last visit to Algiers. On hearing of a British fleet's return on what was plainly a related mission, van Capellan had gone to Gibraltar and came aboard the flagship to place his five frigates at Exmouth's disposal.

While the guns exercised above, Exmouth studied his chart of Algiers, weighing how to deploy his force. When they left Gibraltar on 14 August this consisted of five ships of the line – the 100-gun *Queen Charlotte*, the *Impregnable*, a 98, and the *Superb*, *Minden* and *Albion*, all 74s. His ten frigates were *Leander*, *Severn*, *Glasgow*, *Granicus* and *Hebrus* (British) and *Melampus*, *Frederica*, *Diana*, *Amstel* and *Dageraad* (Dutch). There were four sloops – *Heron*, *Mutine*, *Cordelia* and *Britomart* – and four bombs – *Beelzebub*, *Fury*, *Hecla* and *Infernal*. Then there was his wild card – eight ships' boats, converted at Gibraltar to his specifications in order that their bottoms could sustain the launching of Congreve rockets. These devices were still evolving and generally renowned for wild inaccuracy, but made a spectacular and terrifying display, and could be effective against large targets.

If Exmouth should be killed or incapacitated, command would pass to his second, Rear-Admiral Sir David Milne in the *Impregnable*. This was not a prospect that would have inspired confidence in anyone, for Milne had spent most of his sea life on lesser stations and had minimal experience of action. The man who ought to have been second-in-command was Sir Charles Penrose, but Exmouth's friend was destined for the most bitter disappointment of an honourable career. Orders to join Exmouth, sent overland from England, failed to reach him at Malta, where he remained, agonising, amid reports that an expedition was under way. Eventually he could stand it no more. On 19 August, oblivious to the fact that Exmouth had left Gibraltar four days earlier, Penrose sailed for Algiers himself.

Exmouth had in the meantime received disturbing news. Only hours before the fleet left Gibraltar a sloop arrived from Algiers and Captain James Murray came aft with intelligence of the mission to rescue the McDonell family.

Knowing that British residents would be in danger, Exmouth had sent ahead Captain William Dashwood in the sloop *Prometheus* with orders to extract the consul along with his wife and two children, and to do so 'in the way least likely to create suspicion'.[5] When Dashwood reached Algiers on 31 July it may already have been too late. McDonell remained at liberty but when he came aboard the sloop it was with news that the Algerines had learnt 'thro the French papers' of Exmouth's approach and were preparing for war.

McDonell then refused to come away directly. The Dey's suspicions were already roused, he said, and he had an obligation to pay Sicily's treaty tribute, which had just arrived, or other British citizens and their allies would suffer retribution. *Prometheus* stayed at anchor for days while the consul sought unsuccessfully to arrange a hand-over of the money.[6] Constant military activity was now visible ashore and a guard had been placed on the consul's house. By 6 August even the doughty McDonell was fearful enough to accept that he and his family would have to be covertly evacuated.

Dashwood's difficulty was that the consul's household included not only his wife and teenage daughter but also a baby. He went ashore himself, armed with two midshipmen's uniforms to disguise the women. The ship's doctor, David McManus, who had prepared an opiate, was then to take it to the house, drug the baby and smuggle it out in a basket.

The first part of this daring rescue went off smoothly. Mrs and Miss McDonell duly appeared at the quay as two boyish mids and came off in a gig to *Prometheus*. Ostensibly to obtain provisions, the gig then returned to await Dr McManus's arrival with McDonell and the baby. Instead, janissaries appeared at the marine gate, raced down to the quay and seized and shackled the crew. For reasons that are not clear – either because a member of the household had betrayed them or because the baby started to cry as they left – Dr McManus and the consul had been arrested.

That night eighteen men of the *Prometheus* joined the millions before them who had been taken in chains to the bagnios. McManus was there as well, and also shackled. McDonell, although in irons, had been allowed to stay in his house.[7]

Omar had hostages sufficient to his purposes and sent the baby out to its mother, which Exmouth felt grudgingly obliged to record 'as a solitary instance of his humanity'. With the consul's family safely stowed on *Prometheus*, Dashwood could only set sail in the hope of finding the admiral. Fortunately he chose his course well and on the evening of 16 August came up the *Queen Charlotte*'s side to relate his story. Before a shot had been fired, the Algerines had obtained an advantage.

No more than 500 miles separated Gibraltar from Algiers, which lay due east, but a strong contrary wind baffled progress so that between 20 and 24 August the fleet advanced by just eleven miles. Hands constantly exercised aloft took brief respite below from the heat. Cabin timbers had already been taken down and replaced with canvas in preparation for action, so the main deck ran clear from stern to head.

Among the admiral's usual entourage, two non-naval men were prominent over those final days. Both had been brought on the *Queen Charlotte* for their specific skills, and both were near their moment of trial.

Major William Reid of the Royal Engineers was an artillery expert who had been with Wellington in the Peninsula War. He and Exmouth spent hours in conclave. It may have been at Reid's suggestion that a novel exercise was carried out on a number of ships in which 12-pounder carronades were swayed aloft to the cross-trees and test-fired from various elevations on the fore, main and mizzen masts.[8] A revealing aspect of this experiment was that it involved short-range guns. Exmouth's strategy was to get in close, so the carronades could be depressed to fire down on the open tier of the mole.

This realisation may have contributed to the apprehension felt in the fleet. The phrase 'wooden walls against stone' was on everyone's lips and, Reid recalled,

> many officers doubted the issue ... I spent my whole time endeavouring to impress on others my conviction that we should be entirely successful if we went in close.[9]

Which was all very well but, the sceptics might have asked, how many casualties would be sustained on ships reduced thus to so many sitting ducks.

The second interloper in this naval fraternity was a singular figure who might, in his robes and turban, have been taken for an Algerine himself. In fact, Abraham Salamé was an Egyptian Christian, employed by the Foreign Office, who had joined the *Queen Charlotte* at Portsmouth as Exmouth's interpreter and occupied a privileged cabin beside the admiral's secretary.[10] Salamé's English was almost as good as his Arabic and Turkish, and he would write the most vivid personal account of what followed.[11]

Finally, on 25 August, the wind shifted favourably to the north-west and royals and staysails were set, bringing Algiers just a day away. At noon the Queen Charlottes were mustered by divisions for an address by the admiral, and at 6 p.m. all captains came aboard.

It would seem to have been a businesslike occasion, a sombre spelling out by Exmouth of his intentions. The Dey was to be issued with an ultimatum. If he failed to accept its terms in full within three hours, each ship would take up a position off the mole or the city and engage the batteries: Algiers' defences and its navy were to be bombarded to destruction or until the Dey surrendered. The captains were back on their own ships within two hours. Each had a copy of the map of Algiers compiled by Warde nine months earlier, and specific instructions on where to place his ship and the procedures to be followed.

At dawn they sighted Cape Caxines, the northern tip of Algiers Bay, and Salamé was brought to the admiral's cabin. 'He told me

I was the next day to carry letters to the Dey,' the interpreter recalled:

> His Lordship observed that it would be better for me to change my Turkish costume and to put on European dress; for knowing the Algerines to be a treacherous people [he] thought I should be less exposed in the English costume.[12]

The letters he would take made four demands in the Prince Regent's name: the abolition of Christian slavery; the delivery of all Christian slaves in the country; the repayment to Sardinia, Naples and Sicily of ransoms for the liberation of their subjects; and a peace treaty with the Dutch. A fifth letter, from Exmouth himself, demanded the freeing of McDonell and the *Prometheus* crew and held the Dey 'responsible for any violence that may be offered to them'. A sixth, to the consul, said that if the Dey sent for him, he was not to enter into any negotiations. Exmouth told Salamé he was not to deliver these personally, but to hand them over from a boat 'with a long stick' and wait no more than three hours for a reply.

At 5 a.m. on 27 August, Salamé donned the unfamiliar shirt and trowsers and went up on deck. Algiers lay about ten miles south, 'all of white stone and, being surrounded with gardens and cultivated land, a pretty sight'. One of the officers recalled:

> The morning was beautifully fine, with a haze which foretold the coming heat. As the morning advanced, the breeze failed us, but at nine o'clock we had neared the town to within about five miles; the long line of batteries were distinctly seen, with the red flag flying in all directions, and the masts of the shipping showed above the walls of the mole.[13]

Officers gathered round the interpreter as he prepared to put off from *Queen Charlotte*. One joked: 'Salamé, if you return with an answer that the Dey accepts our demands without fighting, we will kill you instead.'[14] He joined the laughter. But over the next two hours, as a boat with him and a Lieutenant Burgess was rowed towards the city, his gaze turned from the pleasing landscape to the bristling tiers of guns ahead. At 11 a.m. a boat put out to meet them.

The letters with Exmouth's demands were handed to the harbour captain. Salamé asked after McDonell and the captive seamen. Alive and safe, came the reply. Then, while the letters were carried to the Dey, Salamé sat down to wait, and studied the mole.

At anchor were four frigates, five corvettes and about thirty gunboats which between them mustered fewer than 200 guns. To judge from their unseaworthy state, they could only be deployed defensively – along with the real steel of Algiers' resources, which lay ashore.

Access to the mole was controlled by the island of Alghezire itself. This crescent about 250 yards offshore and linked to the city by a causeway, supported a lighthouse and tiers of batteries mounting 18-, 24- and 32-pounders, some 220 cannon in all. These were directed to cover vessels approaching from the north, east or south. On the southern head of the island, the gateway to the mole, were located two monster 68-pounders. Any intruder passing through this formidable arsenal and coming under the city walls, in the west, would be exposed to the batteries located above the fish market and along the shoreline. Although no precise figure was to be had of their strength, Warde was probably not far off the mark in estimating that 600 guns in all could be brought to bear on an enemy fleet from behind narrow embrasures in stone walls five feet thick.

By 2 p.m. Salamé and Lieutenant Burgess had been studying this panorama for three hours and the deadline set by Exmouth had expired. The fleet was advancing into the bay and was within two miles. Ashore men could be seen mustering on Alghezire and around the fish-market battery.

To allow every last chance, they waited another twenty minutes. Then, 'We hoisted the signal "no answer has been given" and began to row towards the *Queen Charlotte*.'[15]

The sight that met William Shaler from his window that morning was impressive, 'the whole western horizon as seen from this house, covered with vessels of war of various classes and sizes, from the terrible three-decker down to the insignificant gun boat'.[16] The fleet's approach had been signalled overnight when distant cannon thundered out warnings. Beacons had been lit up and down the coast, summoning fighters from outlying areas, and as night fell Algiers filled with robed figures, streaming along narrow ways down to the mole. The air of excitement was heightened by the appearance of the Dey, borne on a litter among his people, who responded with chants of devotion and crowded forward to touch his caftan.[17]

Now, in mid-morning, the parapets of the mole and shore batteries were thick with men. It was fine and hot and, Shaler noted, there was scarcely a breath of wind in the air. The fleet seemed to approach on a current, rather than by any controlled influence of sail.

Shaler realised that Exmouth had returned 'with the intention of taking positions of attack'. Even at this stage, however, the Algerines evidently did not. Confidence in their defences was unbounded and, although there is no record of what response the ultimatum had elicited at the Dey's palace, it was never likely to be accepted. The city had confronted at least a dozen serious threats including four naval bombardments over the past 200 years. The last, by a Spanish fleet of 83 ships in 1784, had been an abject failure. Algiers had a history of seeing off foes and its defences were stronger than ever. So far as its inhabitants were concerned, the warlike city was utterly impregnable.

The Navy liked to fight on full stomachs, so men were piped to dinner at noon. On the frigate *Leander*, captain and officers sat down in the gunroom 'to a substantial sea pie and wine was pledged in a bumper to a successful attack and a general expression of hope for an unsuccessful negotiation'.[18]

On the *Queen Charlotte*'s poop Exmouth moved restlessly from one side to the other, an eye aloft to the airs in his sails, weighing distance and speed as the shoreline grew closer. Around noon they came to a mile off the mole.

He had prepared as meticulously as he could. One factor beyond anyone's control now absorbed him. The wind. Nothing

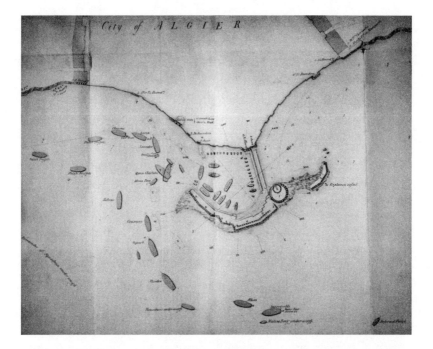

A battle plan based on Charles Warde's sketch of the mole at Algiers.
Each captain was given a copy, indicating where to position his ship.
The *Queen Charlotte* anchored directly off the mouth of the mole.

could be done to avoid the murderous batteries of Alghezire
island. The essential thing was to get past them before they
destroyed him. For that the wind must hold up. Sudden calm of
a kind typical off North Africa in summer – of the kind they had
experienced earlier in the day – could spell catastrophe.

He had not engaged in any real battle since the *Droits de
l'Homme* almost twenty years earlier, had never commanded a
fleet action at all. Yet, as the critical hour approached, an officer
on deck was struck by his composure:

> . . . attired as usual in an undress uniform coat without epaulets,
> white cravat and waistcoat, with nankeen trousers, gaiters and
> shoes, having a spyglass in his hand.[19]

At 2 p.m. the deadline expired and the hands were summoned
aft. The admiral spoke briefly from the quarterdeck – 'in a few

clear and expressive sentences' which touched on duty and pride as well as suffering fellow humans, notably the men of the *Prometheus*, which raised a cheer before they went back to their posts. At 2.20 the boat with Salamé emerged from the mole signalling, 'No answer has been given.'

When the interpreter came on board again he noticed a complete change in Exmouth:

> For I knew his manner was in general very mild, and now he seemed to me *all fightful*, as a *fierce lion*, which had been chained in its cage and was set at liberty.[20]

Salamé expressed his regret at having failed to obtain a reply. Exmouth muttered, 'Never mind, we shall see now.' He turned to the officers, saying, 'Be ready.' Among them was John Gaze, at his side these past twenty-three years. He would direct them through the shallows off Alghezire.

From Exmouth's handling of the *Queen Charlotte* in this, his sole major fleet action, it would appear that he had not only studied Nelson's manoeuvres at the Nile and Copenhagen but had decided to emulate him in the method he had used to come to anchor by the stern. By a complex operation, Exmouth noted, Nelson had been able to stabilise his flagships in both battles, correcting any movement from the recoil of the guns. Though this was the only indication he ever gave of having learnt from his illustrious contemporary, the timing and occasion were significant.[21]

He had resolved that the *Queen Charlotte* would lead in and adopt the most exposed position, at the mouth of the mole, to engage the Algerine fleet. She was followed in line astern by *Superb*, *Impregnable*, *Albion* and *Minden*. The frigates, *Leander*, *Severn*, *Glasgow* and *Granicus*, were to take up places in their midst, joining in the bombardment and towing out any line ship to be disabled. They were all to pass by the south-east of Alghezire and come to off the shore batteries.

The bombs had anchored almost a mile to the east of the island. These four aptly named vessels – *Beelzebub*, *Fury*, *Hecla* and *Infernal* – would hurl their mortars at the lighthouse battery on Alghezire and beyond – 'taking care,' in the admiral's words, 'not to throw their shells over our own ships'. The commanding officer was a man in whom he had the greatest trust – Commander William Kempthorne.

Incendiary fire of another sort would be rained down by the eight boats converted to launch Congreve rockets. Admiral van Capellan's frigates were allocated honourable if less exposed positions, opposite smaller batteries along the south-western shore.

Twenty minutes after receiving Salamé's signal they were about 300 yards from the southern head of Alghezire. Hundreds of men were visible on the batteries' upper tier. At that moment the wind dropped. It had held up just long enough to carry them to their stations.

Events were unfolding so rapidly that the Algerines still stood dumbfounded at their guns. As Exmouth had decided he would not open fire first, the question now was whether they would manage to load while the fleet was still at their mercy.

Captain Brisbane came up to ask whether the hands should take cover. 'If the enemy open any fire they can lie down as we run in,' Exmouth replied. 'I don't think they will.'[22]

Watching from his upper window, the American consul, Shaler, was scribbling notes and, though it irked him to admit virtue in the old foe, he thought Exmouth took his position in a gallant manner:

> The British admiral fills away with a moderate breeze from the north and leads in, in majestic style . . . and to appearance almost brushing the formidable line of marine batteries with his yards.[23]

Exmouth led from the front in all respects. Not only was the *Queen Charlotte* taking up the most dangerous place in the line, he was on the poop, the raised rear deck above the quarterdeck, where he would be conspicuous both for his bulk and admiral's uniform, and a natural target for Algerine riflemen little more than fifty yards away. There was something reckless about his conduct at this moment. It may even have appeared irresponsible – a self-conscious attempt to emulate Nelson, when the man who would then assume command was untested. The truth is, it was the only way he knew.

Still the Algerines remained frozen. Salamé, on the poop with Exmouth, noted the faces staring at them across the water, the 'many thousand Turks and Moors looking on astonished to see so large a ship coming all at once [to] the mole'.[24]

> We gave them three cheers and the batteries as well as the walls being crowded with troops they jumped on the top of the parapets to look at us . . . I am sure [they] were not aware of what they were about, nor what we meant to do . . . They thought we should be terrified by their fortifications, and not advance so rapidly and closely to the attack.[25]

The *Queen Charlotte* had reached the mouth of the mole and was closely followed, with one exception. Exmouth's orders had pointed out that as space to manoeuvre was very limited 'it will require the greatest attention to place the ships well in their respective stations; and it is very desirable to avoid opening any fire if it be possible before they are placed'.[26]

The exception was the *Impregnable*. She had slowed more rapidly than the rest, partly because of the wind's failure, partly because of being poorly handled. While the rest of the line had penetrated beyond most of the Alghezire batteries, she was drifting off to the east and remained exposed to their fire.

At 2.45 the *Queen Charlotte* came to about fifty yards from the mole, directly across the entrance and right in the line of the two giant 68-pounders. One young mid chirruped: 'I dare say the Dey thinks we must be near-sighted, for we seem to think we can't get close enough.'[27]

Now Exmouth demonstrated his familiarity with Nelson's manoeuvres at the Nile and Copenhagen. The concept was simple: anchoring by the stern to stabilise the flagship against the recoil of her own guns; but the execution was taxing and required a highly trained company – to run twin cables weighing up to twenty tons the length of the ship so she could be held by two stern anchors. A mainsail was set to maintain tension against them, while her bowsprit was lashed to the mainmast of a brig.[28] This was to correct movement of the ship from the recoil of the guns, and keep her broadside on to the mole.

A sense of unreality had fallen on the scene as the three-decker's wooden walls came to, level with the stone tiers. One officer noted how 'a vast number of spectators were assembled on the beach, seemingly quite unconscious of what was about to happen'.[29] The lively mid declared they were 'as thick as hops' and marvelled that Exmouth 'had some pity on the poor devils, for he stood on the poop and motioned with his hand for them to get out of the way'.[30]

The Algerine gunners had just recovered themselves and finished loading. Which battery fired first was a point of disagreement; some said the lighthouse, some the fish-market. It was also unclear which ship was the first to be hit, the *Queen Charlotte*, *Superb* or *Impregnable*. But the time, most agreed, was a few minutes before 3.

'That will do,' Exmouth roared. 'Fire, my fine fellows!'

Lighted tapers were already poised over the *Queen Charlotte*'s guns. Their first riposte was directed at those murderous 68-pounders, and Salamé watched transfixed as 'one – a most astonishing thing – was thrown with its carriage into the sea. The other was knocked off its carriage by a shot in its mouth.'[31]

Gunnery on the flagship had been sharpened to a terrible intensity. Fifty guns on the starboard beam, including 32-pounder cannon and carronades, got off three broadsides within six minutes. Seconds after their charges were spewed out, stone battlements erupted in clouds of dust that never quite cleared away afterwards. The 12-pounder carronades which had been swayed aloft into the cross-trees were depressed and fired down on the open tier of the southern battery. Each canister shot discharged about 280 musket balls, and the men below – 'astonished to see the balls falling on them from the *masts* of the ship, like *hail*!' – ducked and scattered like wild creatures, 'upon their feet and hands'.

About 500 defenders were estimated to have died in those opening broadsides. Within a few minutes, Salamé wrote: 'The sky was darkened by smoke, the sun completely eclipsed and the horizon became dreary.'[32]

Admiral Exmouth was transformed into Captain Pellew, as Salamé noted:

> I never saw any body so active and attentive to every point. My astonishment was increased to see his Lordship, who is about sixty-five years old [he was in fact still fifty-nine] and of a stout body, during the battle with a round hat on his head, a telescope in his hand and a white handkerchief round his body, running from one place to another, directing all the people as actively as any young man on board.

Salamé's own emotions were a blend of terror and confusion:

> My ears deafened by the roar of the guns and finding myself in the dreadful danger of such a terrible engagement, I was quite at a loss, like an astonished or stupid man, and did not know where I was.

Exmouth saw the fear on his face and said: 'You have done your duty. Now go below.'

The frigates *Glasgow*, *Severn* and *Leander* had followed in behind the *Queen Charlotte* and passed her. The advance of the 74s was less smooth, because of a signalling error. Exmouth ordered, 'Prepare to anchor'. Instead the flag flown was, 'Anchor'.[33] As a result, the *Superb*, *Minden* and *Albion* came to short of their allotted places off the south-eastern battery and only gradually moved on once the position became clear. That left the *Impregnable*.

The 98-gun three-decker had been ill-handled while approaching the mole, her sails being clewed up too early on the orders of Edward Brace, her elderly and sickly captain. Although drifting out of the line she could still have regained her position, but, at the signal to anchor, Brace brought *Impregnable* to as well – still in her lethally exposed state. There ought to have been no such confusion: each ship, plainly, was to proceed to her originally allocated position. Brace should have been over-ruled by Rear-Admiral Milne, the senior officer on board, but he – inexperienced in action – failed to act. She would remain where she was.

One account of events on *Impregnable*, by Lieutenant Henry Wilson, is a dry series of minutes, recording how she came to, starboard broadside on, about 350 yards from the three tiers of guns of the lighthouse battery, and commenced 'a well directed fire'. There is no mention of the devastation around Wilson, apart from a brief, equally dispassionate reference to 'an explosion on the main deck occasioned by a shell from the Enemy passing through the after hatchway in the Admiral's Cabbin which killed and wounded a number of our men'.[34] Actually, this mortar blast killed and wounded no fewer than fifty hands. But even that was a fraction of her casualties.

The likelihood is that *Impregnable* was more like 450 yards from the battery, where her own fire was less effective, while the Algerine gunners, once they settled to work, became ferociously accurate. Over the next two hours the *Impregnable*'s hull was hit 233 times. Almost every ball represented an explosive charge that released hundreds of oaken splinters, varying in size from a needle to a sturdy branch. While a direct hit from a ball might tear a man in two, flying chunks of timber caused by far the greater number of casualties.

In the midst of carnage, the untested Admiral Milne seems to have come close to losing his head, signalling Exmouth for assistance while declaring 'although the *Impregnable* might sink, she would never surrender'.[35] A three-decker, she could well have been reduced to a bare hulk in battle, but was not likely simply to go down.

Ineffectively though they were led, the Impregnables responded magnificently. For hours they stood to their guns while men around them fell or were swept away. A witness described the aftermath of a ball striking one crew:

Eight men [were] lying between two guns, each in the convulsed attitude in which he had expired. One man had one arm extended, the other close to his breast, both fists clenched in a boxing attitude, whilst his right leg lay by his side, having been cut in two by a cannon-ball close to the hip. Near him was another poor fellow extended on his belly, his face downwards with his back exposed; between his shoulders was buried an 18-pound shot. Legs, arms, blood, brains and mangled bodies were strewn about in all directions.[36]

On the scarcely less exposed *Queen Charlotte*, Salamé was overpowered with admiration for the hands – 'their manners, their activity, their courage and their cheerfulness'.[37] And their devotion to the cause – for when wadding ran out, they tore off their shirts and cut them up to keep the guns firing.

Salamé made his way to the cockpit and, finding the surgeon at his desperate work, volunteered to help, until recoiling from 'the most shocking sight in the world, taking off *arms* and *legs*. I could not bear it and found myself fainting away when the Doctor began sawing the bone.' Among those to come below was Lieutenant John Johnstone with a face wound. This was dressed and he went cheerily aloft saying, 'I am very well now, I must go' – only to be brought down again with his left arm virtually taken off at the shoulder, so 'it hung by a little bit of flesh, all the side of his breast horribly torn'.[38] (Johnstone survived the surgeon's knife and was taken into his own cabin by Exmouth, who described him in a burst of affection as 'an example of animation and courage as I hardly ever before witnessed'. He was there until his death four weeks later.) Also ministering to the wounded was the chaplain, the Rev. J. B. Frowde, a nephew of Susan's.[39]

The first hour was the most intense, and in this time – exposed on the poop to musket as well as cannon fire – Exmouth suffered at least one of his brushes with death that day. His coat was pierced twice, without wounding him, and another shot smashed his telescope. A spent shot hitting his leg drew blood, as did a flying splinter in the face. None of those present saw him take any notice or say anything about these blows although, as one said, he needed a strong jaw 'to have been able to stand such a thump'.[40]

Murderous fire from the *Queen Charlotte* had driven many crews from the southern battery by 3.30; but she was still being hit by musket fire and guns ashore. Exmouth could make out little through the pall that enveloped the ship and so engrossed were his own crews he had difficulty restraining their fire long enough for the smoke to lift. When it did he went with an officer to the starboard gangway where, making himself still more conspicuous, he gestured to one embrasure. 'We are a good deal annoyed by the musketry of these fellows,' he said. 'Try if you can to dislodge them with a few eight-inch shells.'[41]

Sharing the flagship's position at the mouth of the mole was the frigate *Leander*. She had sustained particularly severe casualties, sixty-five wounded having been brought below after the first two broadsides. At around 3.30, as the gun crews fell back from the southern battery, she was confronted by a new threat: about forty gunboats carrying troops were just emerging from the mole, obviously intending to board her and the *Queen Charlotte*. Captain Edward Chetham of the *Leander* directed his guns and Marines to fire on them. As the smoke cleared, 'fragments of boats were seen floating, their crews swimming and scrambling to the shore. Another broadside annihilated them.'[42]

Meanwhile *Leander*'s surgeon, Mr Quarries, was performing miracles on bodies strapped to a table in the confined and crowded cockpit. Working by candlelight, while his assistants held down those whose screams punctuated the grating of his saw and the thundering of guns, Quarries carried out amputations on seventeen men. Ten of them recovered, a phenomenal success rate.[43]

At 4 p.m. smoke still enveloped most of the fleet. From the spurting flames of cannon fire astern Exmouth could make out that the 74s, *Superb*, *Minden* and *Albion*, were engaged with the shore batteries, along with the frigates *Severn* and *Glasgow*.

A third frigate, *Granicus*, at hand in a notionally supporting role, had taken up a place in the line between *Queen Charlotte* and *Superb*, a courageous initiative but one which produced a proportion of casualties almost as high as on *Leander*. However, with the southern battery subdued, Exmouth was able to turn his attention to the Algerine vessels in the mole.

First an order was sent for *Leander* to cease fire while three boats put off from the flagship and were seen to 'push into the mole, running the gauntlet in gallant style. They boarded the outermost frigate, which was found deserted by her crew, and in a few minutes she was in a blaze'.[44] Although the boats' crews, commanded by Lieutenant Peter Richards, took heavy casualties, their endeavour spelled the destruction of the Algerine navy. Flames began to spread from the frigate to other vessels in the mole.

Musket fire from the southern battery was still felling men on the nearest ships, but the principal threats now came from the more distant fish market, and what Exmouth referred to as 'a fort on the upper angle of the city on which our guns could not be brought to bear, which annoyed us excessively with shot and shell during the whole action'.[45] The *Glasgow*, which he had sent to *Impregnable*'s assistance, was taking heavy casualties. The *Severn* suffered less severely and she exemplified that most romantic of naval images – the man of war with women at the guns. (Exmouth, in his report, proclaimed: 'So devoted was every creature in the fleet that even British women served at the same guns with their husbands.'[46] Salamé ascertained that women had carried powder and balls to the *Severn*'s guns.[47])

A different kind of destruction was being rained on the city by mortars and Congreve rockets. Commander Kempthorne in *Beelzebub* and the other three bombs, along with the adapted ships' boats, had been hurling incendiary fire from up to a mile offshore. While their accuracy was variable, the effect was spectacular and, for those ashore, quite terrifying, as Shaler, still taking notes from the American consulate, wrote:

The cannonade endures with a fury which can only be comprehended from practical experience. Shells and rockets fly over and by my house like hail ... The upper part of my house appears to be destroyed, several shells having fallen into it. Whole rooms are knocked to atoms.[48]

Shaler's notes offer probably as reliable an overview of the battle as any. At 5 o'clock, two hours after its commencement, Algerine soldiers were sent back to resume fire from the marine batteries, and although this proved a near-suicidal enterprise, reinforcements arrived at regular intervals. The fish battery kept up a vigorous cannonade, as did the fort at the north-west corner of the town. Algerine resistance was nothing if not resolute. But hour by hour it was lessening while the fury of the ships' guns was undiminished.

As the sun set behind the citadel, a new light arose through the haze. Flames from the Algerine frigate had spread across the mole. By 7.30 every enemy vessel was ablaze, and fires

Wooden walls against stone: 'Shells and rockets fly over my house like hail,' wrote William Shaler, the American consul, during the bombardment.

289

illuminated the scene ashore where 'people were distinctly seen in all their movements by the light of their burning navy, running in crowds from the demolished works to the great gate of the city'.[49] At one point a breeze came up and the flames threatened the *Queen Charlotte* and *Leander* with 'a most intense heat, the flames burning with great power at the mast heads and the loose fire flying about'.[50] Both ships were hauled out on their cables until the breeze dropped.

Nightfall brought a slackening of fire. On most ships the guns 'were so much heated by the incessant fire, we were forced to wait their cooling before reloading'. Powder and ball were all but exhausted. Men, deafened and blackened, slumped in exhaustion at their posts.

When Salamé came up on the poop again it was to an awesome sight. Fire on the Algerine ships had spread to warehouses ashore and 'the blaze illuminated all the bay and the town with the environs almost as clear as in the day time – the view of which was most awful and beautiful'.[51]

Exmouth was outlined against the glow, the great nose like a ship's bow, eyes gleaming with exhilaration, his voice hoarse from shouting. 'Well, my fine fellow Salamé, what think you now?' he rasped. The interpreter noticed slight wounds to his face and leg, but when he looked at the admiral's coat was astonished

> to see how it was all cut up by musket balls and by grape . . . as
> if a person had taken a pair of scissars and cut it all to pieces.[52]

At eleven o'clock, with 'the growling of cannon only heard at long intervals', Exmouth ordered all ships to cut their cables and withdraw to the bay. That was easier said than done for every ship had rigging and sails shot to shreds and some had to be towed out by the sloops.

Before they came to anchor, at about 1 a.m., the human cost was becoming clear – nowhere more so than on the *Impregnable*, which had more than 200 casualties, almost 30 per cent. An officer moving around below could scarcely keep his feet, 'from the slipperiness of the decks, wet with blood' and came on the terrible scene of men and boys caught in the mortar explosion on the main deck:

> . . . crawling about in the most excruciating agony, stark naked, a single feature of whose faces could not be discovered, perfectly blind, uttering the most heart-rending shrieks and calling out to everyone they met to put them out of their misery and put them over-board.[53]

Ashore, in the ruins of the American consulate, Shaler gazed down on a spectacle 'peculiarly grand and sublime . . . every thing in the port in flames, two wrecks on fire drifting out'; and, just then, another phenomenon occurred. Salamé saw 'a tremendous storm, accompanied by thunder, lightning and hail, which was a most extraordinary thing at this season'.[54] Shaler marvelled at the images created by this dramatic illumination of the night and how 'vivid lightning discovers the hostile fleets retiring with the land breeze, and paints them in strong relief on the deep obscurity of the horizon'.[55]

As the *Queen Charlotte* was being towed out, Exmouth assessed his own casualties – 139 dead and wounded. He gave Captain Brisbane orders that no officer or man was to rest until the deck on which the injured would be quartered had been cleaned of debris 'and every wounded man is in his cot'.[56] The experienced John Gaze observed that 'in all probability this saved many lives'.[57]

Admiral van Capellan came on board with congratulations and thanks. The five Dutch frigates had performed admirably off the southern batteries and had 65 dead and wounded; yet, as van Capellan was the first to say, they had been spared higher casualties by 'your gallant position with *Queen Charlotte* which was the safety and protection of our squadron'.[58]

Across the fleet, 'grog was served out and the hammocks piped down, but few men had the strength to hang them up'.[59]

It was after midnight when officers mustered in the flagship's great cabin for the Reverend Frowde to lead them in thanksgiving prayers. Then Exmouth, who had ordered food to be made ready and had madeira brought up, 'gave a grand supper and drank to the health of every brave man in the fleet'. And, Salamé wrote, 'We also drank to his Lordship's health and then every body went to sleep, almost like dead men.'[60]

*

At 10 a.m. Exmouth sent Salamé ashore with his demands, giving the Dey until 1 p.m. to fire three guns in acceptance. Arriving amid the ruins of the mole, the interpreter 'could not now distinguish where the batteries had stood'. The water, blackened with still-smoking timbers, was 'full of the hulks of their navy . . . the dead bodies floating'. Further thunder and lightning added to the apocalyptic pall over Algiers which, Shaler wrote, 'has suffered incredibly; there is hardly a house without some damage and many are ruined'.[61]

Exmouth's letter said: 'England does not war for the destruction of cities. I am unwilling to visit your personal cruelties on the inoffensive inhabitants of the country; and I therefore offer you the same terms of peace conveyed yesterday'; this was conditional on the immediate release of McDonell, unharmed. The consul had in fact been taken in shackles to a bagnio during the bombardment and had he been killed or wounded Exmouth would have faced an awkward dilemma because there was a strong element of bluff in his demand. He had barely enough ammunition left for a broadside from a single ship.

At 1 p.m. three guns thundered out from the citadel.

Over the next two days Exmouth had some time to savour his moment, writing letters to Susan and intimates like Keats at what he called 'this, the happiest point of my fortunate Life'.[62] Final details were left to Penrose, who arrived from Malta on 29 August and who, while mortified to have missed the action, resumed command and took over negotiations. Exmouth, ready to quit the scene at the earliest opportunity, did not go ashore and never met the Dey again. He would stay, though, to see the culmination of his endeavours.

McDonell was released and brought before Omar who was

forced to make a humiliating apology before the whole court 'for the indignities and hardships he had been obliged to endure'. Next to be liberated were the eighteen hands of the *Prometheus* who reported that conditions had been rough, but eased by charitable visits from Shaler, acting in McDonell's absence.

The freeing of 'all slaves presently within the dominion of the Dey, regardless of their nationality', took longer; but on 29 August Exmouth's heart soared when he saw what he estimated to be a thousand of them 'cheering on the mole'. The best figure for those brought from the interior and embarked in the next few weeks for return to their native lands is 1,231. Most were citizens of various Italian states, but they also included Spaniards, Dutch and Greeks.[63] Salamé spoke to some and found they had been held for up to thirty-five years. This brought the total freed on Exmouth's two expeditions to about 3,040. That there were not more may have caused surprise – but then some grotesquely inflated figures for the number held in Barbary had been bandied about, including one of 'no less than forty-nine thousand' published in the *Naval Chronicle* the previous year.

Under the other terms agreed, Algiers renounced Christian slavery once and for all, the ransom money paid by the Italian states earlier was returned, and new treaties of peace were signed with Britain, Holland and the Italian states.

Victory came at a high price. The number of British dead is actually unknown because of the faint distinction between those killed on the spot and the severely wounded. Official figures, cited by the naval historian William James, put total casualties at 143 dead and 726 wounded, when a conservative calculation indicates a death toll of at least 200. To take one example, of the *Impregnable*, the official number of dead was 50 but a further 23 men died in the two weeks after the battle, taking the true figure to 73.[64] The ship to suffer the highest ratio of casualties was the frigate *Leander*, with 17 dead and 118 wounded, a good number of whom would have died subsequently, despite the best efforts of surgeon Quarries.

No specific figure exists for Algerine losses. Salamé, who went ashore afterwards and spoke to officials, could only arrive at a figure of between 4,000 and 8,000. Shaler, reluctant to concede a major British victory, said at first they did not exceed 600, which was absurd. He later settled on about 3,000.

Algiers was certainly the hottest and one of the bloodiest actions in the era of sail. Northcote Parkinson, a naval historian and not given to hyperbole, thought it among the most brilliant victories of the classic age in English naval history, consummately planned and, so far as Exmouth could ensure it, precisely executed. To that might be added what his aide John Gaze always thought was his forte – gunnery. Ultimately, a mighty contest was decided by Exmouth's training of his men, and their courage and endurance over five hours. They paid accordingly. Whatever the total of dead, the British casualty rate at Algiers was roughly 16 per cent, compared with 12.5 per cent at Copenhagen, 11 per cent at the Nile and 9 per cent at Trafalgar.[65]

When these numbers came back to trouble Exmouth – as they did – he might have recalled his feelings, luminously expressed in a letter to the most severely wounded senior officer, Captain John Coode of the *Albion*, a few days after the battle.

> I am proud of having fought in your company. I lament your sufferings from my heart, but I would willingly bear them all in such a noble cause. We did not combat for kings or governments, but for our suffering fellow creatures.[66]

That he grieved is plain. One of the letters he retained among his private papers was from the mother of Lieutenant Johnstone, who had died in Exmouth's cabin four weeks later:

> All that belonged to my dearest son arrived safe, and with a broken heart I viewed these things that had quitted Wimpole Street under such different circumstances. God knows the kindness you heap'd on my departed Angel forms a Pillow of comfort that I lay my head on every night.[67]

There, too, among his papers is a note, translated from the original Spanish, from a freed slave:

May God prosper your precious days and render your name immortal to the remotest nations of the earth.[68]

The bombardment of Algiers did not destroy Barbary power. Omar set to rebuilding the city's defences, putting its Jewish inhabitants to forced labour in the place of Christian slaves, and though he survived just one more year – the janissaries came for him one morning and had him strangled and buried within an hour – a new Dey was soon proclaiming defiance.[69] Nor did the treaty imposed by Exmouth stamp out Christian slavery, any more than the Abolition Act ended transatlantic slavery. But it did significantly constrain the Algerines and it was no fault of Exmouth's that it was not enforced more rigorously. Ultimately, the failure to make more of the opportunity he created on 27 August 1816 was one of political will. Shaler wrote that the Algerines 'had been given a tremendous drubbing and their power should have been broken once and for all . . . They ought to have been forbidden to build another ship, they ought to have been forbidden ever to mount another gun.' But he was also clear in his own mind that the principal objective had been achieved: 'Every captive was set free.'

Of the last services performed by Exmouth as a commander, one concerned his ill-fated protégé, William Kempthorne. The *Queen Charlotte*'s log records that on 1 September, two weeks before she sailed for home, 'Captain Kempthorne succeeded to the command of the ship.' He, too, was about to quit the sea, but Exmouth had seen to it that a worthy officer finally gained the rank of post-captain, denied him since his court martial fifteen years earlier.

The second initiative involved the fifty-six smugglers and poachers who had in effect been impressed from prisons in July. Exmouth wrote to the Admiralty on 12 September, requesting that they be freed as an 'act of grace towards men who have behaved admirably under my observation'. Their Lordships replied sternly that no legal provision existed for such an act, but they were wrong. A month later the Prince Regent marked 'the late splendid transactions' by granting every man a free pardon 'on the recommendation of Lord Exmouth'.[70]

His third wish was that a symbolic salute be extended to every man in the fleet. In October he appealed for a medal 'to raise the spirits of thousands of seamen (at present out of temper because they believe themselves unnoticed). This medal will afford consolation on the bed of sickness and brighten the last moments of departing life.'[71] As usual, the Admiralty declined, but the idea did not die and thirty years later a medal was issued for service at Algiers and two later naval actions, at Navarino and Acre. Although Exmouth was dead by then, the surviving claimants included thirteen of the fifty-six smugglers and poachers.[72]

There are times when the mundane daily routine of a ship's log gives way to a kind of lyricism. On Exmouth's last voyage, Cape St Vincent was passed on 18 September, with light airs and a clear sky, 'sailmakers repairing hammocks, armourers at the forge, carpenters as necessary. At noon ship under topsails, royals and courses. Squadron in company.' Thus she came home to Spithead where, at 9.30 on 8 October, the tops and sides were manned by about 600 men who 'cheered the Commander in Chief on his leaving'. Then, for the last time, he came down the side to a barge and was brought ashore. Of the previous 46 years, he had spent 36 years, 3 months, 2 weeks and 4 days at sea, in a total of 23 ships.[73]

A huge fuss was made of him and for once he felt able to bask in it, having longed, in the words of his friend Penrose, 'to reach England and receive the rewards and applause of a country highly sensible to his merits'.[74] The Prince Regent made him a viscount and from European monarchs – of Prussia, France and Russia among others – tributes poured in, along with honours of whose existence he was not even aware. An outpouring of melodramatic productions followed – a play, an operetta, various ballads and acres of dire verse; one in particular he would have treasured, for its personal if not its poetic content, coming as it did from his former secretary, Thomas Fitzgerald. It went in part:

Humanity sigh'd to see Afric' enslave
The Christians that Fortune had thrown in her hand
And Europe might blush to behold on the Wave
A pirate that plundered both Ocean and Land!

A weightier tribute came from the Duke of Wellington, congratulating Exmouth on:

the most arduous and brilliant operation of service that has occurred for many years . . . No person admired it more than I or was more sensible of how much its success was due to your heroic conduct and example.[75]

Sir Philip Broke, a gallant frigate captain and victor in the *Shannon* of a bloody action against the USS *Chesapeake*, was quite overcome: 'You have raised a shout of triumph through the world that wakens the universal recollection of our ancient grandeur on the seas!'[76]

But perhaps the greatest accolade came from the most reluctant source. Years later, Penrose recalled how Thomas Fremantle, by then an embittered man and near death, said to him:

I know you admire and are a particular friend of Lord Exmouth and therefore, as I am known to dislike him personally very much, I would not mention him could I not say truly that when he had command of the fleet the Admiralty could go to sleep without care. And the noble devotion and skill he took to his station at Algiers would alone immortalise his name.

As Penrose said: 'This does honour to both parties.'[77]

Epilogue

———— ⚬⚬⚬ ————

It was John Wilson Croker who first called Exmouth 'the greatest sea officer of his time'.[1] Croker's is not a name to conjure with these days, but he was First Secretary at the Admiralty for twenty years and knew all of Exmouth's contemporaries. He was also a fair judge of character. 'The better you become acquainted with *heroes* the less you think of them,' he once said.[2] On Exmouth's death he wrote: 'He was a great man and, what is now still more satisfactory to think of, a good man.'[3]

The words, 'greatest sea officer', were a considered choice. After Nelson there was no room for another great admiral, as Sir Edward Codrington made plain. Exmouth, he said, was remarkable for the gifts of resourcefulness and activity essential in a good seaman – but he was not born to be an admiral and 'was not liked by his fleet'. Nelson, on the other hand, was no seaman, but 'was adored by his'.[4] This is curious as Codrington – who had served under Exmouth in the Mediterranean and went on to distinction as a victorious admiral himself, at Navarino in 1827 – did like him. So did Sir Charles Penrose who, echoing Croker, thought he 'deserved the title of first seaman of the age', while adding that 'perhaps plain-speaking prevented Lord Exmouth from enjoying general popularity'.[5] Actually, Exmouth was no more nor less popular than most fleet commanders, and the assumption that his capabilities were diminished because he was less able than Nelson to keep difficult subordinates like Fremantle and King sweet will not bear scrutiny.

The question of popularity arises because Exmouth was being compared with Nelson, which is interesting in itself but misguided; whatever Nelson's genius as a commander, it was his death and the manner of it that made him a quasi-religious figure, beyond comparison or criticism. More to the point is Cuthbert Collingwood, who was cast in the same mould of compassionate paternalism as Exmouth and was much beloved in his own ship, but never won over his fleet as Nelson did; one junior actually called him 'a selfish old bear [with] few if any friends and no admirers'.[6] Nevertheless he was an able successor to Nelson as commander in the Mediterranean.[7] And so far as popularity is concerned, it is just as well that St Vincent's ability was not measured by his talent for soothing awkward customers.

Popularity aside – and the devotion Exmouth inspired among subordinates, as opposed to well-connected rivals, is plain – any assessment of him as a fleet commander must be based on his performance at Algiers. That alone should give the lie to the historians' verdict that he was only suited to single-ship command. Whether as Sir Edward Pellew or Lord Exmouth, he had few deficiencies in the virtues listed by scholars for excellence in naval leadership – seamanship, originality, stamina, aggression, tactical flair, thorough planning, clarity of communication, moral as well as physical courage and a profound concern for the morale of the Navy as a whole.[8] His great misfortune was that his first fleet command took him to India, which made him a rich man while depriving him of the chance to shine when it mattered most, as the war at sea reached its zenith in European waters.

India also cast an enduring shadow on his reputation. The reward he gained for having supported Addington and St Vincent in the 1804 parliamentary debate tainted him to the end of his days and piled political foes on top of an already healthy list of naval ones. They did not disperse, even after his finest hour, for defeat of France had ushered in an age of reform when his old-fashioned views invited fresh abuse from radicals. William Cobbett wrote that victory at Algiers had been 'very easy, but it will form a subject of empty boasting in this country as long as people are able to endure it'.[9] Cobbett's real objection was that the victory had been won by 'a courtier'. Far more vicious was a class-based smear published in *The Real John Bull* in 1822, six years after Algiers, describing Exmouth as:

> a rude, sturdy, boisterous and impudent seaman . . . without any of the genius for war which will immortalize a Nelson . . . Sure to make his way through the world some way or other, he always scents out what is to be got and obtains about double his share of it. His style is between an impudent entreaty and a bullying demand.[10]

Cupidity was the rule among admirals. In Exmouth's case, it was kept in check by Susan. The wealth he did accumulate – which was considerable, amounting to almost £80,000 at his death – was intended largely for their children. The last word on the subject might be left to the fair-minded Penrose, whose view was that Exmouth was neither grasping nor generous with prize money, but rather meticulous in gaining the full benefit of his entitlement. When Exmouth returned to the Mediterranean after Bonaparte's escape in 1815, he superseded Penrose and not only became entitled to the lion's share of prizes, but did so from the moment he entered these seas, rather than (as a more easygoing spirit might have allowed) at the point that Penrose handed over command. 'All his emoluments began from the date of his crossing the boundary line of the station,' Penrose recalled. 'Instead of sharing as CinC, I was only one of the junior admirals.'[11] That translated as a difference between £2,000 and £12,000. Exmouth was within his rights, but those less well disposed than Penrose might understandably have taken offence.

When Exmouth came ashore in 1816, he put all these issues behind him. At the age of sixty, he finally became a landsman.

The homecoming to Teignmouth on 9 November was a triumphal parade. Local gentry rode out in a cavalcade to welcome him. His coach was then borne by a dozen tars through a large floral arch into town. As they hove in sight a band struck up 'Rule Britannia' and – according to a local newspaper reporter – twenty-four maidens in white dresses, carrying laurel branches and baskets of flowers, skipped beside the carriage, scattering petals in the way as it trundled past cheering townsfolk. The procession came finally to a halt outside West Cliffe House where the family awaited him, with Admiral John Schanck, who had been his lieutenant on the American lakes forty years earlier. After a few speeches the crowd gave three cheers, and the newspaper declared that 'the united feelings of joy, respect and honest exultation which burst forth from the spectators formed a scene truly British'.[12]

Viscount Exmouth of Canonteign remained in public life for some years, serving as port admiral at Plymouth and supporting worthy bodies – the Seaman's Hospital Society, the Merchant Seaman's Bible Society and the Institution for the Preservation of Life from Shipwreck. However, he attended the Lords rarely, and only to champion traditionalist causes. He never came round to Catholic emancipation and opposed Queen Caroline's divorce bill – again to the fury of radical opinion, which briefly took her up as a symbol of oppression. In the summer of 1820, *The Times* reported that a mob had descended on a London house where Exmouth was a guest and that he came out 'requesting them as reasonable men to desist and go home'. They hooted and abused him 'until he and the rest of the party sallied forth and the mob were overpowered and dispersed'.[13]

An encounter with another gang in Plymouth ended less happily, leaving him by his own admission 'kicked and torn'. Though now certain that 'the people are mad, and the world is mad, and where it will end the Lord only knows', his spirit was intact as he wrote to Samuel: 'But here I am, quite whole and sound and merry, in spite of them all, poor fools!'[14]

When in London he would see Sir Richard Keats, the closest of his old sea friends, now governor of the seamen's hospital at Greenwich, and pester him with lists of former hands in need of sanctuary. They corresponded to the end, sharing news on shipmates' passing and their common sufferings from rheumatism.[15]

Back at West Cliffe House life revolved around family and friends. Among the latter was Admiral Schanck who might have tried less magnanimous neighbours, being a tiresome old

Cannon from Algiers displayed outside the Exmouths' final home,
in Teignmouth. Formerly West Cliffe House, it became the
offices of the town council.

bore who preened around the Exmouths like an unctuous vicar
but was never treated with less than indulgence.[16] Another of
Exmouth's friends, baffled by his tolerance of Schanck, was told,
'I love the old boy.'

While family remained the centre of his universe, it was also a
continual source of buffeting. One tragedy of his later years was
the death by duel in 1819 of his nephew, Edward Pellew, son of
Israel and a captain in the Life Guards. Edward, aged twenty-six,
took up with the wife of a junior officer and eloped with her to
Paris where her husband, Lieutenant Theophilus Walsh, followed

them and killed him with a single ball to the head before he fired a shot. As Exmouth told Sir Sidney Smith, after receiving a warm letter of condolence from his old adversary, the tragedy was all the more agonising for Edward being his parents' only child; and when Exmouth had to break the news, their grief was intensified by the knowledge 'that he died in the Commission of Sin' and had concealed the affair from them 'previous to his going off with this Wretched Woman'.[17]

Within a year, Exmouth's eldest son too was caught up in scandal. Pownoll had gone back to sea but, still unable to persevere, came ashore in 1818. Canonteign House was not a happy home, his wife Eliza complaining that it was located 'in a very stupid part of the country'. At some point she met a young Army lieutenant and in the summer of 1820, in an elopement with ghastly echoes for the family, she abandoned her husband and three children and fled with him to Ireland. Although the affair animated a debate in Parliament, Pownoll was not one to pursue them in order to obtain satisfaction. Exmouth's letter to her father, Sir George Barlow, could scarcely have been kinder. 'We did all that parents could to secure the happiness of our children,' he wrote. 'I can only assure you, my dear Sir George, that I feel as much distress as you can possibly do.'[18]

Fleetwood had meanwhile been given a ship in 1818 and sent to the Mediterranean – under Thomas Fremantle, once his father's disputatious junior but now C-in-C. Exmouth wrote with understandable apprehension to Fremantle (had he not once said forebodingly 'what goes round comes round'?) to 'request your kindness and protection of my Boy'.[19] It is unlikely to have done much good. Fremantle, according to his predecessor Penrose, was a disillusioned and bitter man who ought never to have been given the command.[20] Fleetwood came home in 1822 and spent the next thirty years on half pay.

The other Pellew children were more blessed in finding contentment. George became Dean of Norwich. Edward, also a scholarly clergyman, ministered to the village of Christow, a few miles from Pownoll's mansion at Canonteign. Emma had eleven children. Julia was childless but exceptionally happy in her marriage. Between them the Pellew siblings had thirty-three children – which was far too many pretty grandchildren, as Susan once said, to leave any time for pets.

Although the old admiral was a benevolent and largely revered patron, he was still capable of inspiring hostility. His contribution to the rebuilding of West Teignmouth Church in 1824 led to a public falling-out with the vicar, a Reverend Salter, who objected that the family pew had been raised fully two inches in the process. This dispute went to Exeter Consistorial Court, which found that Salter had been 'neither courteous nor conciliatory', but agreed nevertheless that the pew should be reduced 'to preserve the uniform appearance of the church'.[21]

Poor health and deaths in the family cast a shadow over Exmouth's last year. The day after Christmas in 1831, his youngest daughter, Julia, died, aged forty-two. Six months later, Israel died, after a week in agony. The excruciating rheumatic pain suffered by Exmouth in making his way to Plymouth for his brother's funeral may have shortened his own days.

He died at 6.30 on the morning of 23 January, 1833, surrounded it was said by his entire family, and holding a large and rather florid silk handkerchief. He was seventy-five. The bedroom on the upper floor of West Cliffe House looked down on the Teign estuary and out to sea where he might have observed the comings and goings of seamen and smugglers, fishermen and shipbuilders, almost to the last.

There was some talk of a big London funeral. Susan demurred, however, and on a hoary winter's day his people came to the tiny Church of St James at Christow, where the tithed folk from the Canonteign estate worshipped, to a service verging on the humble – what a local paper described as 'a disregard of parade and ostentation which distinguished his whole life'.[22] Exactly who attended among all his old friends, followers and foes is not recorded, but the church was able to seat fewer than a hundred souls when his lordship was set down in the vault. The rest stood outside.

Two years later the family was riven by publication of a book. When Susan heard that Samuel Pellew had commissioned a biography of his younger brother she pleaded with him to desist. Edward, she wrote, had 'extracted from me a solemn promise never to allow if I could prevent it any memoir of him to be published during the period of my own life'.[23] The book, an ill-informed and bland hagiography by Edward Osler, came out anyway.

Susan died four years after her husband, aged seventy-one, and was buried beside him in the vault at Christow, also joining Pownoll who had survived his father by less than a year. At this point George Pellew began making notes for a new biography of his father, copying hundreds of letters and consulting some old shipmates, like John Gaze. George had written a life of his father-in-law, Henry Addington, but it seems he was seeking an author to pass the material to, rather than intending to use it himself. At his death in 1866, however, the project lapsed.

West Cliffe House became the offices of Teignmouth town council in 1909. It retains some original features, including two stained glass windows: one shows a British seaman brandishing shackles beneath the legend 'Algiers'; the other resembles a portrait of the Duke of Wellington, who visited his old Peninsula ally there. In recent years the room where Exmouth died has served as a social services unit.

Canonteign, Pownoll's residence and the family estate, was whittled away. Where once labourers tended the soil, a golf course stands. The house built with Exmouth's prize money, repository for portraits, paintings of his victories and other memorabilia, was ravaged by fire. Finally, having devoured the last of the family fortune, Canonteign House was sold in the 1990s.

In researching this book, I passed often through that landscape, pausing at country pubs tucked away on B roads to reflect how these respective worlds had changed: the age of sail a fragment of history, its culture forgotten; everything established by Edward Pellew lost or disposed of, apart from the Exmouth title. It was during one of these visits that I came to the farmyard and the barn of objects which revealed the trunk with George Pellew's notes. It struck another melancholy chord at first, then the image came to mind of a son scratching away night after night in the hope of preserving his father's memory, which seemed apt; and one note in particular was illuminating.

The viscount, it transpired, had come to regret his choice of title as Lord Exmouth, and wished it altered to Lord Pellew. When he was ennobled, Susan wrote of her regret at 'my change of name, which tho' a pretty Title leaves me still to regret that of Pellew', and in time he too seems to have felt that, title or not, he was still more Pellew than Exmouth, closer to the man who had raised himself from the lower deck than the one who had become rich and exalted. Nothing came of it. A letter from Croker at the Admiralty, who had suggested the title in the first place, pointed out that there would be complications and thought it 'more proper that you should carry on with the title under which you performed this eminent service [in Barbary]'; the name of Exmouth, he said, was now hailed around the Mediterranean, while that of Pellew was unknown.[24] Uncertain of himself, still lacking confidence in such matters, Pellew left it there.

It is a pity, for Croker was wrong. The name of Pellew has the greater resonance and he might be better remembered had he followed the examples of Nelson and Anson in using their own names as titles. But then, after all, his real title was not a politician's gift but the one conferred by peers like Penrose. Christopher Cole, a sometimes testy friend, recalled how once, in their frigate days, a hawser running from the ship to a rock needed untying. Pellew, he wrote,

> Called to the men on the forecastle and desired some active fellow to go down by the hawser and cast it off, saying that a boat would soon be there to bring him on board again. The smartest seamen in the ship declined. In an instant the captain was seen clinging to the hawser and proceeding to the rock. The hawser was cast off and to the astonishment of everyone, he swang himself to the side of the ship by the same means, mounted the side and was again directing the duty going on.[25]

There he hoves once more into view: tall, broad, keen-eyed, animated and beaming, master of the quarterdeck and athlete of the tops, welcoming a gallant foe into his cabin, diving to the rescue of a man overboard, or simply fighting the cause of some hapless fellow creature – Pellew of the *Indefatigable*; truly, the First Seaman of the Age.

Appendix

———— ⊗◎ ————

The following list of advice was contained in a notebook written by Pellew for his eldest son in 1804 when was given his first command, the sloop *Fly*. Commander Pownoll Pellew was bound for the West Indies and it is apparent that his father's first concern was for his health and that he should return safely; the note is revealing of Pellew's own precautions in tropical climes. As it turned out, the advice on care of his ship was the more pertinent. Pownoll's weakness was not health but seamanship. He lost his sloop on a reef a few months later.

From your Affectionate Father to his Dutiful Son,

Avoid as certain destruction both of Soul and Body all excess of whatever Nature they may be. In the Climate you are going to you must use great Caution to avoid all the night dews – and when you are exposed by night never permit your breast to be uncovered or your neck exposed without something tied round it. Never stop on Deck unless covered by something to keep off the Dew. It is equally necessary to avoid the Sun in the Middle of the Day from which much danger is to be expected. It may at a moment produce Giddyness of head, sickness and fever. Take great care never to over-heat your blood by drinking or exercise. Never go out shooting on any account or riding in the Sun and be very particular never to check perspiration or sit in a draft of Wind so as to produce it – altho it is so pleasant to the feeling it is almost certain Death.

At night always sleep in Calico. Be you ever so hot, it is a great security against the diseases of that Country. On your first arrival be extremely careful not to indulge in eating too much fruit – and do not go into the water when the Sun is high. Take great care to keep your body regular and never pass a day without Evacuation.

The moment you feel your Body bound take directly a pill or two of those you carry of the size of a large pea. And should you ever feel unwell instantly take a strong Emetic or a good dose of Physic. If you are seized with a flux take directly a large dose of Rhubarb and apply directly to your Surgeon. Always wear a piece of White paper inside your hat.

If you should take prizes I need scarcely recommend you to treat your Prisoners with kindness, but be very careful to keep safe and proper Guards over them. An Officer who suffers his Prisoners to retake his Ship can never recover the Stain on his Character.

Be extremely Cautious and Correct in you Conduct. The first impression of your Character will formed from it and the companions of your choice. Always endeavour to keep in with the Captains and Admiral as much as possible, behaving with quiet Modesty. You will always learn something in their Company and they will soon respect and esteem you.

Never become one of the Tavern parties on shore. They always end in drunkenness and Dissipation.

In your Command be as kind as you can without suffering imposition on your good Nature. Be steady and vigilant. Never neglect any opportunity to write to your Mother who deserves your utmost love and attention for her unceasing goodness to you and all your family. I hope you will believe I shall be equally glad to hear of you. I am sure you will never dishonour yourself or your family or the Service of your King.

In your Expenses be as frugal as you can. You know the situation of your Father and how many calls he has for Money, and should you have any of your own to send to England I recommend your sending it to Wedderburn. Be attentive to your person and dress. Nothing recommends a young Man more to notice. If you meet Capt O'Brien tell him I ordered you to ask his protection. Admiral Dacres will be as a Father to you. Never fail to consult him and ask his advice on any occasion of difficulty. Take great care to examine all papers you put your name to and be satisfied of the truth of them and avoid any accident on this point. Never sign a paper when brought to you in a hurry if it is one of account but desire it be left to your perusal. At least once a month look over your Ship's Books and the different officers expenses – and do not pass by any extraordinary expense without strictly investigating the circumstance, as it is your Duty to be as honest and careful for the King as for your yourself.

Never fail to keep the Ship's reckoning yourself and observe by Day and Night. It is a great Duty for you have in charge the Lives of hundreds. I hope you will never from idleness excuse yourself from this sacred Duty and never lay down to rest without sending for your Master and together with him mark the Ship's place in the Chart. Do not let any false Modesty or Shame prevent you from this or asking his aid in working your Lunars. It is madness to do so in the extreme and must ultimately end in the ruin of any Young Officer who practises it.

Notes

CHAPTER 1: A Turbulent Boy

1. Ellis, pp. 35–7.
2. X871/35, Cornwall Records Office. As these records also show, Constantia and her second husband were eventually forced to turn to her brother for help.
3. Osler, p. 5. This first biography of Pellew was written against the wishes of his widow but at the behest of his older brother, Samuel. Otherwise the family did not cooperate. But in this instance Samuel was probably reflecting, accurately, the sentiments of Constantia's children.
4. Among the Cornish memoirs in which Pellew features are William Bottrell, *Traditions and Hearthside Stories of West Cornwall*, Rev. R. Polwhele, *Reminiscences*, and Walter Tregellas, *Cornish Worthies*.
5. The childhood friend was a girl interviewed in later life by Bottrell, pp. 159–61.
6. Osler, p. 8. The quotation was provided to the author by Pellew's brother Samuel. Details of the trusts established by Edward Langford for the Pellew children are to be found in X871/35 at Cornwall Record Office.
7. ADM 51/496, log of the *Juno*, 26 Dec. 1770.
8. Knight, pp. xxix–xxx.
9. Pellew's first serious biographer, C. Northcote Parkinson, maintained that the Pellews retained influence with the local aristocrat, Lord Falmouth, and that this was brought to bear to find Edward a ship; with such a patron, it followed that he entered the Navy as one of the young gentlemen destined for advancement. There is no evidence for this, as Parkinson himself acknowledged (p. 5), and what there is is against. It is true that Falmouth's patronage would be exerted in Pellew's favour, but that was only after he had proven his ability, some ten years later. Even the case that the Pellew family took an interest in the boy becomes open to question after Constantia's remarriage. In all the family records and accounts, it is the Langfords rather than the Pellews who were involved in the boy's development. See also Chapter 2, Notes 1 & 27, and Chapter 3, Note 32.
10. ADM 51/496, log of the *Juno*, 3 Nov. 1770: 'Recd 10 boys from the

311

Marine Society'. See also ADM 36/7429, muster of the *Juno*.

11. ADM/36/7429, muster of the *Juno*. Parkinson was wrong in saying that Pellew entered as captain's servant.

12. I am grateful to Malcolm Rae for his study in *British Admirals of the Napoleonic Wars*, which first alerted me to the discrepancies between Parkinson's somewhat blithe view of the young Pellew's circumstances and the contrary evidence to be found in the Juno's muster book.

13. Parkinson, p. 7.

14. ADM 36/7429, muster of the *Juno*.

15. This remark, attributed to Lt John Schanck, was written by Pellew's son George, on p. 16 of the densely annotated family copy of the Osler biography.

16. Leech, p. 22.

17. This assessment, and the description of Stott's disciplinary habits, are based on a reading of his logs.

18. Saunders Island, the first of the Falkland group claimed by Britain (in 1765), is among the western isles and one of the smallest.

19. Woodis is almost entirely absent from the family records, but it seems clear from papers in the Cornwall Record Office that he and Constantia had to borrow money from her brother (X871/41). One of Constantia's second pair of twins, Frances Woodis, went on to a splendidly scandalous career as a femme fatale.

20. ADM 36/7749, muster of the *Alarm*.

21. ADM 51/3759, log of the *Alarm*, 4 Aug. 1772.

22. ADM 36/7749 & 7750, muster of the *Alarm*.

23. Davis, p. 23.

24. Colley, p. 49. Over two decades in the seventeenth century, Colley records, Cornwall and Devon lost a fifth of their shipping to North African corsairs.

25. Colley, pp. 93–6 points out the ambiguities in Pellow's account.

26. Parkinson, p. 32.

27. Osler, p. 9. As with most of Osler's source material, this story was provided by Pellew's elder brother, Samuel.

28. The family's copy of the Osler biography, annotated by Pellew's son George, has this story written on the page opposite the above, and attributes it to John Gaze, Pellew's long-serving right-hand man.

29. ADM 36/7751, muster of the *Alarm*, May 1774–Aug 1775.

30. ADM 107/7.

CHAPTER 2: War for the Lakes

1. ADM 36/9232, muster of the *Blonde*. This is further evidence against Parkinson's conclusion that Pellew had a family connection with Lord Falmouth to thank for being placed under Pownoll's command.

2. Pownoll's share of the prize money came to the equivalent of £5 million.

3. Osler, pp. 11–12.

4. ADM 36/9232, muster of the *Blonde*. George van Heyden, a Dutchman, sufficiently impressed Pownoll to stay on as a midshipman.

5. ADM 51/118, log of the *Blonde*, 12 August.

6. This anecdote was related by Schanck himself to Pellew's son, George, who inscribed it on p. 16 of the family copy of Osler.

7. ADM 51/118, log of the *Blonde*, 7 July 1776. General Charles Lee was not captured until five months later.

8. Parkinson, p. 29.

9. Mahan, p. 437, quoting Douglas's report.

10. Ibid., p. 439.

11. Parkinson, p. 38.

12. ADM 36/8784, muster of the *Garland*. Although Parkinson thought it unlikely that Pellew was ever on the *Garland*, he is listed as not only receiving his pay through her, but his victuals.

13. ADM 51/387, log of the *Garland*, 3 Dec. 1776.

14. Private Collection, John Schanck testimonial for Alexander Broughton, 18 Aug. 1790.

15. It was said in family history that John Pellew was an ensign, a rank which indicated he had money behind him. I am grateful to Malcolm Rae for telling me of his research, showing John Pellew was a plain foot soldier.

16. There is no family record touching on John Pellew's fate. Insofar as Edward Pellew's distant relationship with Samuel is concerned, it was said that his 'intercourse and correspondence with his eldest brother were only occasional and became more and more rare'.

17. This story is another of George Pellew's inscriptions in the family copy of Osler, at p. 38.

18. The letter was reprinted in Parkinson, p. 45, and Osler, pp. 37–8. The original appears to have been lost.

19. Osler, p. 20. This personal letter, too, has been lost.

20. Ibid.

21. Parkinson, p. 46.

22. Most of Broughton's letters to Pellew were destroyed or lost, but Pellew's were retained by Broughton's widow and subsequently returned to the Exmouth family.

23. Suckling helped the young Nelson once he became Comptroller of the Navy Board. Knight, pp. xxix–xxx, 32–3, 38–9.

24. ADM 51/737, log of the *Princess Amelia*.

25. ADM 107/7.

26. X871/37/1, Cornwall Record Office. This amount also included a one-fifth share of John Pellew's legacy, which was shared among the surviving

siblings on his death.

27. Caird Library, AGC/P/13, Constantia Pellew to Henry Lee-Warner, September 22, 1778. Lee-Warner was a wealthy eccentric whose father had been a benefactor to Pellew's father, helping him to obtain command of one of the Dover packets. The letter tends to confirm that Pellew had no patronage, for if he indeed had the backing of Lord Falmouth at this time it is unlikely that his mother would have approached someone with lesser influence.

28. ADM, 51/536, log of the *Licorne*, 31 May 1779.

29. Ibid., 23 March 1779.

CHAPTER 3: Patronage Lost and Won

1. ADM 51/52, log of the *Apollo*, 15 June 1780.

2. Ibid., 30 May 1780.

3. Osler, p. 47.

4. Ibid., p. 50. The description comes from a letter drafted by Pellew to the Admiralty but evidently never sent. The original – now lost – was reprinted by Osler.

5. Ibid., p. 51.

6. Ibid., p. 52.

7. See Rodger, pp. 388–9.

8. See Note 4 above. Two of Pellew's sons noted in the margins of the Osler biography their belief that the letter had not been sent, and there is no surviving copy in Admiralty records.

9. Osler p. 11.

10. Exmouth Papers, Box 26, Sandwich to Pellew, 20 June 1780.

11. The 'tarpaulin or gentleman' debate, as to whether captains and admirals should be appointed from the aristocracy or professional seamen, had raged in Samuel Pepys's time, and had been largely overtaken by patronage and influence. However, class continued to play a role.

12. ADM 1/2306, Captains Letters, undated July 1780. This is his first recorded letter as a captain.

13. This was recalled by Pellew's right-hand man, John Gaze, who wrote it on p. 56 of the family's Osler.

14. ADM 51/441, log of the *Hazard*, 6 Nov. 1780.

15. Caird Library, AGC/P/13, Pellew to Henry Lee-Warner, 8 April 1782.

16. ADM 1/2306, Captains Letters, 14 Feb. 1781.

17. Caird Library, AGC/P/13, Constantia Woodis to Henry Lee-Warner, 9 Dec. 1780.

18. Ibid., Pellew to Henry Lee-Warner, 8 April 1782.

19. ADM 1/2306, Captains Letters, 14 Feb. 1781.

20. ADM 51/710, log of the *Pelican*, 21 April 1782.

21. Private Collection, Viscount Keppel to Pellew, 25 May 1782.

22. ADM 1/2307, Captains Letters, 1 July 1782.
23. Knight, p. 82.
24. ADM 1/2307, Captains Letters, 27 Nov. 1783.
25. Although Parkinson believed that Pellew spoke no French, and that his correspondence was translated, many French papers were among his letters, while the nature of his friendship with Jacques Bergeret bespeaks some knowledge of the language.
26. Exmouth Papers, Box 22, Pellew to Broughton, 22 July 1807.
27. Ibid.
28. Polwhele.
29. Even those letters that escaped did so seemingly by accident. While Susan preserved her husband's official correspondence with an eye to history, she had burned all their private correspondence. There are a handful of her own that she seemingly overlooked and which form part of the NMM collection.
30. Exmouth Papers, Box 22, Pellew to Broughton, 22 July 1807.
31. X871/41, Cornwall Record Office. Langford's eldest son inherited the fortune but on his death it was squandered by his widow. This had an impact on Constantia, who was asked to repay a loan which, it seems, she was unable to do.
32. As noted in Chapter 1, the case made by Parkinson was that Edward Pellew had, from the start, a claim on the protection of Lord Falmouth. While conceding that 'what the claim was is not known', Parkinson believed that it came through another Cornish seaman, Admiral Edward Boscawen. The evidence indicates more convincingly that Pellew really did start without influence, and that although Lord Falmouth played a significant part in the family's rise to prominence, the primary beneficiary was Samuel Pellew. It is only from this point that Falmouth's influence on Edward's behalf becomes clear.
33. Pellew's son, George, wrote that Samuel had assisted Osler 'in direct opposition to the remonstrances of surviving members of the family'.
34. Exmouth Papers, Box 22, Pellew to Broughton, 22 July 1807.
35. Ibid., Box 2, Pellew to Broughton, 2 May 1801.
36. Polwhele.
37. Mahan, p. 445.
38. Osler, pp. 60–8.
39. ADM 1/2308, Captains Letters, Pellew to Admiralty, 21 Dec. 1786.
40. Parkinson seemingly failed to examine the logs of Pellew's ships, apart from the *Impetueux*, which was a special case, and did not have available comparative disciplinary records which set Pellew's practices in context.
41. ADM 51/1065, log of the *Winchelsea*, 23 Nov. 1786.
42. Ibid., 11 Jan. 1789.
43. Osler p. 72. The anecdote of the cow was inscribed by George Pellew on

the following page.

44. Exmouth Papers, Box 22, Broughton to Pellew, 26 Nov. 1789.
45. Private Collection, Falmouth to Pellew, 22 July 1792.
46. Rodger, p. 363.
47. Private Collection, Falmouth to Pellew, 3 Jan. 1793.
48. Ibid., Pellew to Falmouth, 17 Dec. 1792.

CHAPTER 4: A Cornish Chief

1. Gaze's account was inscribed by George Pellew opposite p. 77 of Osler. Gaze also contributed to many subsequent annotations in the family volume 'as an eyewitness of almost all my father's services'.
2. ADM 1/2130, Captains Letters, 3 March 1793.
3. Buckingham, p. 16.
4. The Cornish language fell into disuse during the Industrial Revolution and died out in the 1890s.
5. ADM 36/13161, muster of the *Nymphe*.
6. Osler, annotation facing p. 77.
7. See Rodger, pp. 420–1.
8. ADM 1/2310, Ibid., 15 Jan. 1793.
9. Osler, annotation facing p. 82.
10. ADM 51/514, log of the *Nymphe*.
11. Rodger, p. 391.
12. ADM 51/514, log of the *Nymphe*, 25 May 1793.
13. ADM 36/13161, muster of the *Nymphe*, records the desertion and pressings. Israel Pellew's presence is recorded only in the log as he was not officially entered.
14. Osler, annotation facing p. 80.
15. Pellew's own account of the battle, in *Nymphe*'s logbook, is spare to the point of barrenness. Osler's account is the most full, based on what Pellew had told his family, and, because it does not have any of the corrections that were added by Gaze when – as he often did – he found fault with the biographer's facts, it can be taken as accurate.
16. Private Collection, Edward Pellew to Samuel Pellew. See also Parkinson, p. 90.
17. Ibid.
18. Exmouth Papers, Box 22, undated, Pellew to Madame Mullon.
19. Ibid.
20. Osler, p. 402, Appendix B. The original has been lost.
21. Osler, p. 92.
22. Exmouth Papers, Box 22, Raffe to Pellew, 26 July 1793.
23. Ibid., Pellew to Raffe, 28 July 1793.
24. Parkinson, p. 90.
25. In his most intimate letters to Broughton he wrote of being moved to

tears by his son Fleetwood's exploits.

26. ADM 1/2310, Captains Letters, 19 June 1793.
27. Mahan, p. 450.
28. *The Times*, 22 June 1793.
29. Parkinson, p. 89.
30. *The Times*, 28 June 1793.
31. Osler, annotation by George Pellew facing p. 91.
32. Exmouth Papers, Box 22, Samuel Pellew to Edward Pellew, 22 June 1793.
33. Ibid.
34. What has become of the portrait is not known.
35. Rae, p. 279. This was the share system as laid down by regulation. Individual captains sometimes made private agreements with their crews.
36. Wareham, *The Star Captains*, p. 56. The claim was made on Samaurez by a relatively lowly official and was not pursued.
37. Parkinson, p. 320.
38. Parkinson, p. 108.
39. Exmouth Papers, Box 22, Warren to Pellew, 23 April 1794.
40. Wareham, *The Star Captains*, pp. 61–2.
41. *The Times*, 31 Oct. 1835.
42. ADM 1/2311, Captains Letters, 24 Oct. 1794.

CHAPTER 5: Indefatigables

1. Exmouth Papers, NMM, Box 22, Private Collection, Chatham to Pellew, 27 Nov. 1794.
2. Ibid., Spencer to Pellew, 10 Jan. 1795.
3. See Gardiner, pp. 41–3. Also Parkinson pp. 117–25.
4. ADM 1/2311, Captains Letters, 17 Jan. 1794.
5. Ibid., 8, 12, 21 May.
6. Quoted in Osler, p. 165. The family annotation identifies Gaze as the source.
7. Hay, pp. 156–7. A full account of this incident is to be found in Chapter 12.
8. *The Times*, 6 Aug. 1793.
9. I have been unable to ascertain what punishment Welch did receive.
10. ADM 36/11471, muster of the *Arethusa*, is unusually clear among ships' musters in showing the comings and goings of hands.
11. Osler, p. 165. Shore leave was among the most contentious issues among hands and very often the captains who were least likely to grant it suffered the highest rates of desertion. See Rodger, pp. 499–500.
12. Buckingham, pp. 8–9.
13. Ibid., p. 41.
14. ADM 1/2318, Pellew to Nepean, 14 Dec. 1799; ADM 36/13145, muster

of the *Indefatigable*.

15. In India, where he was Commander-in-Chief, the press would report on Admiral Pellew's zeal as a dancer.

16. ADM 51/1109, log of the *Indefatigable*, 9 & 11 March 1795.

17. Ibid., 7 May 1795.

18. This note was inserted by John Gaze, master of the *Indefatigable*, opposite p. 111 of the annotated Osler.

19. Buckingham, p. 167.

20. ADM 36/13142, muster of the *Indefatigable*.

21. Buckingham, pp. 168–9.

22. ADM 36/12827, muster of the *Impetueux*, shows Emidy's progress. He would have been entitled to claim a discharge on leaving the *Indefatigable*, so his presence on *Impetueux* was plainly voluntary.

23. The incident is described in Hazlitt, pp. 280–4.

24. Osler, pp. 112–14. Gaze attested to the veracity of both incidents.

25. This story was inscribed by George Pellew on p. 166 of Osler.

26. See Note 23 above.

27. Private Collection, Jeremiah Coghlan to Fleetwood Pellew, 26 Jan., 1833.

28. See Note 23.

29. Teignmouth Museum collection, Pellew to Edward Locker, 13 July 1811.

30. *The Times*, 5 Oct. 1835, letter from James Thompson. Both this and a letter from 'Fair Play' dated 26 Sept. confirm the accuracy of the account in Osler.

31. *The Times*, 11 June 1796. This reference to the lower class was in fact a somewhat clumsy way of expressing the society's aim of, rather, fostering consciousness of philanthropic ideals in quarters where they were not generally practised.

32. Private Collection, Spencer to Pellew, 19 Feb. 1796.

33. The words are attributed to Louisa in *Persuasion*, but Austen's ties to the Navy through her brothers make the sentiments her own.

34. There is an echo here with one of the great partnerships of maritime fiction: Pellew is cast as mentor to Horatio Hornblower in C. S. Forester's novels; Coghlan's exploits resonate as those of a real-life Hornblower.

35. Hay rose to command an East Indiaman, the *Astell*, in which he distinguished himself in a stout defensive action against French frigates in the Indian Ocean in 1810. His letter to *The Times* in January 1836 after Pellew's death, properly vindicated himself, and then rather spoilt his case by casting aspersions on Pellew who, he said, 'was sent on shore at his own entreaty by myself'. This led to a flurry of letters to the paper, including one from a former *Dutton* hand, James Thompson, confirming that Pellew had been among the last to leave.

CHAPTER 6: French Foe, French Friend

1. ADM 51/1171, log of the *Indefatigable*, 15 March 1796.
2. Parkinson, pp. 144–5.
3. Ibid.
4. See Nicolson, pp. 22–8.
5. Exmouth Papers, Box 22, Pellew to Spencer, 20 Dec. 1796.
6. ADM 1/2316, Captains Letters, Pellew to Nepean, 17 Aug. 1798. These faults persisted until a refit in 1799.
7. ADM 51/1109 and ADM 51/1171 are the respective logs on which these figures are based.
8. These figures represent punishment rates of between 2 per cent and 4 per cent. In his close study of discipline in the Navy between 1784 and 1812, John D. Byrne found ships in which 10 per cent and up were the norm, with a high in a single year of 26 per cent. Low levels of 2 per cent were found, but for periods of less than a year. See *Crime and Punishment in the Royal Navy – Discipline on the Leeward Islands Station*.
9. Osler, pp. 61 & 64, quoting Christopher Cole and unnamed hands.
10. ADM 51/1171, log of the *Indefatigable*, 13 April 1796.
11. ADM 51/1111, log of the *Revolutionnaire*, 12 April 1796.
12. Linois acquired a certain notoriety in the Indian Ocean at the so-called Battle of Pulo Aor in 1804 where he became probably the only admiral in history to flee with his squadron from a fleet of richly laden merchantmen, albeit armed Indiamen of the East India Company.
13. ADM 51/1166, log of the *Revolutionnaire*, 20 April 1796.
14. Parkinson states that they covered 168 miles in fifteen hours, but the *Indefatigable*'s log for this period gives the distance as 115 miles in eleven hours.
15. Exmouth Papers, Box 22, Bergeret to Admiral Villaret, 21 April 1796. Bergeret's full description of the action is also to be found on pp. 147–9 of Parkinson.
16. ADM 51/1171, log of the *Indefatigable*, 21 April 1796.
17. Exmouth Papers, Box 22, Bergeret to Admiral Villaret, 21 April 1796.
18. This anecdote was inscribed by George Pellew into the family copy of Osler opposite p. 128.
19. Quoted in Price, p. 9.
20. Exmouth Papers, Box 22, Spencer to Pellew, 30 April 1796.
21. Ibid., Bergeret to Pellew, undated [May 1796].
22. Ibid., Bergeret to Pellew, 23 June 1798.
23. It was Parkinson's contention that this censorship related to the ill-fated career of Richard Broughton, and in some instances that is the case, but there are also other letters which have no bearing on 'Dick', such as that dated 21 May 1801, in which the only discernible words are St Vincent.
24. ADM 1/2318, Captains Letters, Pellew to Nepean, 14 Dec. 1799.

25. Private Collection, Spencer to Pellew, 22 May 1804. This letter makes explicit the connection as Spencer was writing to ask Pellew to take Cadogan with him when he took up the East Indies command.
26. ADM 36/13143, muster of the *Indefatigable*.
27. Cordingley, p. 25.
28. Exmouth Papers, Box 22, Pellew to Broughton, 2 June 1798.
29. The Broughton family were at pains to cross out some passages in Pellew's letters in which his troubles with the boy are mentioned.

CHAPTER 7: 'The Most Important Crisis of My Life'

1. ADM 51/1171, log of the *Invincible*, 9 Dec. 1796.
2. Private Collection, Pellew to Spencer, 13 June 1796.
3. Quoted in Rodger, p. 437.
4. ADM 51/1171, log of the *Indefatigable*, 12 Dec. 1796.
5. See Morriss, pp. 163–5.
6. Osler, p.137.
7. Quoted in Rodger, p. 439.
8. ADM 51/1171, log of the *Indefatigable*, 16 Dec. 1796.
9. Quoted in Parkinson, p. 167.
10. Ibid., p. 169.
11. Gaze, who inveighed frequently against Colpoys, inscribed this story opposite p. 136 of the Osler biography. Pellew's son George added: 'this letter to be carefully sought for'. I believe he did not find it, and nor have I.
12. These further notes by Gaze are opposite pp. 136 and 142.
13. Gaze inscribed this entry opposite p. 136 of Osler.
14. Parkinson, p. 171.
15. Exmouth Papers, Box 22, Minutes of the Action on the night of 13 Jan. 1797.
16. ADM 1/2314, Captains Letters, Pellew to Evan Nepean, 17 Jan. 1797. This is the most complete account of the action.
17. Parkinson, p. 175.
18. ADM 1/2314, see note 16 above.
19. Parkinson, pp. 179–80.
20. Inscribed by Gaze opposite p. 151 of Osler.
21. Exmouth Papers, Box 22, Minutes of the Action on the night of 13 Jan. 1797.
22. ADM 1/2314, see note 16 above.
23. Ibid.
24. Ibid.
25. Exmouth Papers, Box 22, Minutes of the Action on the night of 13 Jan. 1797.
26. A certain licence has been used here. The observation comes from John

Hunter, *A Historical Journal of the Transactions at Port Jackson and Norfolk Island, 1793.*
27. Wareham, *Frigate Commander*, p. 256
28. Exmouth Papers, Box 22, Spencer to Pellew, 25 Jan. 1797.
29. Lieutenant Elias Pipon's account is contained in the *Naval Chronicle*, Vol. III.
30. See Rodger p. 438, footnote.
31. Exmouth Papers, Box 22, Lacrosse to Pellew, Undated [March 1797].
32. See Hague, p. 386.
33. Exmouth Papers, Box 2, Pellew to Broughton, 1 Dec. 1799.
34. *The Times*, 4 March 1797.
35. Ibid.
36. Private Collection, Lady Spencer to Pellew, 26 Jan. 1797.
37. Exmouth Papers, Box 22, Broughton to Pellew, 24 Jan. 1797.
38. See Wareham, *The Star Captains*, pp. 56 & 160.
39. Wareham, *Frigate Commander*, p. 123.
40. These figures are taken from a study of *The Times* database.

CHAPTER 8: A Protest Too Far

1. Jervis, then about to be ennobled as Lord St Vincent, played up the poverty of his boyhood, passing over the fact that his father had Admiralty connections and was related to the mighty Lord Anson; and while Collingwood was poor, his father managed to pay £30 for him to enter the ship of a family friend as a midshipman.
2. Wareham, *The Star Captains*, p. 45.
3. Morriss, pp. 184–5.
4. Exmouth Papers, Box 22, Pellew to Broughton, 2 June 1798.
5. ADM 36/13143, muster of the *Indefatigable.*
6. Exmouth Papers, Box 22, Pellew to Broughton, 12 March 1798.
7. Ibid., Pellew to Broughton, 2 June 1798.
8. Ibid., Pellew to Spencer, August 1796.
9. Ibid., Spencer to Pellew, 16 Feb. 1797.
10. Ibid., Pellew to Spencer, 31 Jan. 1797.
11. ADM 51/1210, log of the *Indefatigable.*
12. The Greyhounds were not subjected to court martial, so there is no reliable record of these events.
13. Private Collection, Pellew to Spencer, 31 May 1797.
14. NMM, Exmouth Papers, Box 22, Spencer to Pellew, 3 June 1797.
15. Rodger, p. 518.
16. Exmouth Papers, Box 22, Pellew to Spencer, undated.
17. Quoted in Knight, pp. 259 & 264.
18. Quoted in Parkinson, p. 194.
19. This was not only Pellew's opinion. The decision to restrict the frigate

captains' freedom was attributed by most commanders to 'the Jealousy and avarice of Lord Bridport'. See Wareham, *Frigate Commander*, p. 144.

20. See Morriss, pp. 163–8.
21. Exmouth Papers, Box 22, Spencer to Pellew, 14 & 28 March 1797.
22. Private collection, Lady Pellew to Pellew, 27 Aug. 1797.
23. Exmouth Papers, Box 22, Lady Pellew to Pellew, 19 Nov. 1813.
24. Exmouth Papers, Box 22, Pellew to Broughton, 12 March 1798.
25. Parkinson, pp. 197–8.
26. Morriss, p. 266.
27. NMM, Exmouth Papers, Box 22, Pellew to the Rev. Dr Cole, 3 May 1798.
28. See Parkinson, pp. 210–18.
29. Exmouth Papers, Box 22, Pellew to Spencer, undated.
30. Ibid., Spencer to Pellew, 21 Feb. 1799.
31. Ibid., Pellew to Spencer, 24 Feb. 1799.
32. ADM 51/1246, log of the *Indefatigable*, 1 March 1798–28 Feb. 1799.
33. Ibid., 27 Feb. 1799.
34. Exmouth Papers, Box 22, Pellew to Spencer, 28 Feb. 1799.
35. Ibid., Chatham to Pellew, 4 March 1799.
36. Ibid., Pellew to Broughton, 2 June 1798.
37. The exchange is covered in ADM 1/2318, Captains Letters, Pellew to Evan Nepean, 25 Feb., 1799. The final figures are from ADM 36/12827, muster of the *Impetueux*.

CHAPTER 9: A Ship in Revolt

1. Apart from the clear indication that Pellew was there to bring them to heel, the company appear to have resented the fact that he had kept his squadron at Falmouth during the Great Mutiny, thereby preventing the frigates from becoming involved. 'They took against me . . . considering me the cause of preventing the *Indefatigable* from joining them,' he wrote to Broughton afterwards.
2. There were a number of trials of thirty-three captured Hermiones, of whom twenty-four were executed. The proceedings of this particular case are in ADM 1/5348, 13–15 March 1799. A false account of Pellew's part in this hearing was given by Osler, and has found its way into a number of histories, to the effect that when one of the men was found guilty Pellew insisted that he be executed immediately, without reference to the Admiralty. This story was related to Osler by Samuel Pellew, to show his brother's resolve in a crisis. However, it is not substantiated by the trial record, and was dismissed as untrue by one of Pellew's fellow captains, Sir Robert Barlow.
3. Apart from London, only seven English towns had populations of more

than 10,000. About 800 had populations of between 1,000 and 2,000.
See Porter, p. 54.

4. ADM 51/1241, log of the *Impetueux*, 13 May 1798–9 Feb. 1799.

5. ADM 1/5349, ff. 806–28, court martial 19–20 June 1799. Ross was
   described as a father figure in the crew's letter to Lord Bridport. His
   weakness is apparent from his conduct in the mutiny.

6. ADM 51/1282, log of *Impetueux*, 26 March 1799.

7. Morriss, pp. 366–7.

8. Bonaparte always rued his decision, writing after Waterloo: 'If instead
   of Egypt I had undertaken that against Ireland, what could England
   have done?' Although the French Army continued to go from strength to
   strength, the Nile marked arguably the end of France as a naval power.
   (Hague, *William Pitt the Younger*, pp. 430–2.)

9. ADM 51/1282, log of the *Impetueux*.

10. Wareham, *Frigate Commander*, p. 132. The captain was Graham Moore.

11. Ibid., p. 185.

12. ADM 51/1282, log of the *Impetueux*.

13. Hazlitt, p. 239.

14. ADM 1/5349, Evidence of Lt Stokes.

15. Ibid., Pellew's report, 8 June.

16. Ibid.

17. Ibid., Evidence of Capt. Boys.

18. Ibid., Evidence of Midshipman Kinsman.

19. Ibid., Evidence of John Evans.

20. Ibid., Evidence of Lt Stokes.

21. Ibid., Petition to Lord Bridport. The figure for floggings is fairly accurate
    – forty-four dozen lashes had been inflicted rather than forty-nine – but a
    story of a seaman drowning while trying to swim ashore is not borne out
    by the log. The 'father figure' was, of course, Lieutenant Ross.

22. Ibid., Evidence of George Morley.

23. See Osler, pp. 191–4. This work is riddled with errors, none more
    persistent than the remark attributed to St Vincent that although Pellew
    was 'an excellent and valuable officer, the most important service he ever
    rendered to his country was saving the British fleet in Bantry Bay'.

24. Mostert, p. 348.

25. ADM 51/1282, log of the *Impetueux*, 16 June 1799.

26. ADM 1/5349, Pellew's report of the mutiny, 8 June 1799.

27. Quoted in Parkinson, p. 221.

28. ADM 1/5349.

29. ADM 51/1282. The account of Pellew's petition to St Vincent is
    contained in Osler who was often inaccurate, but on this occcasion it
    chimes with Pellew's character reference for Sidney at the court martial.

30. Exmouth Papers, Box 2, Pellew to Broughton, 11 Oct. 1799.

31. ADM 1/2318, Captains Letters, Pellew to Evan Nepean, 2 Nov. 1799.
32. Exmouth Papers, Box 2, Pellew to Broughton, 1 Sept. 1799.
33. Ibid., Pellew to Broughton, 1 Dec. 1799.
34. See Parkinson, pp. 227–35.
35. Quoted in Rodger, p. 464.
36. Quoted in Parkinson, p. 241.
37. See Wareham, *The Star Captains*, pp. 93–4. The author shows how the percentage of frigate captains drawn from titled and gentrified families increased from 45 per cent in 1793–1800 to almost 70 per cent in 1801–14.
38. See Parkinson, p. 245.
39. Digby Papers, Box 22a, Digby to St Vincent, 6 Aug. 1800, and St Vincent to Digby, 18 Aug. 1800. Details of quite what the act of 'abominable disrespect' was do not appear to have survived.
40. Exmouth Papers, Box 2, Pellew to Broughton, 1 Dec. 1799.
41. Ibid., Pellew to Broughton, 11 Oct. 1799.
42. Private Collection, Coghlan to Fleetwood Pellew, 26 Jan. 1833.
43. Parkinson, p. 241.
44. Private Collection, Pellew to Broughton, 6 July 1800. I have been unable to trace this letter in the Exmouth Papers but it is quoted in full by Parkinson, pp. 243–4.
45. Exmouth Papers, Box 22, Pellew to Chatham, 1 Sept. 1800.
46. Rodger, p. 466.
47. Exmouth Papers, Box 2, Pellew to Broughton, 12 May 1800.
48. Buckingham, pp. 135–6.
49. See Rodger, pp. 464–5.
50. Davidson, p. 170.
51. ADM 1/2322, Captains Letters, Pellew to Nepean, 31 Oct. 1801.

CHAPTER 10: St Vincent's Anchor

1. Private Collection, Willaumez to Pellew, October 1801.
2. ADM 1/2324, Captains Letters, Pellew to Evan Nepean, 15 April 1802.
3. Exmouth Papers, Box 2, Pellew to Broughton, 21 May 1801.
4. Knight, pp. 421–4.
5. Exmouth Papers, Box 2, Pellew to Broughton, 21 May 1801.
6. Ibid., Box 22, Susan Pellew to Pellew, 19 Nov. 1813.
7. Ibid., Pellew to Broughton, 22 July 1807.
8. Ibid., Box 2, Pellew to Broughton, 21 May 1801.
9. Ibid., Box 22, Pellew to Broughton, 22 July 1807.
10. Ibid., Julia Harward to Sir Edward Pellew, 6 May 1814.
11. Ibid., Box 22, Pellew to Broughton, 1 Sept. 1803.
12. Ibid., Box 2, Pellew to Broughton, 11 Oct. 1799.
13. Ibid., Box 2, Pellew to Broughton, 21 May 1801.

14. *Naval Chronicle*, Vol. 18, p. 462.
15. Exmouth Papers, Box 22, Pellew to Broughton, 25 Feb. 1803.
16. Ibid.
17. Ibid., Box 2, Pellew to Broughton, 21 May 1801.
18. Parkinson, p. 363, quoting Pellew to Markham, 23 Aug. 1806.
19. Exmouth Papers, Box 22, Pellew to Broughton, 25 Feb. 1803.
20. Ibid.
21. Ibid., Pellew to Broughton, 5 March 1804.
22. Ibid.
23. Rodger, pp. 478–80.
24. Quoted in Hague, p. 521.
25. See Rodger pp. 476–9, Knight p. 471.
26. Quoted in Parkinson, p. 310.
27. Ibid., p. 320.
28. *The Times*, 18 May 1802.
29. George Pellew married a daughter of Addington and wrote on p. 208 of the family copy of the Osler biography of Addington's statement that Pitt had never forgiven his father.
30. Exmouth Papers, Box 22, Pellew to Broughton, 31 March 1804.
31. Quoted in Lambert, p. 239.
32. Quoted in Parkinson, p. 317.
33. Because of the lengthy delay in his promotion he skipped a rank, Rear-Admiral of the Blue.
34. Exmouth papers, Box 22, Pellew to Broughton, 31 March 1804.
35. Ibid., Box 24, Pellew to Charles Yorke, 21 July 1810.
36. Ibid.

CHAPTER 11: Storm in the East

1. Exmouth Papers, Box 2, Pellew to Broughton, undated.
2. Ibid., Box 7, From Sir Edward Pellew to Officers of the British Navy, 10 April 1802.
3. ADM 1/176, Admirals Letters, Lambert to Rainier, 17 Feb. 1805.
4. Ibid., Pellew to Decaen, 26 March 1805.
5. ADM 51/1527, log of the *Culloden*, 22 May 1805.
6. Quoted in Parkinson, p. 335.
7. Exmouth Papers, Box 2, Pellew to Broughton, 10 Jan. 1807.
8. ADM 1/176, Admirals Letters, Pellew to Marsden, 29 April 1805.
9. Exmouth Papers, Box 2, Bergeret to Pellew, 13 Aug. 1805.
10. Charles Decaen, Governor of the Île de France, suspected that Flinders was a spy, and Pellew's appeal to the Admiralty to negotiate directly with Paris had no beneficial outcome. See ADM 1/177, Admirals Letters, Flinders to Pellew, 13 Aug. 1805 & Pellew to Marsden, 13 Feb. 1806.
11. Exmouth Papers, Box 2, Pellew to Broughton, 22 July 1807.

12. Ibid., Susan Pellew to Pellew, 5 Jan. 1814. This letter, like the others from Susan to have survived, is from his service in the Mediterranean, but he had also cut down his drinking in the Indies, hence its use here.

13. Ibid., Box 2, Pellew to Broughton, 10 Jan. 1807 & Box 22, Pellew to Broughton, 22 July 1807.

14. Taylor, p. 23. The reference to Lady Barlow's 'shapes' is contained in a letter from Pellew to the lady dated 15 Aug. 1810, in the Barlow papers.

15. Quoted in Parkinson, p. 332.

16. Exmouth Papers, Box 2, Pellew to Broughton, 10 Jan. 1807.

17. Knight, pp. 477–8.

18. ADM 1/176, Admirals Letters, Troubridge to Marsden, 1 Sept. 1805.

19. Exmouth Papers, Box 2, Pellew to Broughton, 10 Jan. 1807.

20. ADM 1/176, Admirals Letters, Pellew to Marsden, 8 Sept. 1805.

21. Quoted in Knight, p. 191.

22. ADM 1/176, Admirals Letters, Pellew to Marsden, 30 Sept. 1805.

23. Private Collection, Pellew to Sidmouth, 5 Sept. 1806.

24. ADM 1/176, Admirals Letters, Troubridge to Pellew, 26 Sept. 1805. This file contains all the correspondence.

25. Ibid., Troubridge to Marsden, 5 Oct. 1805.

26. Ibid., Pellew to Marsden, 1 Nov. 1805.

27. ADM 51/1607, Log of the *Culloden*.

28. RNM 500/88/57, Penrose journal, f. 153.

29. Bentinck Papers, PW Jd 219/2.

30. One incident, recorded in the Bentinck Papers, PW Jd 219/1–2, may be illustrative. Early in his command, Pellew had good cause to rebuke a captain named Proctor over tactics that enabled a French frigate, *Semillante*, to escape the Bay of Bengal, and let his temper get the better of him. Proctor, instead of simply accepting the admonition, sought a court martial. On being acquitted, he was invited to dine with Pellew who said he had never doubted his zeal or honour. Proctor asked for a copy of the court-martial record, then pushed matters further by requesting it be published. Pellew replied that he might have it printed in England 'but he could not permit it within his command where it would have the appearance of an appeal to the public'. That was probably the right response, but it is hard somehow to imagine Proctor daring to presume so with other admirals. Nelson would have charmed him into humility; St Vincent would have terrified him into subservience.

31. Private Collection, Spencer to Pellew, 22 May 1804.

32. Smyth did not live to enjoy his patronage, dying at Madras in 1805, but left further evidence of Pellew's warmth, describing him as 'a humane, jolly tar'. On the boy's death Pellew wrote to his father that he had 'endeared himself to us all by a thousand ways and is regretted . . . by none more than myself'.

33. ADM 1/176, Admirals Letters, f. 297.
34. ADM 1/2318, Captains Letters, Pellew to Nepean, 14 Dec. 1799.
35. ADM 1/5358, Court martial of Lt Kempthorne, 28 Sept. 1801. Kempthorne had been repeatedly challenged by the captain about his veracity before finally he 'looked him in the face and put his hands on his hips'.
36. ADM 1/2322, Captains Letters, Pellew to Nepean, 3 Dec. 1801.
37. ADM 1/176, Admirals Letters, Pellew to Marsden & Pellew to Melville, 25 Jan. 1805.

CHAPTER 12: Fortunes of War

1. ADM 1/175, Admirals Letters, Pellew to George Udney, 4 Jan. 1806.
2. Barlow Papers, Pellew to Sir George Barlow, 4 Jan., 1806.
3. See Parkinson, *War in the Eastern Seas*, pp. 288–90.
4. In addition to their respective flagships, the two admirals had between them five ships of the line, a dozen frigates and four sloops. The officer most experienced at blockading, Captain John Osborn of the *Tremendous*, believed an effective cordon would require two ships of the line, six frigates and four sloops, operating in two squadrons, relieving one another every ten weeks. These resources were simply not available.
5. Fremantle Papers, D/FR/32/4, Troubridge to Fremantle, June 1806.
6. Private Collection, undated. Recipient unknown, but possibly Lieutenant-General Hay Macdowall.
7. Quoted in Parkinson, p. 359. Pellew to Nepean, 1 June 1806. Although no longer Admiralty Secretary, Nepean remained a member of the government and Pellew was probably using him as a conduit.
8. Exmouth Papers, Box 2, Pellew to Broughton, 10 Jan. 1807.
9. Ibid.
10. Quoted in Parkinson, p. 363.
11. Exmouth Papers, Box 2, Pellew to Broughton, 10 Jan. 1807.
12. Ibid.
13. Parkinson, pp. 362–3.
14. Parkinson, p. 364.
15. Exmouth Papers, Box 2, St Vincent to Pellew, 11 Jan. 1806.
16. Parkinson, p. 355.
17. The difference between Troubridge's letter to Fremantle, quoted above, and another to Lord Sidmouth is revealing. In the first he did not hesitate to suggest corruption by Pellew, while in the latter he merely spoke of a dereliction of duty.
18. Private Collection, Captain Edmund Palmer to Viscount Exmouth, 16 Jan. 1818.
19. Exmouth Papers, Box 2, Pellew to Broughton, 10 Jan. 1807.
20. Ibid., Box 22, Susan Pellew to Edward Pellew, 12 Oct. 1813.

21. Ibid., Box 2, Pellew to Broughton, 1 May 1807, and 1 June 1808.
22. Many of these letters are contained in Box 26.
23. Ibid., Box 22, Lord Exmouth to Pownoll Pellew, 20 July 1816.
24. One action, involving George Hardinge in the 36-gun *San Fiorenzo* after intercepting the 44-gun *Piemontaise*, was fit to rank with Pellew's exploits. Hardinge was among sixty-two men to die in a battle that ended with the surrender of *Piemontaise*.
25. The memorial was compiled clandestinely and sent to London without Pellew or the authorities in India being informed.
26. Osler, pp. 252–3.
27. Private Collection, Lord Minto to Lord Mulgrave, 28 May 1808.
28. Taylor, pp. 8–9. In 1805 Pellew pressed 818 hands out of 6,155 men on arriving Indiamen.
29. ADM 1/176, Pellew to Wellesley, 29 July 1805.
30. Private Collection, Lord Minto to Lord Mulgrave, 28 May 1808.
31. Barlow Papers, Pellew to Barlow, 23 June 1811. Pellew was told that young Barlow had fallen after going into the tops to sleep in hot weather with two men from his mess.
32. Ibid., Pellew to Lady Barlow, 15 Aug. 1810.
33. Rae, p. 288. Pellew's secretary, Edward Locker, noted that he left £300,000 on his death, but this included earnings from his days in frigates and as commander in the Mediterranean.
34. Corbet was killed in a frigate action off Bourbon two years later. See Taylor, *Storm and Conquest*.
35. Hay, pp. 93, 102, 156.
36. Ibid., pp. 155–6.
37. Exmouth Papers, Box 2, Pellew to Broughton, 10 Jan. 1807.
38. Ibid., Pellew to Broughton, 1 June 1808.
39. Ibid., Box 22, Pellew to Broughton, 22 July 1807.
40. Taylor, p. 152.
41. Osler, p. 259.
42. Hay, pp. 166–7.
43. Pellew was never called upon to account for himself, though there were complaints by Indiamen captains, some of whom testified at an internal inquiry to being concerned at the course. The proceedings of the inquiry are to be found in L/MAR/1/23 of the British Library's collection of East India Company papers.

CHAPTER 13: The Last Command

1. Parkinson, p. 413.
2. Teignmouth Museum, Pellew to Locker, 13 Sept. 1809.
3. Barlow Papers, Pellew to Lady Barlow, 15 Aug. 1809.
4. Barlow was wrongly blamed for a mutiny by senior officers of the

Madras Army in 1809. See Taylor, *Storm and Conquest.*

5. Martin Wilcox, 'This Great Complex Concern', in *The Mariner's Mirror,* May 2011.

6. Exmouth Papers, Box 22, Hoseason to Pellew, 27 Sept. 1810.

7. Ibid., Box 24. There are a number of memorials and letters dealing with this affair. The most important are Fitzgerald's own memorial to the Duke of Clarence, dated 10 Sept. 1827; Pellew to Charles Yorke, 21 July 1810; and Exmouth's memorial, 13 Sept. 1827.

8. Private Collection, Pellew to Yorke, 15 Dec. 1810.

9. Bentinck Papers, PW Jd 4476–8, Pellew to Bentinck, January 1811.

10. Exmouth Papers, Box 22, Pellew to Sir Richard Keats, 22 Jan. 1813.

11. Ibid., Box 24, Report of Victualling Board.

12. Ibid., Exmouth to the Duke of Clarence, 13 Sept. 1827.

13. Ibid., Thomas Fitzgerald to the Duke of Clarence, 10 Sept. 1827.

14. There are a dozen or so letters from Jane Smith dated between 1811 and 1814 contained in Box 22 of the Exmouth Papers.

15. Ibid., Box 22, Pellew to Broughton, 22 July 1807.

16. On Pellew's assumption of the command it consisted of 25 ships of the line, 20 frigates and 22 sloops.

17. Crawford, p. 152.

18. Fremantle Papers, D/FR/35.

19. Nelson reportedly wanted Keats rather than Sir Thomas Hardy as his right-hand at Trafalgar. Knight, pp. 647–8.

20. Private Collection, Pellew to Yorke, 18 July 1810.

21. Parkinson, p. 413.

22. Wynne Diaries, Vol 1, p. 148.

23. Fremantle Papers, D/FR/39/1.

24. Ibid., D/FR/235/4, Pellew to Fremantle, 12 June 1811.

25. Ibid., Pellew to Fremantle, 15 Nov. 1811.

26. Parkinson, p. 241.

27. Fremantle Papers, D/FR/39/1, Pellew to Fremantle, 11 July 1811.

28. Bentinck Papers, PW Jd 4516, Pellew to Bentinck, 10 May 1812.

29. Exmouth Papers, Box 3, Barrow to Pellew, 20 July 1812.

30. Bentinck Papers, PW Jd 4518, Pellew to Bentinck, 29 May 1812.

31. Fremantle Papers, D/FR/39/1, Pellew to Fremantle, 7 Aug. 1812.

32. Bentinck Papers, PW Jd 4551, Wellington to Pellew, Undated [August 1812].

33. Ibid., PW Jd 4484.

34. Fremantle Papers, D/FR/235/4, Pellew to Fremantle, 17 Nov. 1812.

35. Parkinson, p. 317.

36. Exmouth Papers, Box 4, Rowley to Pellew, 4 Sept. 1812. Rowley had previously proved his ability by turning around a dangerous situation in the Indian Ocean and securing the invasion of Mauritius.

37. Ibid., Box 2, Codrington to Pellew, 12 Sept. 1813.
38. Ibid., Box 22, Pellew to Keats, 22 Jan. 1813.
39. Ibid., Box 4, Bell to Pellew, 29 July 1812.
40. Ibid., Box 10, Pickmore to Pellew, 8 June 1812.
41. Bentinck Papers, PW Jd 4521, Pellew to Bentinck, 29 May 1812.
42. Exmouth Papers, Box 22, Pellew to Keats, 12 Sept. 1813.
43. Ibid., Pellew to Keats, 5 March 1814.
44. Ibid., Pellew to Keats, 10 Dec. 1812.
45. Most of Fremantle's letters to Pellew are contained in Box 9 of the Exmouth Papers.
46. Fremantle Papers, D/FR/235/4, Pellew to Fremantle, 12 Aug. 1811.
47. Exmouth Papers, Box 22, Pellew to Keats, 12 Sept. 1813, indicates that Fremantle was among two or three admirals with local mistresses.
48. Nicolson, pp. 101, 312–13.
49. RNM 500/88/57, ff. 153–4. This is the private journal of Admiral Penrose, hand-written and bound. The contents are in three sections. All folio numbers cited here are from the final section.
50. Ibid., f. 232.
51. Bentinck Papers, PW Jd 4518, Pellew to Bentinck, 22 May 1812.
52. Exmouth Papers, Box 26, Bentinck to Pellew, 19 June 1812.
53. Bentinck Papers, PW Jd 4552, Pellew to Bentinck, 27 Aug. 1812.
54. Exmouth Papers, Box 4, Drury to Pellew, 10 Jan. & 6 July 1810.
55. Ibid., Drury to Pellew, 22 Oct. 1810. Pellew had his revenge when a dispute with Drury over prizes found in his favour and he was able to write sweetly: 'You will not hesitate to return any money paid to you.'
56. Ibid., Pellew to Drury, Jan. 1811.
57. ADM 51/2767 & ADM 1/5437, Court martial of Peter Lawless and others, 16–22 July 1813.
58. The case was referred back to the Admiralty for a ruling on a legal technicality, but Pellew went further with a plea for a pardon, referred to the Prince Regent. Exmouth Papers, Box 3, Croker to Pellew, 28 Sept. 1813
59. Exmouth Papers, Box 22, Susan to Pellew, 12 Oct. 1813.
60. Ibid., Susan to Pellew, 13 March 1814.
61. *Monthly Magazine*, Vol. 30, Part 2, 1810.
62. Exmouth Papers, Box 22, Susan to Pellew, 10 April 1814.
63. Ibid., Box 26, Lady Nelson to Pellew, 6 Aug. 1812.
64. Jane Smith's letters are in Box 22 of the Exmouth Papers.
65. Ibid., Jane Smith to Pellew, 13 May 1814.
66. Ibid., Susan to Pellew, 10 April & 30 May 1814.
67. Ibid., Pellew to Keats, 5 March 1814.

CHAPTER 14: White Knights

1. Exmouth Papers, Box 1.
2. Bentinck Papers, PW Jd 4499, Pellew to Bentinck, 24 Feb. 1812.
3. Ibid., 4501, Pellew to Bentinck, 25 Feb. 1812.
4. See Paul Baepler (ed.), *White Slaves, African Masters, an anthology of American Barbary Captivity Narratives*.
5. Bentinck Papers, PW Jd 4509–13, various letters.
6. Fremantle Papers, D/FR/39/1, Pellew to Fremantle, 19 May 1812.
7. Pocock, pp. 8–9.
8. Bentinck Papers, PW Jd 4516, Pellew to Bentinck, 10 May 1812.
9. Fremantle Papers, D/FR/39/1 Pellew to Fremantle, 22 & 29 May 1812. The reference to Tartus is to the Ottoman source of Barbary provisions.
10. Bentinck Papers, PW Jd 4555, Report of Captain Adam, 12 Sept. 1812.
11. Fremantle Papers, D/FR/32/7, Pellew to Fremantle, 27 Aug. 1814.
12. Perkins & Douglas-Morris, p. 38.
13. Bentinck Papers, PW Jd 2066, Pellew to Bentinck, 1 May 1815.
14. Fremantle Papers, D/FR/32/9 Pellew to Fremantle, undated.
15. RNM 500/87/57, Penrose journal, f. 94.
16. Ibid., f. 91.
17. Perkins & Douglas-Morris, p. 161.
18. Pellow's account of his experiences was published soon after his return as *The History of the Long Captivity & Adventures of Thomas Pellow* and became a bestseller. This subsequently became the subject of another best-selling if rather simplistic book – Giles Milton's *White Gold*.
19. Exmouth Papers, Box 21, Castlereagh to Bathurst, 29 Jan. 1816,
20. Private Collection, Melville to Pellew, 26 Dec. 1815.
21. Ibid.
22. Ibid.
23. Exmouth Papers, Box 18, Instructions to Captain Warde, 25 Jan. 1816.
24. RNM 500/87/57, Penrose journal, f. 97.
25. Ibid., f. 94.
26. Shaler, p. 45.
27. Ibid., pp. 47–8.
28. Perkins and Douglas-Morris, pp. 66–7.
29. FO 113/4; ADD MS 64075, f. 66.
30. Exmouth Papers, Box 10, McDonell to Pellew, 28 Sept. 1813.
31. FO 3/18, McDonell to Bathurst, 7 April 1816.
32. Shaler, p. 18.
33. FO 113/4, f. 21.
34. Ibid., f. 3.
35. FO 3/18, McDonell to Bathurst, 7 April 1816.
36. Shaler, p. 141.
37. RNM 500/87/57, Penrose journal, f. 105.

38. ADD MS 41528, William a'Court to Lord Exmouth, 27 Feb. 1816.
39. Exmouth Papers, Box 21.
40. FO 3/18, McDonell to Bathurst, 7 April 1816.
41. RNM 500/87/57, Penrose journal, f. 109.
42. Exmouth Papers, Box 18, contains various letters between Exmouth and the Princess.
43. Ibid. The request was refused.
44. RNM 500/87/57, Penrose journal, f. 112–13.
45. Exmouth Papers, Box 21.
46. Private Collection, Exmouth to Sidmouth, May 1816.

CHAPTER 15: Massacre at Bona

1. FO 113/4, Shaler to State Department, 29 June 1816.
2. Ibid., Report of William Shaler, 30 Aug–5 Nov 1815.
3. Exmouth Papers, Box 18, Exmouth to Croker, 18 June 1816.
4. FO 3/18, McDonell to Bathhurst, 20 May 1816.
5. Exmouth Papers, Box 18, Exmouth to Croker, 18 June 1816.
6. FO 3/18, McDonell to Bathurst, 20 May 1816.
7. Exmouth Papers, Box 18, Exmouth to Croker, 18 June 1816.
8. Ibid.
9. FO 113/4, Shaler to State Department, 29 June 1816.
10. ADM 51/2164, log of the *Boyne*.
11. Exmouth Papers, Box 18, Exmouth to Croker, 18 June 1816.
12. ADM 51/2164, log of the *Boyne*.
13. FO 113/4, Shaler to State Department, 29 June 1816.
14. FO 3/18, McDonell to Bathurst, 14 Sept. 1816.
15. Ibid., McDonell to Bathurst, 7 April 1816.
16. ADM 51/2164, log of the *Boyne*.
17. Exmouth Papers, Box 18, Exmouth to Croker, 18 June 1816.
18. Ibid.
19. Ibid., Box 21, undated report of Captain Dundas.
20. FO 3/19, McDonell to Bathurst, 9 Sept. 1817.
21. FO 113/4, Exmouth to McDonell, 20 May 1816.
22. FO 3/18, McDonell to Bathurst, 20 May 1816.
23. Osler, p. 303.
24. Exmouth Papers, Box 18, Castlereagh to Exmouth, 30 Sept. 1816.
25. FO 3/18, Report of Mr Escudero, 13 June 1816.
26. Ibid., Report of Hugh McDonell, 30 June 1816.
27. Ibid., 21 July 1816.
28. Parkinson, p. 435.
29. Ibid.
30. *Caledonian Mercury*, 5 Aug. 1816. The substance of the report was that the Bey at Tunis told Exmouth 'he had no fear of threats and would repel

force by force . . . but on a moment of reflection said he would refuse nothing to her Royal Highness the Princess of Wales'.

31. *The Times*, 24 June 1816.
32. Ibid., 1 July 1816.
33. Exmouth Papers, Box 24, A Statement of Lord Exmouth's Proceedings at Algiers.
34. Penrose's statement on the state of the fleet tends to discredit Northcote Parkinson's conclusion that Exmouth's failure to win volunteers signalled unpopularity.
35. Perkins & Douglas-Morris, pp. 76–7.
36. Ibid., p. 86.
37. Osler, pp. 366–7.
38. Four years later Eliza Pellew eloped with an Army officer.
39. Exmouth Papers, Box 18, Exmouth to Pownoll, 20 July 1816.
40. This opinion was picked up and published in Exmouth's local paper, the *Exeter Flying Post*, on 1 Aug. 1816.
41. Exmouth Papers, Box 23, Croker to Sir Fleetwood Pellew, 27 Jan. 1833.
42. Ibid., Box 18, Exmouth to Sidmouth, 11 Aug. 1816.

CHAPTER 16: 'Wooden Walls Against Stone'

1. Perkins and Douglas-Morris, p. 87.
2. ADM 51/2720, log of the *Queen Charlotte*; Perkins and Douglas-Morris, pp. 90 & 95.
3. Exmouth Papers, Box 18, Exmouth to Sidmouth, 10 Aug. 1816.
4. Fremantle Papers, D/FR/39/1 Pellew to Fremantle, 29 May 1816.
5. ADM 1/432, Narrative of Captain Dashwood.
6. Ibid.
7. Salamé, p. 15.
8. See for example ADM 51/2811, log of the *Severn*, 21–24 Aug. 1816.
9. Exmouth Papers, Box 23, Reid to Exmouth, 24 Feb. 1824.
10. Exmouth had earlier set Salamé a test, giving him a prepared statement 'Declaration for the Abolition of Christian Slavery' to translate, and then comparing it with a translation from a second source. Salamé, pp. 5–6.
11. Salamé's *Narrative* provides a candidly admiring record of Exmouth's final action and might be thought to have been written with his approval if not encouragement were it not for the differences with his account, for example as to the source of the opening broadsides, and which ship was first hit.
12. Salamé, p. 20.
13. The unnamed officer was on the *Leander*. His memoir was published in *The Mirror of Literature, Amusement, and Instruction*, 27 June 1829.
14. Salamé, p. 25.
15. Ibid., p. 34.

16. Shaler, p. 279.
17. Perkins and Douglas-Morris, p. 107.
18. See note 13 above.
19. Parkinson, p. 455.
20. Salamé, pp. 35–6.
21. Knight, pp. xxxii–xxxiii. I am grateful to Professor Knight for bringing this point to my attention.
22. Parkinson, p. 455.
23. Shaler, p. 280.
24. Salamé, p. 36.
25. Ibid., p. 38.
26. Perkins and Douglas-Morris, p. 93.
27. *Exeter Flying Post*, 31 Oct. 1816, 'A Letter from a Midshipman on the Princess Charlotte'.
28. Knight, p. xxxii.
29. See note 14.
30. See note 28.
31. Salamé, p. 32.
32. Ibid., p. 40.
33. William James, *Naval History of Great Britain*, Vol. VI, 1826, p. 402.
34. ADD, MS 457264, British Library.
35. Perkins and Douglas-Morris, p. 159.
36. Ibid., p. 132.
37. Salamé, p. 41.
38. Ibid., p. 44.
39. Ibid.
40. See note 28.
41. Parkinson, p. 461.
42. See note 13.
43. Exmouth Papers, Box 2, Testimony of A. Baird, 17 Oct. 1816. Quarries's skill won praise at the Admiralty.
44. See note 14.
45. Private Collection, Admiral Exmouth's diary.
46. ADM 1/432, Exmouth to Croker, 28 Aug. 1816.
47. Salamé, p. 49.
48. Perkins and Douglas-Morris, p. 129.
49. See note 14.
50. Ibid.
51. Salamé, p. 51.
52. Ibid., pp. 52–3.
53. Perkins and Douglas-Morris, p. 132.
54. Salamé, p. 166.
55. Shaler, p. 281.

56. Osler, p. 337.
57. Gaze inscription in Osler, p. 330.
58. Salamé, p. 53.
59. See note 14.
60. Ibid.
61. Perkins and Douglas-Morris, p. 152.
62. Private Collection, Exmouth to Sidmouth, 29 Aug. 1816.
63. There has been some confusion about the figure, which was probably inflated in the immediate aftermath. The number arrived at by Salamé in a process in which he was closely involved is probably the most accurate, although even his arithmetic was faulty at times.
64. Exmouth Papers, Box 18, *Impregnable*, Return of Killed and Wounded.
65. Parkinson, pp. 468–9.
66. RNM 500/88/122 Exmouth to Coode, 9 Sept. 1816.
67. Exmouth Papers, Box 18, Mrs Johnstone to Exmouth, 26 Nov. 1816.
68. Ibid., Box 21, A narrative of Antonio Higuero, 5 Sept. 1816.
69. FO 3/19, McDonell to Bathurst, 8 Sept. 1817.
70. Perkins and Douglas-Morris, pp. 188–9.
71. Private Collection, Exmouth to Melville, 21 Oct. 1816.
72. Perkins and Douglas-Morris, p. 190.
73. This calculation was made by his third son, George.
74. RNM 500/88/57, f. 153.
75. Exmouth Papers, Box 21, Wellington to Exmouth, 8 March 1817.
76. Private Collection, Broke to Exmouth, 11 Oct. 1816.
77. RNM 500/88/57, ff. 153–5.

Epilogue

1. Exmouth Papers, Box 23, Croker to Fleetwood Pellew, 27 Jan. 1833.
2. Knight, p. 548.
3. See note 1.
4. Quoted in Parkinson, pp. 470–1.
5. RNM 500/88/57, Penrose journal, ff. 153–4.
6. Davidson, pp. 147–8.
7. See Rodger, pp. 525–6.
8. Ruddock Mackay and Michael Duffy, *Hawke, Nelson and British Naval Leadership, 1747–1805*.
9. Cobbett, *Weekly Political Register*, 21 Sept. 1816.
10. *The Real John Bull*, 17 Aug. 1822.
11. RNM 500/88/57, Penrose journal, f. 39.
12. *Exeter Flying Post*, date unclear, Nov. 1816.
13. *The Times*, 20 June 1820.
14. Exmouth to Samuel Pellew, 29 Nov. 1820, quoted in Osler, pp. 350–1.
15. Exmouth Papers, Box 23, contains these letters and others from

Exmouth's later years.

16. Ibid., Box 7, contains Schanck's letters to Exmouth.
17. Teignmouth Museum, Exmouth to Sir Sidney Smith, 17 Oct. 1819.
18. Taylor, p. 343.
19. Fremantle Papers, D/FR/32/15 Exmouth to Fremantle, 23 Jan. 1819.
20. RNM 500/88/57, Penrose journal, f. 232.
21. *Morning Chronicle*, 31 March 1824.
22. Rae, p. 293.
23. Exmouth Papers, Box 23, Lady Pellew to Samuel Pellew, undated.
24. Private Collection, Croker to Exmouth, 26 Sept. 1816.
25. Osler, p. 64. George Pellew identified the unnamed officer as Cole.

Bibliography

—————⌘—————

Manuscript sources

The Caird Library at the National Maritime Museum, Greenwich, is the repository for the vast collection of documents, principally letters, known as the Exmouth Papers, MSS/92/027. There is little system to the manner in which they are boxed, which is as Cecil Northcote Parkinson left them. When I began my research, work had started on cataloguing these for the first time, but this was suspended during the moving of the library to new quarters in a major refurbishment of the museum. Although the cataloguing is to resume and the papers may be reordered, the references cited in footnotes here should not become obsolete, and future researchers ought to have the additional benefit of a comprehensive catalogue.

The Devon Record Office at Exeter now holds other Exmouth family papers, referred to in the footnotes as Private Collection. In the main these consist of copies made by George Pellew of original letters to be found at the Caird Library. However, there are also some original documents.

The National Archives at Kew holds the Admiralty records. These include: ships' logs, (the ADM 51 series); musters (ADM 36 – a valuable and sometimes neglected source of information on manning and individual transfers between ships); Captains Letters and Admirals Letters (ADM 1); and court martial proceedings (ADM 1). The archives also hold the records of the Foreign Office (FO) for the Algiers campaign.

The Centre for Buckinghamshire Studies at Aylesbury contains the papers of Sir Thomas Fremantle.

The University of Nottingham, Department of Manuscripts and Special Collections is the repository for the papers of Lord William Bentinck.

The Royal Naval Museum (RNM) Library, Portsmouth, holds the journal of Admiral Sir Charles Penrose.

The Teignmouth and Shaldon Museum has on display a range of memorabilia on loan from the Exmouth family as well holding items of correspondence cited in the footnotes.

The Cornwall Records Office in Truro contains the records of the Langford family, which cast light on Pellew's background, his childhood and youth.

The British Library contains among its manuscript collections the papers of Hugh McDonell and William a'Court, and Lieutenant Harry Wilson's account of the bombardment of Algiers.

Lord Digby and Anthony Barlow hold private papers of their ancestors.

Selected books

Adams, Max, *Admiral Collingwood – Nelson's Own Hero*, London, 2005

Bottrell, William, *Traditions and Hearthside Stories of West Cornwall* (pub. 1873, Internet Archive)

Buckingham, James, *Autobiography of James Silk Buckingham* (pub. 1855, Internet Archive)

Byrne, John D., *Crime and Punishment in the Royal Navy – Discipline on the Leeward Islands Station 1784–1812*, Aldershot, 1989

Colley, Linda, *Captives – Britain, Empire and the World 1600–1850*, London, 2002

Cordingley, David, *Cochrane the Dauntless*, London, 2007

Crawford, Captain Abraham, *Reminiscences of a Naval Officer*, London, 1999

Davidson, James, *Admiral Lord St Vincent*, Barnsley, 2006

Davis, Robert C., *Christian Slaves, Muslim Masters – White Slavery in the Mediterranean 1580–1800*, London, 2004

Dugan, James, *The Great Mutiny*, London, 1966

Ellis, Kenneth, *The Post Office in the Eighteenth Century*, London, 1958

Fremantle, Alice, ed., *The Wynne Diaries 1789–1820*, Oxford, 1953

Gardiner, Robert, *Frigates of the Napoleonic Wars*, London, 2006

Hague, William, *William Pitt the Younger*, London, 2005

Harvey, Robert, *Cochrane – The Life and Exploits of a Fighting Captain*, London, 2000

Hay, M. D., ed., *Landsman Hay – Memoirs of Robert Hay, 1789–1847*, London, 1953

Hazlitt, William, *Conversations of James Northcote*, London, 1830

Ingrams, Richard, *The Life and Adventures of William Cobbett*, London, 2005

Knight, Roger, *The Pursuit of Victory – The Life and Achievement of Horatio Nelson*, London, 2005

Lambert, Andrew, *Nelson – Britannia's God of War*, London, 2004

Lavery, Brian, *Nelson's Navy – The Ships, Men and Organisation, 1973–1815*, London, 1989

Leech, Samuel, *A Voice From the Main Deck*, London, 1999

Lewis, Michael, *A Social History of the Navy 1793–1815*, London, 1960

McCullough, David, *1776 – Britain and America at War*, London, 2005

Mahan, A. T., *Types of Naval Officers* (pub. 1901, Gutenberg)

Milton, Giles, *White Gold – The Extraordinary Story of Thomas Pellow*, London, 2004

Morriss, Roger, *The Channel Fleet and the Blockade of Brest, 1793–1801*, Ashgate, 2001

Mostert, Noel, *The Line Upon a Wind – An Intimate History of the Last and Greatest War Fought at Sea Under Sail 1793–1815*, London, 2007

Nicolson, Adam, *Men of Honour – Trafalgar and the Making of the English Hero*, London, 2005

Osler, Edward, *The Life of Admiral Viscount Exmouth*, London, 1835

Padfield, Peter, *Maritime Power and the Struggle for Freedom 1788–1851*, London, 2003

Parkinson, C. Northcote, *The Life of Edward Pellew, Viscount Exmouth*, London, 1934

Perkins, Roger and Douglas-Morris, K. J., *Gunfire in Barbary*, Havant, 1982

Pocock, Tom, *Breaking The Chains – The Royal Navy's War on White Slavery*, Barnsley, 2006

Polwhele, Richard, *Reminiscences in Prose and Verse*, London, 1836

Pope, Dudley, *The Black Ship*, London, 1963

Porter, Roy, *English Society in the 18th Century*, London, 1991

Price, Anthony, *The Eyes of the Fleet – A Popular History of Frigates and Frigate Captains*, New York, 1996

Rae, Malcolm, *Sir Edward Pellew, First Viscount Exmouth*, in *British Admirals of the Napoleonic Wars* (ed. Peter Le Fevre), Barnsley, 2004

Rodger, N. A. M., *The Command of the Ocean – A Naval History of Britain, 1649–1815*, London, 2004

Salamé, Abraham, *A Narrative of the Expedition to Algiers in the Year 1816* (pub. 1819, Internet Archive)

Shaler, William, *Sketches of Algiers – Political, Historical and Civil*, Boston, 1826

Southam, Brian, *Jane Austen and the Navy*, London, 2005

Taylor, Stephen, *Storm & Conquest – The Battle for the Indian Ocean, 1809*, London, 2007

Tregellas, Walter, *Cornish Worthies* (pub. 1884, Internet Archive)

Wareham, Tom, *The Star Captains – Frigate Command in the Napoleonic Wars*, Rochester, 2001

Wareham, Tom, *Frigate Commander*, London, 2004

Woodman, Richard, *The Sea Warriors*, London, 2001

Zamoyski, Adam, *Rites of Peace, The Fall of Napoleon and the Congress of Vienna*, London, 2007

Articles

Arthur Pinhey, 'Portraiture of Edward Pellew', *Mariners' Mirror*, July 1936

A. Temple Patterson, 'A Protégé of Pellew', *Mariners' Mirror*, Vol. 63, 1977

Acknowledgements

Authors need help, but never more than when they enter unfamiliar or difficult waters. I have been ruthless in seeking guidance from those more knowledgeable about the maritime world than I, and their freedom in giving it leaves me with much to be grateful for.

I owe a special debt to Professor Roger Knight who, despite the demands of his own work, read the manuscript and saved me from errors of fact and judgment. Malcolm Rae shared the fruits of his own considerable research and enlivened with his company visits to Teignmouth. Martin Salmon offered information gleaned from his cataloguing of the Exmouth papers at the Caird Library. Richard Harding made available his research on Pellew's biographer, Cecil Northcote Parkinson.

My own research benefited immeasurably from the help of the 10th Viscount Exmouth who encouraged the work and entrusted me with the collection of papers compiled by George Pellew, along with the family's copy of the Edward Osler 'life' containing the revealing annotations made by George Pellew and John Gaze.

Anyone who has conducted research at the National Archives at Kew knows how much the knowledge and enthusiasm of the staff there contributes to the work of professional and amateur historians alike. We owe a great deal to this outstanding institution.

Matthew Sheldon and Graham Naylor assisted with information held at the Royal Navy Museum in Portsmouth and Plymouth Library respectively. Anthony Barlow sent me letters from his family papers. The Lord Digby gave me access to the private collection of his ancestor's papers.

Others whom I would like to thank for various acts of kindness are Pat Warner and Lin Watson of the Teignmouth and Shaldon Museum, Michael Murray and Johanna Moriarty of Penzance, and Anthony Claydon.

This book would not have been written but for the support of Starling Lawrence at W. W. Norton. As always, Julian Loose at Faber gave valuable creative advice. Donald Sommerville was an informed and sharp-eyed copy editor. The efforts of my agent, Caroline Dawnay, brought to mind Pellew's favourite ship.

Authors may need the help of specialists, but we would be lost without the candid opinions of those to whom we are closest. My biggest debt is to the readers whose comments have most influenced this and previous books – my friend, Tom Fort, my children, Wil and Juliette, and the constant in my life and every endeavour, my wife Caroline.

Index